Mrs Oscar Wilde

Mrs Oscar Wilde
A Woman of Some Importance

ANNE CLARK AMOR

SIDGWICK & JACKSON
LONDON

First published in June 1983 in Great Britain
by Sidgwick and Jackson Limited

First Paperback Edition October 1988

ISBN 0 283 99743 5

Printed in Hong Kong
for Sidgwick and Jackson Limited
1 Tavistock Chambers, Bloomsbury Way
London WC1A 2SG

To my husband

Acknowledgements

The author wishes to acknowledge with gratitude the help of the following people: Mr Edward Bainbridge, Mr Robert Bancroft, Miss Lindsay Fulcher, Sir Rupert Hart-Davis, Mr H. Montgomery Hyde, Mrs J. Kenealy, Mr Richard Jones, Miss Sarah Millard, Mr M.A. Pounde; and that of Mr Merlin Holland, who has kindly permitted the use of copyright material from the writings of his grandparents, Constance and Oscar Wilde, and of his great-grandmother, Lady Wilde.

Contents

List of Illustrations   8
1   Many Relations   9
2   The Aesthete   21
3   Loved by a Poet   33
4   Honeymoon   45
5   The House Beautiful   53
6   The Modern Woman   63
7   Family Life   85
8   The Decadent   98
9   The Gilt-headed Youth   107
10   Deception   126
11   The First Attack   138
12   The Constant Wife   151
13   Revelations   165
14   Separation   175
15   Mrs Holland   185
16   Incomprehension   194
17   The Last Summer   206
18   Requiescat   220
    Epilogue   229
    Bibliography   232
    Notes   235
    Index   244

List of Illustrations

Frontispiece (Estate of Vyvyan Holland)

Between pages 34 and 35
Constance, aged about twenty-six (Edward Bainbridge)
Oscar, aged thirty (M.A. Pounde)

Between pages 50 and 51
'Speranza' (reproduced in *The Real Oscar Wilde* by Robert Sherard)
Sir William Wilde, Oscar's father (Edward Bainbridge)
St James's, Sussex Gardens (from an old print)
Constance and Cyril, about 1891 (M.A. Pounde)
The House Beautiful (reproduced in *The Life of Oscar Wilde* by Robert Sherard)

Between pages 114 and 115
Vyvyan (Edward Bainbridge)
Ellen Terry (the author)
Robert Ross and Reginald Turner (Edward Bainbridge)
Lady Sandhurst (*Pall Mall Gazette Extra*, no. 49, 1889)
Lord Alfred Douglas, aged twenty-three (Richard Jones)
Oscar in 1894 (Edward Bainbridge)

Between pages 178 and 179
Constance, about 1894 (reproduced in *The Real Oscar Wilde* by Robert Sherard)
Oscar and Lord Alfred Douglas (reproduced in *Oscar Wilde: His Life and Confessions* by Frank Harris)
The Marquess of Queensberry (Richard Jones)
Reading Gaol (reproduced in *The Life of Oscar Wilde* by Robert Sherard)
Oscar's grave at Bagneux (reproduced in *The Life of Oscar Wilde* by Robert Sherard)

1

Many Relations

'It's a ridiculous attachment,' twittered the other
Swallows, 'she has no money, and far too many
relations.'

'The Happy Prince'

A large crowd of people stood outside St James's Church, Sussex
Gardens, muttering with discontent. They were used to society
weddings, but this one promised to be something very special.
Word had got around that the celebrated Oscar Wilde was about to
be married, and they were eager to see all that went on. To their
extreme annoyance, they found that they were to be excluded from
the church, on the express orders of the bridegroom. Only invited
guests were to be allowed in.

The residents of Sussex Gardens were not easily defeated. For a
full half-hour they remonstrated angrily with the officials. The
ushers finally relented, the doors were opened, and the public
poured in to take their places with leading contemporary figures in
the world of art and literature. Oscar Wilde was the most
talked-about man in the country, yet the woman he had chosen to
be his wife was unknown. Some said that she had been their
neighbour as a child, and that she was half Irish. All of them
speculated about the wedding dress, none more so than the
journalists who had come to report the occasion to the world. The
man about to be married was, after all, an apostle of beauty and the
acknowledged arbiter of taste in the realm of fashion. Surely his
bride would be remarkable.

Suddenly there was a buzz of excitement, and a gasp, and then
the congregation rose. At the door of the church, dressed in cowslip
yellow, crowned with myrtle and looking radiantly happy, stood
Constance Mary Lloyd.

The bride on Oscar's arm came from the same social class as he did, yet her strictly conventional home background was very far removed from Oscar's own bohemian environment. Her English ancestors were exemplars of middle-class respectability. Her great-grandfather was John Lloyd, a banker of Stockport and Cheshire, who became Town Clerk of Stockport and married Mary, daughter of James Watson of Swinton. Their eldest son, Constance's grandfather, was born in Stockport on 1 September 1798, and was baptized John Horatio, after his father and Lord Nelson, who was the popular hero of the day.

John Horatio was educated at Stockport Grammar School, where he quickly proved himself a scholar of outstanding ability with a strong leaning towards the classics. Already he showed signs of that eloquence which was to prove remarkable in later life. He was very close to his father, a man of phenomenal energy passionately devoted to the Church and the King; a Tory of the old school, with whom any notions of personal popularity were strictly secondary to his sense of public duty. He took an active role in quelling the second wave of Luddite insurrections, those riots of the working classes directed against the machines which were taking away their livelihoods, and in due course was appointed Prothonotory of the Counties of Cheshire and Flint. Among the local labouring classes he was disliked, even hated. One night an angry mob set out to kill him, but he was in another part of town and they shot the wrong man. Young John Horatio was sent to warn him to return home by the back alleys, but he refused, and marched with his son through the main thoroughfares pursued by the hostile rabble. The Lloyds were never short of courage.

Constance's great-grandfather was not a wealthy man. He could not have afforded to send John Horatio to college had not Lord Sidmouth, a minister of the Crown, and William Hobhouse come forward to pay the fees. John Horatio matriculated at Queen's College, Oxford in 1818, and four years later attained a double first in mathematics and classics. He became a Fellow of Queen's and Brasenose Colleges and was called to the Bar of the Inner Temple in 1826.

On 1 September 1826, his twenty-seventh birthday, John Horatio married his cousin Caroline, daughter of Holland Watson, a magistrate of Chester and Lancaster, and a major in the Stockport Volunteers. Holland Watson was a notable antiquary and a keen ornithologist, who at his death in 1829 left a splendid library and a collection of about eighty stuffed British birds. John Horatio and Caroline had eight children, four boys and four girls, but two sons and one daughter died in infancy.

John Horatio had a long and very distinguished career. As a frequent speaker at the Oxford Union debating society he had been associated with such famous personalities as John Stuart Mill, Charles Buller and Lord Clarendon. He eschewed his father's political views, and when Stockport was enfranchised after the passing of the Reform Bill in 1832 he was elected to Parliament as a Radical. His tender concern for the poor and afflicted and his essential fair-mindedness were readily apparent. In 1833 he spoke against giving magistrates power of summary conviction for felony, and he supported a petition for an enquiry into the conduct of the Benchers of the Inns of Court relating to the admission of students to the Bar. He took a leading part in the Patent Bill of 1833, and in the following year introduced a bill to abolish the death sentence for arson where life was not endangered. He was a man of great human sympathy and worked for the mitigation of the severity of sentences in the courts. Any bill which was designed for the better government of Ireland automatically received his full support. Though he used his term as a Member of Parliament so well, the strain of so much work coupled with the demands of his legal practice began to erode his health, and he did not stand for re-election.

His legal practice had always been a busy one, but with the development of the railway system from 1845 onwards he became even more active, becoming the country's leading authority on railway matters and acting as Counsel for almost all the railway companies in England. He retained his interest in banking, inherited from his father, and perhaps it was this which encouraged him to solve the financial problem of developing railways by inventing 'Lloyd's Bonds.' These overcame the reluctance of private investors to tie up their capital in debentures which they could not compel the railway companies to buy back as long as the interest payments were not in default. Purchasers of Lloyd's Bonds could get their capital back through court action if need be. It has been said that without Lloyd's Bonds most of the railway development that went ahead at that period would have been impossible. His reputation was such that when the promoters of a scheme to form a company for the laying of a transatlantic cable reached deadlock, it was to him that they turned for advice and he who found a way out of the difficulty. He was greatly interested in patents, and also came into contact with all the leading engineers of his day.[1]

Constance's father, Horace Lloyd, was born in 1828, and was very close to his brother, Frederick Watson Lloyd, a year younger than himself. With so many legal eagles on the branches of the family tree it was hardly surprising that both Horace and Frederick followed their father into the legal profession. Horace was educated at Caius College, Cambridge, where he took his Bachelor's degree in 1850, and was called to the Bar in 1852. Instead of teaming up with his father and brother at 1 King's Bench Walk in the Temple, he set up in independent practice a few doors away at number eleven where he quickly gained a considerable practice at *nisi prius* (trial before a judge and jury) and also in private arbitration cases.

In 1855, when he was twenty-seven years old, Horace Lloyd married Adelaide Barbara Atkinson in Dublin. Adelaide, usually called Ada, was a daughter of army agent John Atkinson, formerly of the 6th Rifles, who with his wife Mary and another unmarried daughter lived at 1 Ely Place, Dublin. Initially Horace and his bride set up home at 3 Harewood Square, in Marylebone, London, and it was here that their first child, a boy baptized Otho Holland, was born on 10 November 1856.[2] The family was completed when Constance Mary Lloyd was born in the same house on 2 January 1858.[3] Saturday's child, she was baptized on 9 June 1858 at Christ Church, Cosway Street, Marylebone.[4] Although registration of birth was already compulsory, Constance's birth was never registered. This seems a curious omission on the part of a barrister. Perhaps Horace was too busy, and Ada too preoccupied with social and domestic affairs to remember to comply with the law; or perhaps this failure on their part was indicative of a more serious malaise in the household.

For the Lloyds' marriage was not a happy one. In the main Horace and Ada pursued separate social lives, and often went away leaving Otho and Constance alone in the house with only the servants to care for them. In the early years there were four servants, including the butler, but by 1871 the establishment had increased with the recruitment of a cook. The turnover of servants was high and this, too, may have been due to some extent to the friction between Constance's parents. Despite these problems, Horace's career flourished, and in 1866 he moved his chambers to 1 Brick Court, in the Temple. The family moved house too, to Sussex Gardens, near Hyde Park; first to number nine, where they lived from 1865 until 1866, and finally to a large and distinguished-looking house at number forty-two.

Meanwhile, marital relations between Horace and Ada were deteriorating. Though Horace was fond of his wife, it would appear that he was not a very faithful husband. Whether this was a cause or effect of their disharmony is unclear. He was very much the successful man-about-town, and often forsook his wife for the popular continental resorts frequented by the Prince of Wales and his set. Hamburg and that fashionable watering place, Baden-Baden, were his particular favourites. At chess and billiards he was a formidable opponent, and he haunted the Whitehall Club and Simpson's Divan. Ada shared little in his social activities, and after the first few years of marriage tended to go her own way. She was excessively attached to her Irish relatives, and spent a good deal of her time in Dublin, sometimes taking Constance and Otho with her.

Ada Lloyd is, at best, a shadowy figure. It is difficult to say how much of the blame for the differences with her husband lay at her door. Though in some ways an amiable woman, she seems to have been weak-willed and self-indulgent. Certain areas of immaturity in her character made it difficult for her to adapt to life in London. Throughout her early years she had been dominated by her mother, Mary Atkinson, a woman of forceful yet kindly personality who was universally liked. Unlike Ada, Mary had highly developed maternal instincts and cushioned her children and grandchildren alike in a protective coating of love and sympathy. Her husband, John Atkinson, died in 1862, when Constance was only four years old, but the loneliness which might otherwise have overtaken Mary was eased by the continual comings and goings of her singularly united family. A handsome and wealthy woman, she never contemplated remarriage, though she lived on for twenty-six years after her husband's death in the large, imposing house in Ely Place. John Atkinson's death was not the only tragedy that befell Constance's family in that year. On 23 November Constance's uncle, Frederick Watson Lloyd, died suddenly at Worthing. He was only thirty-three years old, a young barrister of great promise who had seemed set for a brilliant future.

As often happens with children whose parents are in dispute, Constance and her brother were exceptionally close, and idolized each other. Educationally, Constance derived considerable advantage in their early years from the relationship. Although boys of their social class were normally sent to public school, it was customary for girls to be educated at home. The doors of Oxford and Cambridge were not yet open to young women, who were considered too frail in physical terms to withstand the rigours of university life. In later years Constance would have argued that through tight lacing and the weight of their normal apparel they were indeed too frail. Otho, on the other hand, was destined for a full academic career, and his parents' arrangements for his studies took account of this. Until he was ready to sit the entrance examination for Clifton, a public school near Bristol, he and Constance would have been educated together. Whatever intellectual paths he trod were automatically followed by Constance, with her quick, eager mind and ready enthusiasm. From the outset it was assumed that Otho would enter the legal profession, but from his earliest days he developed a passion for the classics which was to last him all his life. Constance matched his love of languages; but it was to French and Italian that she turned with greatest pleasure and in later life much of her reading was in those tongues. Horace Lloyd proudly described his daughter as a scholar, and so she was, in the broadest sense of the word. He was even prouder of Otho, whose academic brilliance was clearly apparent from earliest childhood. One day Horace was returning home by train when he heard his fellow passengers describing 'a boy who had passed such a wonderful exam'.[5] To his amazement he discovered that they were speaking of his own son, who had just sat the entrance examination for Clifton. Yet Otho's ability had its disadvantages, too, for he was placed immediately in the Lower Fifth, with boys much older than himself. This he always felt was a mistake, particularly since he was totally ignorant of public-school life.

Like all girls of her era, Constance would have been taught to draw. There is no record of whether she achieved any degree of proficiency with pencil or brush, but she certainly possessed an eye for colour and form, and a highly developed critical faculty. Later she haunted art galleries and museums, and as she grew older her love of art developed until it became one of the major pleasures of her life.

High on the list of social accomplishments thought desirable for girls in the Victorian era was music. Constance proved an apt and gifted pupil, and her skill at the piano delighted all who listened to her. Inevitably as she grew older the pleasure of her audiences was heightened by Constance's personal grace and beauty. She was slim and ivory-complexioned, with candid violet eyes, abundant long chestnut hair, and an engagingly modest bearing. In short, she was graceful, intelligent and accomplished, and well loved by all who knew her.

When Constance was still a child her father was involved in a scandal. Though the history is cloudy, it would seem that Horace was suspected of sexual offences. In *Oscar Wilde: His Life and Confessions*,[6] Frank Harris, who knew Wilde personally, claimed that Horace Lloyd was a homosexual. After consulting Oscar's intimate friend Robert Ross, however, he wrote in a subsequent edition[7] that it was not of homosexual offences that Constance's father had been suspected. According to Ross, 'The charge against Horatio [*sic*] Lloyd was of a normal kind. It was for exposing himself to nursemaids in the gardens of the Temple.'[8] The use of the word 'normal' in this context may seem inappropriate. An accusation of indecent exposure cannot have helped Horace's ailing marriage, and could have had disastrous effects on his career. Nevertheless, to his contemporaries suspicions of homosexuality would have been infinitely worse; for although homosexual activities in private between consenting adults were not a crime before the passing of the Criminal Law Amendment Act in 1885, they were regarded as more heinous than murder in Victorian England. As Wilde's confidant and friend of many years and his literary executor, Robert Ross was uniquely able to comment, and it is clear that whatever the truth of the matter, something unsavoury occurred. The Lloyds were, however, able to sweep the whole episode under the carpet and forget that it had ever happened. At the time of Oscar's trial, Constance's family, with the sole exception of Otho, were able to unite in self-righteous, unpitying and unforgiving disgust at his sexual 'crimes', without any regard to the scandal that had once surrounded their own relative.

All Horace Lloyd's problems, marital and otherwise, were resolved once and for all when he died of natural causes at the family home on 30 March 1874. He was only forty-six years old. No hint of any scandal can be found in his obituary notice in the *Law Times*, which gives a dignified account of his career and adds, 'He attained the honour of a silk gown in 1868, and had been for some years a Bencher of his Inn.'[9]

Horace's death markedly changed the family fortunes, for the substantial income from his prosperous legal practice died with him. In capital terms, however, Ada now found herself richer to the tune of some £12,000, for under the terms of his will his widow inherited his entire fortune, and was appointed legal guardian of Otho and Constance. It is difficult to see why Ada thought it necessary to desert the house which had been their home for the last three years, but dispose of it she did, perhaps because she wished to put behind her for ever any reminders of her former married state.

The house in which Ada Lloyd started her new independent life was at 1 Devonshire Terrace, Hyde Park, only a short distance away from the old home. Constance moved with her, and Otho too, though in practice Constance saw little of her brother, for he was still at Clifton, and returned home only during the holidays. In 1876 he gained a 'demy' scholarship at Oriel College, Oxford. Coincidentally, Oscar Wilde was at Oxford at that time, and his mother wrote and told him to look out for the brilliant young Otho Lloyd. Old John Lloyd was so pleased to see his grandson following in his own footsteps that he decided to leave him all his classical and mathematical books, as well as his prize volumes, when he died. Constance was delighted for her brother's sake, and immensely proud of him; yet she cannot have failed to realize that their paths would henceforth take totally different directions, and that their former daily companionship was gone for ever.

Meanwhile, with an excellent house in a fashionable part of London and a substantial nest egg in her pocket, Constance's mother had become a highly desirable acquisition on the marriage market. In the winter of 1878 she quit the Lloyd family for good when she married George Swinburn King, from the Accounts Department of the Admiralty. Nor was it enough for her simply to shed a load of in-laws with whom she had never been much in sympathy. It now seemed to her necessary to divest herself of her children also. Much may be inferred concerning the respective characters of Ada and her new husband from their inability to share their roof with Constance, gentle, shy and lovely, and Otho, who was rarely at home. It would appear from the scant evidence that exists that Mr King, a widower with one daughter, regarded his new step-children with a certain distrust that was never dispelled. To Constance and Otho he always remained simply Mr King. Fortunately at this juncture John Horatio Lloyd, bereft of the last of his sons, came to the rescue and offered to provide a home for his grandchildren. Ada accepted with alacrity, thus deftly disencumbering herself of all her maternal responsibilities.

Constance's new home was a large and rather splendid house at 100 Lancaster Gate, to which her grandfather had moved in 1866. Old John Horatio Lloyd had two married daughters, Caroline Kirkes and the Hon Louisa Mary Napier. Aunt Carrie was the widow of a physician who had had a large house and practice at 2 Lower Seymour Street, Portman Square. His death in 1865 left her childless and somewhat lonely, but rich. She lived at various addresses in Lower Seymour Street for the next twenty-seven years, was deeply religious, fond of travel to the last, and much attached to her nephews and nieces. Louisa Napier, or 'Aunt Mary', as the family called her, had made the most socially advantageous match of all John Lloyd's children. Her husband was William, second son of the Baron Napier, ultra Scottish and very proud of it. They had seven children, including Eliza, who never married and was one of the best loved of all Constance's family. The Baron, Aunt Mary's father-in-law, was particularly distinguished, having served in the Battle of Trafalgar. He had been Lord of the Bedchamber to King William IV, and Special Trade Commissioner at Canton. His wife Elizabeth was the only daughter of the Hon Andrew James Cochrane Johnson, with whose descendants Constance remained on intimate terms throughout her life. The Napiers and Johnsons were deeply wedded to tradition, totally averse to change and highly suspicious of anyone who departed from the accepted social customs of the day. Constance's distant cousin Adrian Hope formed a part of this family and his adherence to social acceptability was one of the factors which impeded the reunion of Constance and her husband in later years.

Equally kind but less popular with Constance was Aunt Emily, who never married, and who had been running John Lloyd's home for him ever since the death of his wife Caroline. Aunt Emily was a typical Victorian spinster, and had been nurtured in the bosom of the legal profession to boot. Inevitably this had left its mark on her. A stickler for propriety with a rigidly middle-class set of values, she had a passion for orderliness and could be decidedly difficult when the mood took her. Truth to tell, Constance was somewhat afraid of her caprices and her by no means infrequent fits of cold disapproval. Aunt Emily in fact typified the kind of spinster whom Oscar's mother, Lady Wilde, had in mind when she wrote, 'Nothing can be more dreary than rows of opaque black bundles along the walls of the drawing-room. Englishwomen have a fatal predisposition towards black, and when they reach middle life generally retire into black alpaca for the remainder of their days. This voluntary adoption of the symbol of doom is depressing.'[10]

Old John Lloyd was no less middle-class and conventional in his attitudes than his daughters. He had continued in active legal practice with his nephew Horatio Lloyd well into old age, but the death of his two adult sons and of his wife, who died in 1875 and was buried alongside them in Hendon cemetery, finally proved too much for him. He retired in the following year. Although he was seventy-nine years old when Constance went to live with him, his superior mental faculties were in no way impaired. She loved her grandfather dearly, but it can hardly be denied that his household was no longer a lively establishment. He was a genial character who had always enjoyed having young people around him; still, it is a sad thing to outlive one's wife and sons, and he suffered greatly from gout into the bargain.

Constance and her grandfather had a similar sense of humour and also many common interests. Both loved music and painting; both loved English poetry and Shakespeare in particular. John Lloyd excelled above all as a reader of Shakespeare, and could quote vast quantities at will. The library at 100 Lancaster Gate was a fine one, and Constance found much to interest her there. John Lloyd was particularly proud of his wide selection of classical and mathe-matical works; proud, too, of the presentation silver goblets, vases and cups that had belonged to his father, and his father-in-law, Holland Watson. The Watsons were connected by marriage with the Hollands of Lancashire, whose family tree could be traced back to Edward the Confessor. Among the many romantic names on the family tree was that of Sir Otho Holland, one of the original Knights of the Garter, after whom Constance's brother was named. John Lloyd's nineteenth-century copy of the family tree, on parchment, was eventually handed down to Otho, who shared his grandfather's interest in genealogy.

Altogether the atmosphere in the house at Lancaster Gate was somewhat fossilized. The servants went about their business in an unobtrusive fashion, and Henry Riches, the butler, saw to it that nothing disturbed the ordered routine of the master and his family. Life for a young girl of seventeen between those walls was just about as animated as the marble bust of her grandfather, and she was never sorry to escape from Lancaster Gate's restricting influence.

Far less inhibiting was the house in Ely Place, Dublin, where Constance enjoyed frequent holidays with her maternal grandmother, Mrs Atkinson, or Mama Mary, as Constance liked to call her. Mama Mary was naturally gregarious, and in the friendly and relaxed atmosphere of Ely Place kept open house to a constant stream of visitors. No caller was more welcome than her brother, Charles Hare, first Baron Hemphill, a distinguished classical scholar who was called to the Bar in 1860, and became a serjeant-at-law and sat on the King's Bench in 1882. Ultimately he became Solicitor-General for Ireland, Member of Parliament for Tyrone, and a member of the Privy Council for Ireland. He had several children, all of whom Constance adored, but her clear favourite was Stanhope, who ultimately succeeded to the barony.

Most romantic figure on the Hemphill family tree was Constance's great-grandmother, the novelist Barbara Hare Hemphill. Barbara was the youngest daughter of the Reverend Patrick Hare, Rector of Golden and Vicar-General of the Diocese of Cashel. She married Constance's great-grandfather, John Hemphill, in 1807. Best of her books was *Lionel Deerhurst, Or, Fashionable Life Under the Regency*, a pleasant novel written with lots of wit and charm. It was published anonymously in three volumes in 1846 under the editorship of Lady Blessington, but despite its readable style it never ran into a second edition. *The Nun's Niece, Or, The Heiress of Barnulph*, By the author of *Lionel Deerhurst*, also in three volumes, followed in 1855. Her last book, *Frieda the Jongleur*, was more serious in style and less successful. Constance never knew her great-grandmother, who died on 6 May 1858, when Constance was only four months old. Nevertheless the memory of her slight achievement lingered on with the family in Ely Place, and doubtless helped to fill Constance's mind with romantic notions of literary pursuits.

All too little unfortunately remains on record to throw light on Constance's activities in her late teens and early twenties. She was a prolific letter-writer but nobody saw fit to keep these accounts of her daily life. There would surely have been suitors, but who they were remains a mystery. Probably Constance dreamed of marriage, like other young women of her era for whom matrimony was the only acceptable career, yet it is unlikely that she could ever have imagined just how spectacular a marriage she was destined to make.

2

The Aesthete

Duke: But who is the gentleman with the long hair?
Colonel: I don't know.
Duke: He seems popular!
Colonel: He *does* seem popular!

W. S. Gilbert: *Patience*

In 1881 Constance's grandfather and Aunt Emily took a long holiday. Constance, now in her twenty-fourth year, took advantage of their prolonged absence to go and stay with Mama Mary in Dublin, leaving the house in Lancaster Gate to the servants and, when term ended, to Otho. As usual she saw a great deal of her great-uncle, Charles Hemphill, and his family, who lived in Merrion Square. It was the Hemphill connection that led to her being invited to a young people's party given by Lady Wilde for her two sons at her home at 1 Merrion Square.

Willie Wilde was an engaging young man, liked by everyone. Frank Harris describes him as 'a tall, well-made fellow of thirty or thereabouts, with an expressive, taking face, lit with a pair of deep blue laughing eyes. He had any amount of physical vivacity, and told a good story with immense verve, without for a moment getting above the commonplace.'[1]

Oscar, twenty-six years old, was less physically attractive, yet it was he who dominated the party. Constance may possibly have known him as a child, but this meeting was the first of real significance between them. Oscar, attracted by her flower-like beauty, suggested that they take a turn about the square together, and there in the summer twilight they exchanged confidences. Both loved poetry deeply, but Constance was a little disconcerted when she discovered that he cared nothing for Mrs Hemans or Eliza Cooke, who at that time were among her favourite poets. One love they did have in common, though: Keats. When Constance was nineteen years old she had been given a volume of Keats' poems. She kept it permanently by her bedside, and whenever she went on holiday she took it with her. Oscar had already written his sonnet 'The Grave of Keats', which included the lines:

> O sweetest lips since those of Mitylene!
> O poet-painter of our English Land!
> Thy name was writ in water – it shall stand:
> And tears like mine will keep thy memory green[2]

He thought of Keats as a Priest of Beauty killed before his time by the arrows of an unjust tongue.

That night when Constance returned to Ely Place she lay awake listening to Mama Mary wheezing and coughing, and thinking of the young genius with whom she was already in love. On 6 June 1881 Oscar called on her at Lancaster Gate. She afterwards confessed that she was shaking with fright in anticipation of the visit. He begged her to go and call on his mother again, a request which she confided to nobody except Otho. She couldn't help liking him because in her company he was natural and unaffected, and used better language than most people. Constance's Irish relatives were quick to notice the signs of growing attachment between the couple, and actively encouraged notions of matrimony. Her English relatives, however, had decided misgivings on the subject, partly because of Oscar's flamboyant personality and lack of fortune, and partly because of his home background. Oscar's parents, Lady Wilde and her late husband, Sir William, were greatly loved in Ireland, but they were also notorious for their eccentricities.

Oscar's father had been a prominent ear and eye surgeon in Dublin and Honorary Surgeon Occulist to Queen Victoria. He was an antiquarian with twenty books to his credit. He was also an incurable womanizer. Though he was often described as ugly his photographs belie this, and he certainly seems to have had an irresistable appeal to women. Before he succumbed to matrimony he had already fathered three illegitimate children. The eldest was a boy, Henry Wilson, who was always described as his nephew. Henry followed him into the medical profession and ultimately became his partner in his flourishing medical practice. The other two were girls, Emily and Mary, who took their father's surname, and whose mother used to keep a shop in Dublin. These girls were brought up by Sir William's brother, a country parson called Ralph Wilde.

Oscar's mother was even more celebrated than his father. She was Jane Francesca Elgee, daughter of a Dublin solicitor who died unaccountably in Bangalore two years before her alleged date of birth. An ardent patriot, she was a writer who, under the pseudonym 'Speranza' contributed inflammatory articles to the Irish revolutionary weekly, *The Nation*. Her articles were partly responsible for the suppression of the newspaper, and when its editor, Charles Gavan Duffy, was tried for sedition Speranza leapt to her feet in the crowded courtroom and claimed responsibility for the articles. It was a useless gesture, but typical of the dramatic effects in which she specialized.

It is said that Sir William wanted to marry the actress Helen Faucit, a nobly proportioned actress who played Shakespearean and classical roles and had achieved a remarkable success with her Antigone. But in April 1851 Helen married someone else, and he turned instead to Speranza, equally tall and distinguished, and endowed in real life with the qualities of a tragedy queen. Her head was filled with romantic notions; in a letter to a friend she wrote of her ideals of love, 'I would not let him love midnight or the moon, nor seem conscious they existed. I must be his Universe, terrestrial and celestial. I would not have a thought, a word, stolen from me, they would all be my just right, and mine only.'[3] She and Sir William were married on 12 November 1851 in St Peter's Church, Dublin.

Speranza described her new husband as 'a Celebrity – a man eminent in his profession, of acute intellect and much learning, the best conversationalist in the metropolis, and author of many books'.[4] But marriage was not all that she had hoped, for she claimed that Sir William had a strange hypochondriacal nature which he revealed only to her, and which she found it difficult to cope with. 'I do not know how to deal with fantastic evils though I could bear up grandly against a real calamity . . . I love and suffer – this is all I am conscious of now and thus at last my great soul is prisoned within a woman's destiny – nothing interests me beyond the desire to make *him* happy – for this I could kill myself.'[5] On 26 September 1852 their first child, William Charles Kingsbury Wilde, was born at their home in 21 Westland Row, Dublin. There was no longer time for literature in Speranza's life. A friend who saw her busy with tiny saucepans in the nursery remarked

> Alas! the Fates are cruel
> Behold Speranza making gruel![6]

While her husband was in Sweden removing a cataract that had blinded King Oscar for years, Speranza gave birth on 16 October 1854 to their second child. King Oscar consented to be godfather, and the boy was baptized on 26 April 1855 by his uncle, Ralph Wilde, in St Mark's Church, Dublin. His name was Oscar Fingal O'Flahertie Wills Wilde. 'Behold me – me, Speranza – also rocking a cradle at this present writing in which lies my second son – a babe of one month old the 16th of this month and as large and fine and handsome and healthy as if he were three months. He is to be called Oscar Fingal Wilde. Is not that grand and Ossianic?'[7]

It is commonly believed that Speranza, having hoped for a girl, kept Oscar in petticoats for years. Boys and girls alike wore skirts in those days until the age of about four, but a photograph of Oscar at two years old wearing an off-the-shoulder blue velvet gown shows him looking provocatively feminine. There is not the slightest evidence that this produced female characteristics. Oscar grew up healthy, phenomenally strong, and fond of traditional male pursuits. In other words, he was entirely normal, except in one important respect: he happened to be a genius. Any disappointment Speranza had felt was forgotten in 1858, when the birth of her little daughter Isola completed the family. However, in the early years at least, it would appear that Speranza favoured Willie above Oscar, and this may have predisposed Oscar in later years to favour his own elder son: 'Oscar is a great stout creature who minds nothing but growing fat. Willie is slight, tall and spirituelle, looking with large beautiful eyes full of expression. He is twined round all the fibres of my heart'[8] Speranza wrote.

In the very year of Oscar's birth his father began a disastrous association. It began innocently enough when a colleague referred to him the nineteen-year-old daughter of the professor of Medical Jurisprudence at Trinity College, Dublin. Mary Josephine Travers was suffering from inflammation of the ear which seemed likely to leave her permanently deaf. Wilde cured her and accepted no payment. Instead he began taking an interest in her education, and he and Speranza began inviting her to dinner and including her in family 'shilloos' and excursions.

In time Sir William's interest changed from disinterested philanthropy to frank indiscretion, and Mary began to entertain notions of ousting Speranza. To her chagrin, she discovered she was unable to do so, and in revenge began a campaign against her. After many private insults, she published an infamous pamphlet under Speranza's name in which she described how a fictitious Dr Quilp violated a young female patient. She then hired newsboys to sell the pamphlets and to display a placard advertising the names 'Sir William Wilde and Speranza'. A copy was delivered to Merrion Square, whereupon Speranza went to stay at Bray, where Sir William had built four houses, taking the children with her. Here the situation was repeated. Speranza confiscated copies of the pamphlet from a newsboy and Mary promptly took out a summons against her. In desperation Speranza wrote to Mary's father:

> Sir, you may not be aware of the disreputable conduct of your daughter at Bray where she consorts with all the low newspaper boys in the place, employing them to disseminate offensive placards in which my name is given, and also tracts in which she makes it appear that she has had an intrigue with Sir William Wilde. If she chooses to disgrace herself, it is not my affair, but as her object in insulting me is in the hope of extorting money for which she has several times applied to Sir William Wilde with threats of more annoyance if not given, I think it right to inform you, as no threat of additional insult shall ever extort money from our hands. The wages of disgrace she has so basely treated for and demanded shall never be given her.[9]

A few weeks later Mary ransacked her father's drawers and found the letter. Realizing that Speranza had played into her hands she served a writ on her claiming £2,000 damages for libel. Under the law as it stood, Sir William was automatically responsible in law for his wife's torts and was thus technically co-respondent.

The trial proved disastrous. Nobody believed Mary's claim that Sir William had chloroformed and then raped her, particularly since she had continued to see him. What weakened the Wildes' position was that Sir William failed to appear in court to deny the charges, which tended to suggest that he had enjoyed a guilty association with a compliant female patient. Finally the verdict went against the Wildes. The damages awarded to Mary were one farthing; but the entire costs of the action, amounting to some £2,000, were to be borne by Sir William. He had reached the peak of his career in 1864 when he was knighted, but his reputation was severely damaged by the affair and after his trial he largely retired from public life.

In a sense Speranza was the innocent victim of the court case; yet it would appear that she was responsible for not settling out of court. The whole family suffered as a result of the decision to see the thing out in a full trial. That fighting spirit set a dangerous precedent for the future. Oscar and his wife were one day to stand an even greater test; but Speranza's future daughter-in-law was an altogether gentler spirit who could not comfort herself by posing as a magnificent tragedy queen.

In the spring of 1867, while on a visit to Edgeworthstown, where her uncle, the Reverend William Noble, was rector, Oscar's sister Isola died. The family was inconsolable. To Lady Wilde, who had suffered greatly from the Mary Travers affair, it was a bitter sorrow. Oscar was deeply affected, and almost a decade later wrote a poem in five stanzas to her memory, called 'Requiescat'. At his death his friends found in his possession a little envelope, decorated with mourning symbols, labelled 'My Isola's Hair'.

A further tragedy overtook Sir William Wilde in November 1871. His two illegitimate daughters, Emily and Mary, then aged twenty-four and twenty-two respectively, went to a ball at Drumaconnor, County Monaghan. It was a cold night, with snow on the ground, and a fire burned brightly on the hearth. The two girls were among the last remaining guests, when their host asked Emily to take a turn about the floor with him. As they danced her whirling skirt brushed the grate and burst into flames. Mary, seeing the danger, rushed to her aid and her dress was also enveloped by fire. Their host got them out of the house and rolled them in the snow but though his prompt action extinguished the flames they were too badly burned to survive. Yeats' father described the tragedy in a letter. 'After all was over, even to the funeral, Sir William came down and old Mrs Hime told me his groans could be heard by people outside the house. There is a tragedy all the more intense, because it had to be buried in silence. It is not allowed to give sorrow words.'[10] They were buried together in Drumsnatt churchyard and their tombstone was inscribed

In Memory of Two Loving and Loved Sisters, Emily Wilde aged 24 and Mary Wilde aged 22 who lost their lives by accident in this parish November 10, 1871. 'They were lovely and pleasant in their lives and in their death they were not divided.' II Samuel I, v.23.

Sir William, already a broken man from the Travers affair and the death of Isola, was stunned by this terrible event, which marked the beginning of a long decline in his physical powers. He was now rarely to be seen in Merrion Square, and spent most of his time at Moytura House, the villa he had built for himself near Lough Corrib, or at Ilaunroe, in Connemara, where he had a fishing lodge. His son, Henry Wilson, was now carrying on the medical practice virtually single-handed while Sir William passed his days in academic research. Early in 1876 he began to grow visibly frailer, though without any organic complaint. In March he took to his bed, where he remained for six weeks, finally reaching a state of near unconsciousness. On 19 April he died peacefully. Oscar later described his father's last days and his mother's conduct at that time:

She was a wonderful woman, and such a feeling as vulgar jealousy could take no hold on her. She was well aware of my father's constant infidelities, but simply ignored them. Before my father died in 1876, he lay ill in bed for many days. And every morning a woman dressed in black and closely veiled used to come to our house in Merrion Square, and unhindered by my mother, or anyone else, used to walk straight upstairs to Sir William's bedroom and sit down at the head of his bed and so sit there all day, without ever speaking a word or once raising her veil. She took no notice of anybody in the room, and nobody paid any attention to her. Not one woman in a thousand would have tolerated her presence, but my mother allowed it, because she knew that my father loved the woman and felt that it must be a joy and comfort to have her there by his dying bed. And I am sure that she did right not to grudge that last happiness to a man who was about to die, and I am sure that my father understood her indifference, understood that it was not because she did not love him that she permitted her rival's presence, but because she loved him very much, and died with his heart full of gratitude and affection for her.[11]

Despite the scandals in his family history, Oscar's childhood had been a happy one. He loved and revered both his parents and his respect for them was in no way lessened by the Travers affair. They were generous to a fault and incapable of cowardly conduct. Both these characteristics emerged strongly in his own personality. At the age of eleven he joined his brother Willie as a boarder at Portora Royal School, Enniskillen. Willie, at least initially, was regarded as the better scholar. In due course both boys proceeded to Trinity College, Dublin. At the end of his third year Oscar won the Berkeley Gold Medal for Greek, the highest award at Trinity for Classics, and finally, in June 1874, a demy scholarship in Classics worth £95 a year at Magdalen College, Oxford. After matriculating in October 1874 he went into residence at Oxford. 'I was the happiest man in the world when I entered Magdalen for the first time'[12] he recalled later.

Sir William's death left the Wilde family considerably worse off than they had anticipated. Even allowing for the reduction in his income due to his withdrawal from active medical practice he had been able to count on £3,000 a year. Unknown to Speranza, he had been supplementing this from capital for years, and his entire estate was worth no more than about £7,000. He had made a recent withdrawal of £1,000, which Speranza was unable to account for at all, perhaps to take care of the mother of Emily and Mary.

Under their father's will, Willie inherited the house in Merrion Square and Oscar received four houses built by his father in Esplanade Terrace, Bray and shared the fishing lodge at Ilaunroe with his half-brother, Henry Wilson; but Lady Wilde's jointure was inadequately secured on Moytura House. She knew that her husband had intended her to enjoy the interest on her capital sum of £2,500, which had been used for the purchase of the house; he had not foreseen that it would be her sole means of support. Not one of the properties was free from mortgage. Speranza's financial situation was now critical. Willie was obliged to sell 1 Merrion Square. Fortunately, Henry Wilson bought it from him for £2,500 and allowed Speranza and Willie to stay on there, though Speranza calculated that it would cost at least £500 a year to keep up the house. After the outstanding mortgage had been paid off Willie was left with £1,500.

Oscar's position was rather better than that of Speranza and Willie, though he complained to his mother that a suitable marriage to a rich woman might be the way out of his difficulties. Speranza was not sympathetic. She objected violently to the notion of his throwing away the chance of a fellowship by rushing into matrimony, and his tales of poverty did not impress her. She pointed out that he had ample cash to tide him over till the spring when he could sell his houses at Bray, which would fetch £3,000.

In the event, the sale of Oscar's houses brought him considerably less than he had expected. Disputes about the contracts resulted in a lawsuit and although the court found for Oscar he had to pay the costs, so that when the mortgage had been discharged very little remained. As for Ilaunroe, the situation was even more complicated. In 1877 Henry Wilson caught a chill while out riding. Pneumonia set in and he died, aged only thirty-nine. Oscar was grieved at his death and unpleasantly surprised by his will. He and Willie had supposed themselves to be Henry's heirs, but he had left £8,000 to his father's hospital, £2,000 to Willie and £100 to Oscar on condition of his remaining a Protestant. Even the half share in Ilaunroe which ought to have reverted automatically to Oscar was to be forfeited if he embraced the Roman Catholic faith within five years. A further problem arising out of Henry Wilson's death was that the house in Merrion Square would now have to be put on the market. An account, by an acquaintance of Speranza, of the last hours in Merrion Square has survived:

> There were two strange men . . . sitting in the hall, and I heard from the weeping servant that they were 'men in possession'. I felt so sorry for poor Lady Wilde and hurried upstairs to the drawing-room where I knew I should find her. Speranza was there indeed, but seemed not in the least troubled by the state of affairs in the house. I found her lying on the sofa reading the *Prometheus Vinctus* of Aeschylus, from which she began to declaim passages to me, with exalted enthusiasm. She would not let me slip in a word of condolence, but seemed very anxious that I should share her entire admiration for the beauties of the Greek tragedian which she was reciting. [13]

Despite Oscar's careless attitude towards authority his career at

Oxford was nothing short of brilliant. He not only attained the distinction of a first in the final 'Greats' examination but also took the Newdigate Prize with his poem 'Ravenna', inspired by a recent visit to Italy. Though he was pleased with his achievement, his pleasure was diminished by the fact that his father had not lived to see it. He felt that God had dealt very hardly with them in the matter. 'I have not sufficient faith in Providence to believe it is all for the best − I know it is not,'[14] he wrote to his friend William Ward. To Ward he also wrote 'The dons are "astonied" beyond words − the Bad Boy doing so well in the end!'[15]

Even at Oxford Oscar attracted a vast amount of attention. He wore his hair longer than other undergraduates. His clothes were modish. The chequered patterns of his suits were larger than those of other men and he wore his hat at a jauntier angle. Though he devoted himself to literature and cultural pursuits, he adopted a careless pose which often deceived those who did not know him thoroughly. He was large, pale, and languid looking; yet when he applied himself to sporting pursuits he enjoyed a surprising degree of success. Any assailant who attacked him was likely to find himself at a disadvantage, for the aesthetic pose could disappear in an instant, revealing physical strength that was prodigious. His hair, though worn long, was always immaculately groomed, and he had a degree of self-assurance remarkable for his years.

His friend and biographer, Robert Sherard, contrasted certain aspects of Oscar's character with those of his mother. He felt that she possessed a trait best described by the German word, *schwaermerisch*.

This adjective describes a state of gushing exaltation, a somewhat too ready enthusiasm, a capacity for discovering romance in what is trite and commonplace. The word conveys mild and tolerant censure, and generally suggests that the person to whom it is applied is too much taken up in daydreams to give much attention to orderliness and the other domestic virtues . . .

There was nothing of the *Schwaermer* in Oscar's composition. He had no penchant for enthusiasm, exaltation he never displayed; and though as a writer he enrolled himself under that *drapeau romantique des jeunes guerriers* of which Théophile Gautier speaks, as a man of the world he avoided romance. He was for precision, for the absolute, for rule and proof. He was at one and the same time a perfect grammarian and an excellent logician. And that, in spite of the restraint of his reason, he gave way to promptings so illogical as those that led to his catastrophe shows that at times, and under certain conditions, his reason failed him.[16]

Not long after leaving Oxford, Oscar moved into rooms in Thames House, Salisbury Street, London, with his friend the artist Frank Miles. Miles, who was two years older than Oscar, had homosexual tendencies, but there is no suggestion of any such relationship between the two men. Such notions seemed distinctly abhorrent to Oscar at the time, and although he seems to have acknowledged the right to personal choice, he believed firmly in discretion. In August 1876 he wrote to his friend William Ward that he had seen a mutual friend in a private box at the theatre with a choirboy. 'I wonder what young Ward is doing with him. Myself I believe Todd is extremely moral and only mentally spoons with the boy, but I think he is foolish to go about with one, if he *is* bringing this boy about with him.'[17]

Once established in London, Oscar began to entertain in style. Laura Troubridge, who later married Constance's cousin Adrian Hope, 'fell awfully in love with him, thought him quite delightful'.[18] In her diary she described a visit to his rooms: 'Met Tardy, and went together to tea at Oscar Wilde's – great fun, lots of vague "intense" men, such duffers, who amused us awfully. The room was a mass of white lilies, photos of Mrs Langtry, peacock-feather screens and coloured pots, pictures of various merit.'[19] Oscar was well known for his devotion to certain famous actresses of the day; Lillie Langtry, Ellen Terry and Sarah Bernhardt, all of whom found him charming, and to whom he dedicated poems.

In the summer of 1880, Miles, who had substantial private means, commissioned the architect E. W. Godwin to design a house for him at 1 Tite Street, Chelsea. Here Wilde joined him. As yet he had very little regular income, and was experiencing some difficulty in the letting of his Irish property.

Such was Oscar's situation when Constance met him in Dublin; brilliant, bohemian, friend of actresses; without adequate financial resources, and with a closet full of family skeletons. It would appear that her family, though not positively rejecting him as a suitor, wanted to see some evidence that he could provide for Constance, and that their feelings for each other would stand the test of separation. They were now, so to speak, on probation.

3

Loved by a Poet

Happy girl! Loved by a Poet!

W. S. Gilbert: *Patience*

In the months that followed, Oscar called on Constance as often as propriety and his various commitments permitted. Her grandfather liked him, and always enjoyed his visits, but was adamant that he must establish himself before any formal arrangement for Constance's future could be made. She was, after all, a beautiful and accomplished girl with no shortage of suitors. Indeed, it is said that over the next two years she received offers of marriage from three eligible men, all of whom she rejected. She was determined to marry for love and romance, and not for money. Oscar, too, found the notion of a marriage of convenience abhorrent, and found it absolutely necessary to arrange his affairs on a firm financial basis before making a formal proposal.

Oscar was now one of the established leaders of the Aesthetic Movement, and increasing publicity attached to all his activities. As an undergraduate he had attended a fancy-dress ball dressed as Prince Rupert, in a braid-edged black velvet coat, knee breeches, silk shirt and buckle shoes. This was such a triumph that he later adopted the costume for soirées in London, thereby drawing considerable attention to himself. Two plays had already been performed in London in which the leading character was a burlesque of Wilde. In *Where's the Cat?* by James Albery, the character of Scott Ramsey was based on Wilde. The play had opened in 1880 at the Criterion Theatre, with Herbert Beerbohm Tree playing Scott Ramsey. In February 1881 Tree again took the part of Wilde, thinly disguised as Lambert Streyke in *The Colonel* at the Prince of Wales's. The author of this play was Frank Burnand, editor of *Punch*, which now began to satirize Oscar regularly; and when

Gilbert and Sullivan's *Patience* opened in London on 23 April 1881, the characters of Archibald Grosvenor and Reginald Bunthorne each portrayed some of Oscar's eccentricities. Oscar took it all with typical good humour, and went to see a performance at the express invitation of Richard D'Oyly Carte. According to the latter, the Aesthetic Movement was a vehicle for

> the outpourings of a clique of professors of ultra-refinement, who preach the gospel of morbid languor and sickly sensuousness, which is half real and half affected by its high priests for the purpose of gaining social notoriety. Generally speaking the new school is distinguished by an eccentricity of taste tending to an unhealthy admiration for exhaustion, corruption and decay. [1]

Patience was a runaway success, and toured the provinces after more than a year in London. It also created a sensation in America and Australia.

People could no longer ignore Oscar Wilde. On 2 July 1881 the *Athenaeum* advertised the first publication of his *Poems*, parchment-bound and printed on Dutch handmade paper. Most of the poems had already appeared in periodicals and journals, including *The World*, edited by Edmund Yates, who had a high opinion of his work. Oscar had had to bear the cost of publishing his book himself, but it went through four editions in as many weeks, and consequently proved highly profitable. An American edition followed within a matter of weeks and prompted the reviewer of the *New York Times* to call for an amnesty in the 'persecution' of Wilde by the Press. On 7 December the *New York Times* carried an article under the headline 'Oscar Wilde at Oxford' which described how Oscar had been invited by the Library Committee of the Oxford Union to present a copy of his book to them. When the usual motion for acceptance was brought before the House, there was 'great opposition, based on everything except argument'. The objection, voiced by an undergraduate called Oliver Elton, was that they were, for the most part, 'not by the putative father at all, but by a number of better-known and more deservedly reputed authors'. The motion to accept the book was defeated by eight votes in a House of 268 members, and for the first time in the history of the Oxford Union the presentation copy was returned to the author.

If Constance felt alarm at reading such adverse notices, she need

Constance, aged about twenty-six

Oscar, aged thirty

not have worried, for they tended to enhance rather than damage Oscar's reputation. On 2 January 1882, her twenty-fourth birthday, he arrived in New York, where he was immediately surrounded by journalists. The object of the tour was to lecture on aesthetics, which Oscar described as the science of the beautiful; but he took an early opportunity of going to see *Patience*, dressed in the velvet outfit, with red silk handkerchief, which the audience expected of him. When Bunthorne walked on to the stage in identical costume, all eyes turned to Oscar's box. If he minded the burlesque, he gave no sign of it. 'Caricature is the tribute which mediocrity makes to genius,'[2] he remarked affably.

Oscar was, in fact, delighted with his reception, which was nothing short of princely. He described rooms decorated with lilies in his honour. They appointed him three secretaries, and a Negro 'slave' into the bargain. All these were to deal with the great volume of correspondence and army of callers with whom he was besieged. But though Oscar's tour was triumphant, it had its ups and downs. Richard D'Oyly Carte had seen Oscar's conquest of America as ideal publicity for *Patience*. 'Carte thought he had got hold of a popular fool. When he found that he was astride of a live animal instead of a wooden toy, he was taken aback,'[3] wrote Dion Boucicault, the Irish dramatist and actor. Boucicault was concerned at Oscar's lack of business acumen.

> I do wish I could make him less Sybarite – less Epicurean. He said this morning 'Let me gather the golden fruits of America that I may spend a winter in Italy and a summer in Greece amidst beautiful things.' Oh dear – if he would only spend the money and the time amongst six-per-cent bonds! I think I told him so, but he thinks I take 'a painful view of life'.[4]

When Oscar lectured in Boston, sixty Harvard graduates in velvet jackets and knee breeches filled the front rows. Evidently Oscar had got wind of their plans, and made them all look foolish by appearing in conventional evening dress. At his next lecture, in New Haven, two hundred Yale undergraduates arrived with red neckties and sunflowers; but by now the Press was tiring of college pranks and took little notice. Oscar remained, however, acutely aware of the effect of his clothes on his audiences, and when he found in Cincinnati how disappointed his audience was that he had not worn knee breeches he responded by ordering quantities of extra clothes: silk stockings, tight velvet doublets with large flowered sleeves, little cambric ruffs, and so on. In Montreal from his hotel suite he could see his name on the placards six feet high.

Financially Oscar's American tour was a great success. He returned to England at the end of December 1882, having ended what he regarded as the first period of his life. Dion Boucicault had expressed the opinion that Oscar 'might make a fair income . . . if he would reduce his hair and take his legs out of the last century'.[5] Oscar now set off for three months in Paris where, perhaps regrettably, he permanently discarded those knee breeches that had suited him so well. Those long locks which the ladies of America had coveted were now cropped and curled in the manner of a bust of Nero in the Louvre. His new style of attire was strictly à la mode. He reported to Robert Sherard that nobody recognized him, that everyone was amazed by his Neronian coiffure, which they said made him look younger.

Not everyone approved of his new image. Laura Troubridge, who had abandoned her earlier naïve adulation and whose comments about Oscar and his family were henceforth always acid, wrote in her diary: 'Went to a tea-party at Cressie's [Cresswell Cresswell, a family friend] to meet the great Oscar Wilde. He is grown enormously fat, with a huge face and tight curls all over his head – not at all the aesthetic he used to look. He was very amusing and talked cleverly, but it is all monologue and not conversation. He is vulgar, I think, and lolls about in, I suppose, poetic attitudes with crumpled shirt cuffs turned back over his coat sleeves!'[6] Constance and her Irish relatives did not share this view of him, considering him much improved in appearance.

During Oscar's absence from England, Constance had family troubles on her mind. Despite his great age, her grandfather had continued to travel abroad each year to the fashionable watering places of Europe. Usually Aunt Emily went with him. In the autumn of 1882, while on holiday at Spa, in Belgium, he had an attack of congestion of the liver. It is not known whether or not Constance had accompanied her grandfather. Foreign travel was regarded as part of the education of any lady or gentleman, and opportunities for visiting Europe would no doubt have been seized upon whenever they presented themselves.

In the same year Constance's great-uncle, Lord Hemphill, made a visit to England and called on Speranza, who by now had given up the house in Merrion Square and was living with Willie in Park Street, Mayfair. He had obtained her address from Constance, whom he praised immensely. Speranza thought the visit looked encouraging, and was tempted to tell him that she would like Constance for a daughter-in-law, but in the end she did not do so. It would seem that Oscar's fame impressed him, for he remarked that Oscar was quite a celebrity.

These polite exchanges of family courtesies were all very well in their way but they did not succeed in bringing matters to a head. Oscar was well on the way to achieving that position in society which they had all felt would be necessary to enable the couple to entertain a serious courtship. At the same time, he was a long way away and daily surrounded by wealthy and attractive women who were competing for his favour. What Constance needed now was some way of meeting Oscar and re-establishing their earlier relationship.

In October 1883 Constance's grandfather, who had never fully recovered from his illness, suffered a relapse and went into a sharp decline. He had to be kept as quiet as possible, and the house at 100 Lancaster Gate became as silent as the grave. Constance closed the lid of her piano, packed her things and went to stay with Mama Mary in Dublin. On 21 November she learned that Oscar was coming to Dublin for a few days to give a couple of lectures at the Gaiety Theatre, and would be in town that very evening. The Hemphills, eager to advance Constance's cause, left a note at Oscar's hotel, the Shelbourne, inviting him to call. He responded immediately, and although Constance noticed that nervousness in the presence of her relatives made him much more affected, they found him generally most agreeable. Next day Constance went with a family party to hear him lecture on 'The House Beautiful'; they were all delighted with him. They brought Oscar back to tea, and afterwards joined him in his box at the Gaiety for a comic opera, *The Merry Duchess*. 'Personal Impressions of America' for which Constance took a two-shilling seat on 23 November seemed to her less interesting than Oscar's previous lecture – perhaps because she already entertained hopes of becoming mistress of his own House Beautiful. 'Stanhope has started on a new tack and chaffs my life out of me about O. W., such stupid nonsense',[7] she confided to Otho.

Only three days later Constance wrote again to Otho:

37

Prepare yourself for an astounding piece of news! I am engaged to Oscar Wilde and perfectly and insanely happy. I am sure you will be glad because you like him, and I want you now to do what has hitherto been my part for you, and make it all right. Grandpapa will, I know, be nice, as he is always so pleased to see Oscar. The only one I am afraid of is Aunt Emily . . . Now that he is gone, I am so dreadfully nervous over my family, they are so cold and practical. Everyone in this house is quite charmed, especially Mama Mary who considers me very lucky. Mind you write to me soon, dear old boy, and congratulate me. I am longing to know how you will all take it. I won't stand opposition, so I hope they won't try it.[8]

Otho duly responded, in a letter to Oscar, 'I am pleased indeed: I am sure that for my own part I welcome you as a new brother . . . if Constance makes as good a wife as she has been a good sister to me your happiness is certain; she is staunch and true.'[9] Speranza, who was genuinely delighted, wrote to Oscar praising his constancy of feeling, and expressing the hope that he would take a small house in London, which the families could furnish, and live the literary life there. Constance, she felt, could be taught to correct proofs, and Oscar himself could eventually go into Parliament.

To his friend Lillie Langtry Oscar wrote:

I am going to be married to a beautiful girl called Constance Lloyd, a grave, slight, violet-eyed little Artemis, with great coils of heavy brown hair which make her flower-like head droop like a blossom, and wonderful ivory hands which draw music from the piano so sweet that the birds stop singing to listen to her. We are to be married in April. I hope so much that you will be over then. I am so anxious for you to know and to like her.

I am hard at work lecturing and getting rich, though it is horrid being so much away from her, but we telegraph to each other twice a day, and I rush back suddenly from the uttermost parts of the earth to see her for an hour, and do all the foolish things that wise lovers do.[10]

Constance, too, found Oscar's absences irksome, and on 21 December 1883 wrote to Otho's fiancée, Nellie Hutchinson, 'I am with Oscar when he is in town, and I am too miserable to do anything while he is away. He and I are going to Norwood to lunch today as he lectures at the Crystal Palace, and after that he has a week's holiday, which will be much joy for me.'[11]

During this week's holiday Oscar's great friend the artist James McNeill Whistler gave a lunch to two newly engaged couples; Oscar and Constance, described in *The World* as 'the lady whom he has chosen to be the chatelaine of the House Beautiful',[12] and Viscount Garmoyle and his 'fairy queen', otherwise actress Emily Fortescue. Garmoyle never did marry his fairy queen. The engagement was broken off, leaving her richer by the £10,000 awarded to her in a breach of promise action.

There were now a number of business arrangements to be sorted out, including the important question of Constance's marriage settlement. It has often been said that Oscar's motive in marrying Constance was not love at all, but hard cash. Constance was frequently described as old John Lloyd's heiress, but this is a gross simplification of the true situation. Under the terms of John Lloyd's will, which was dated 20 February 1880, his daughters Emily, Caroline and Louisa were to have certain personal effects, such as silverware, pictures and furniture, and Otho was to receive all his prize books and such classical and mathematical books as he cared to select. All the remainder of his property was to be sold. The money raised was to be divided into four and invested, a quarter for each of the three daughters and the remaining quarter divided equally between Otho and Constance. Each beneficiary would receive the income from the separate investments. There was therefore never any question of a capital bequest for Constance. When the will was eventually proved, the estate stood at £92,392 4s. 1d, of which Constance's share was one eighth of the income.

All the same, by the custom of the day Constance was in need of some form of marriage settlement. What John Lloyd arranged, therefore, was the transfer of £5,000 to a trust fund, so that the trustees could advance to Oscar and Constance the interest on the capital, thus affording them a secure annual income. The capital sum would be deducted from Constance's ultimate share from her grandfather's will. Oscar and Constance were signatories to the codicil to her grandfather's will in which these arrangements were made on 10 January 1884.

On 29 April Constance saw her grandfather's solicitors again, this time accompanied by Otho. On this occasion, since each was about to be married, and neither stood to gain any capital sum, their grandfather arranged an advance of £500 to each of them, to be paid into the Union Bank of London. This formed Constance's so-called dowry, which she and Oscar proposed to use for the purpose of purchasing the lease of their marital home.

Oscar was commonly reputed to have been waiting on John Lloyd's death in order to get his hands on Constance's inheritance. Willie Wilde was also reported as saying 'Old Lloyd was dying but the news of the marriage revived him and he took on a new lease of life.'[13] It is clear, however, from the foregoing, and from Oscar's participation in the legal agreement, that he could never have had any such expectations. Since Constance's grandfather died, moreover, within seven weeks of the marriage, both these rumours were demonstrably untrue.

Constance was very comfortably circumstanced, it is true, and her income was secure. Her means were not, however, adequate to meet the needs of a young couple determined to lead a life of elegance and style, to entertain and generally cut a dash in society. Her income has to be looked at in relation to the lifestyle of a man who could command £200 for an hour's lecture, as Oscar had in America, and who generally spent money as fast as he came by it. Oscar had the most eligible women on both sides of the Atlantic at his feet. Had money been his object, he could have done much better by marrying elsewhere.

Given that the common belief that Oscar married Constance for her money is therefore false, and that Oscar could have had his choice of many ladies, rich, beautiful and intelligent, it is natural to ask why in fact he chose to marry Constance. The fact is that, quite simply, he fell in love with her. She was a very lovely young woman, exceedingly gentle in disposition, and possessed of an engaging eagerness to please. She had a naïve belief in the essential goodness of human nature, she was fond of those with whom she came in contact, and she shared with Oscar a love of beauty and simplicity of form. Her high intelligence and deep knowledge of art and literature made her an ideal companion at theatres, art galleries and social gatherings, yet she combined this with a clinging trust in Oscar which was very endearing. Despite her simple charm there were considerable strengths in her character, and she was capable of exceptional loyalty. She was also in every sense Oscar's true disciple, a characteristic which was, perhaps, essential to him. Oscar was much in sympathy with the Pre-Raphaelite artists, many of whom seemed to have a subconscious urge to instruct and reform the women of their choice. It was unthinkable that Oscar, with his notions of the ideal and the beautiful, could have chosen to marry a prostitute or shop assistant, like some of the Pre-Raphaelites; the notion of saving a 'fallen woman' had no appeal for him. Yet he, like them, needed a didactic role, and Constance, with her eagerness to learn and her lively intellect, was the ideal subject. Asked why he fell in love with her, Oscar once said, 'She never speaks, and I am always wondering what her thoughts are like.'[14]

Constance's letters to Oscar indicate quite clearly how desperately she was in love with him. In those early days she addressed him as 'My darling Love' and 'My Own Darling Oscar'. As far as any past amours were concerned, she said, 'Let the past be buried; it does not belong to me'.[15] 'I have no power to do anything but just love you,' she wrote, 'my whole life is yours to do as you will with . . . Do believe that I do love you most passionately with all the strength of my heart and mind.'[16] As to their future together, 'When I have you for my husband, I will hold you fast with chains of love and devotion so that you shall never leave me, or love anyone as long as I can love and comfort.'[17] When he was away she read his letters over and over again until she knew them by heart. They made her 'yet more mad to see you and feel once again that you are mine, and that it is not a dream but a living reality that you love me'.[18] When he left her she wrote, 'I wish you would not take all my sleep away with you.'[19]

Meanwhile, news of the engagement was spreading. Oscar's friend, Waldo Story, heard rumours of the impending marriage and wrote to Oscar for confirmation. On 22 January 1884 Oscar replied from Sheffield, where he was lecturing:

Yes! my dear Waldino, yes! Amazing of course — that was necessary.

Naturally I did not write — the winds carry tidings over the Apennines better than the 2½d. post: of course it accounts for the splendid sunsets about which science was so puzzled . . . Well, we are to be married in April, as you were, and then go to Paris, and perhaps to Rome — what do you think? Will Rome be nice in May? I mean, will you and Mrs Waldo be there, and the Pope, and the Peruginos? . . .

Her name is Constance and she is quite young, very grave, and mystical, with wonderful eyes, and dark brown coils of hair: quite perfect except that she does not think Jimmy [Whistler] the only painter that ever really existed: she would like to bring Titian or somebody in by the back door: however, she knows I am the greatest poet, so in literature she is all right: and I have explained to her that you are the greatest sculptor: art instruction cannot go further.

We are, of course, desperately in love. I have been obliged to be away nearly all the time since our engagement, civilising the provinces by my remarkable lectures, but we telegraph to each other twice a day, and the telegraph clerks have become quite romantic in consequence. I hand in my messages, however, very sternly, and try to look as if 'love' was a cryptograph for 'buy Grand Trunks' and 'darling' a cypher for 'sell out at par'. I am sure it succeeds.[20]

Constance by this time was deep in her wedding arrangements, and preparing her trousseau. Her grandfather, by now in his eighty-fifth year, was very frail, and for this reason it was decided to keep the wedding fairly simple. Even so, six of her cousins were to be bridesmaids, and much care was lavished on the choice of the dresses. Speranza hurried over to Messrs Jay of Regent Street and ordered an outfit for the wedding, which they designed specially for her. Oscar's gifts to Constance included some beautiful lace, and an intricately worked silver girdle which she decided to wear on her wedding dress. The marriage was to be by special licence, which the upper classes tended to prefer, as the business of having the banns read was considered somewhat undignified in Victorian England. Meanwhile, the couple had been looking round for a suitable house and on 30 March 1884 Constance was able to write to a friend, 'We have been looking at a house in Tite Street, which I think we are likely to take.'[21]

On 29 May 1884 at 2.30 p.m. Constance and Oscar were married in St James's Church, Sussex Gardens, by the Reverend Walter Abbott. Witnesses were their respective mothers, Constance's great-uncle, Lord Hemphill, and Oscar's brother Willie. Otho, who was due to be married on 10 June, appears not to have been present. The ceremony was widely reported in the Press, and much attention was paid to Constance's dress. Robert Sherard wrote:

The bride's rich creamy satin dress was of a delicate cowslip tint; the bodice, cut square and somewhat low in front, was finished with a high Medici collar; the ample sleeves were puffed; the skirt, made plain, was gathered by a silver girdle of beautiful workmanship, the gift of Mr Oscar Wilde; the veil of saffron-coloured Indian silk gauze was embroidered with pearls and worn in Marie Stuart fashion; a thick wreath of myrtle leaves crowned her frizzed hair; the dress was ornamented with clusters of myrtle leaves; the large bouquet had as much green in it as white.[22]

The *Irish Times* described the bridesmaids, who were dressed in two styles:

Four young ladies wore pale terra cotta surah skirts, round the bottom of which fans of printed nun's cloth in pale electric blue were set in knots of ribbon of pale flowerpot colour, deep yellow and sage green were placed at intervals heading the flounce. Over the skirts were worn bodices and tunics, looped up behind, of pale blue nun's cloth, with large chintz flowers printed over it; white hats with large leaves, cream lace and terra cotta feathers. Two children who closed the procession wore pale terra cotta surrah frocks, with canary coloured sashes; very short waists, and very large puffed sleeves; hats with canary and terra cotta feathers. The bridegroom looked less like George IV than usual as, though his hair was fully curled, the modern blue morning frock coat and grey trousers rather took away from the character. A number of ladies and gentlemen well known in literary and artistic circles were present and friends of the two families. With the exception of one or two dresses of startling brilliancy – flame coloured plush is a vivid colour on a May afternoon – the ladies' toilettes were exceedingly subdued, in no way differing from the ordinary everyday dresses for morning wear. Lady Wilde wore grey satin, trimmed with chenille fringe; a high-crowned hat, broad leaf, turned up at one side, trimmed with grey velvet and a luxuriant plume of ostrich feathers. The bride's bouquet and also the bridesmaids' were of lilies and maidenhair fern.[23]

Robert Sherard was convinced that Oscar had designed the whole thing himself, and that it boded ill for their marriage. 'No woman who was not blindly convinced of the superiority of her bridegroom's taste would have consented to such a masquerade. It may have occurred to some of the onlookers that a union so initiated could not contain the elements of happiness. Where the woman is entirely hypnotised and subjugated her marriage is not often a happy one for her.'[24] No doubt Oscar was indeed consulted; but though Constance was wildly in love with her husband, she had a will of her own in such matters and, as her son Vyvyan later pointed out, would never have submitted to that kind of dictatorship.

There was one notable absentee from the ceremony: Oscar's great friend Jimmy Whistler. A telegram was handed in at the church door which read: 'From Whistler, Chelsea, to Oscar Wilde, St James's Church, Sussex Gardens: Fear I may not be able to reach you in time for the ceremony – Don't wait.'[25]

After the ceremony a small reception was held at 100 Lancaster Gate. The top layer of the cake, which was designed by Messrs Bolland and Sons of Chester, was put aside for a party which Aunt Carrie Kirkes proposed to give in honour of Otho and his bride, Nellie Hutchinson, on their return from honeymoon. Despite its decorations of real flowers, Constance disliked the cake. 'I think it is disgusting stuff,'[26] she said. After the wedding breakfast Constance changed into a 'travelling dress of rich mahogany-coloured voile, trimmed with marabout of the same shade, and large hat to match'.[27] At four o'clock Giles, the Lloyd family coachman, drove the couple to Charing Cross Station, where their friends assembled to see them off on the boat-train for Paris, via Dover and Calais. For better or worse, Constance was now Mrs Oscar Wilde.

4

Honeymoon

But surely it is something to have been
The best beloved for a little while.
'Apologia'

The couple began their honeymoon in Paris, where they booked into the Hotel Wagram in the Rue de Rivoli. Their suite of three rooms, for which they paid twenty francs a day, was on the third floor, and afforded them a splendid view of the gardens of the Tuileries.

No sooner had they arrived in Paris than they began to socialize. An early caller was Oscar's friend, Robert Harborough Sherard, great-grandson of the poet Wordsworth and an author in his own right. Sherard's father, the Reverend B. Sherard Kennedy, was believed to be a millionaire, but Robert, who did not get on with his father, had apparently repudiated the family fortune, as well as the name, and lived a frugal existence in a Parisian garret. Early in 1884 he published a volume of poems called *Whispers*, which he dedicated to Oscar. Intrigued by his romantic story and handsome young face — he was then twenty-three years old — Constance took to him immediately, and likened him to Chatterton, with whom he shared many characteristics. The attraction was mutual, and Sherard always spoke of Constance with affection.

Sometimes Oscar strolled about Paris with Sherard, while Constance busied herself with her letters. In later years Sherard recalled how Oscar extolled the joys of matrimony. Basically a rather shy young man, Sherard was rather embarrassed by Oscar's raptures about his marriage. 'We were passing through the Marché St Honoré at the time, and here he stopped and rifled a flower-stall of its loveliest blossoms and sent them, with a word of love on his card, to the bride whom he had quitted but a moment before.'[1]

Sherard was not the only person to publish Oscar's comments on matrimony. The *New York Times* found a place on its front page for the following:

Oscar Wilde, who was married last Tuesday to Miss Constance Lloyd, has written a silly and thoroughly characteristic letter to a friend, in which he says he has not been disappointed in married life. He feels confident of his ability to sustain its labours and anxieties, and sees an opportunity in his new relations of realising a poetical conception which he has long entertained. He says that Lord Beaconsfield taught the Peers of England a new style of oratory, and similarly he intends to set an example of the pervading influence of art in matrimony.[2]

Perhaps the *New York Times* was right to call the letter 'silly'. Yet the fact remains that Oscar was passionately in love with his bride, and found consummate happiness in his new married state. As for Constance, her joy was infinite. To her, marriage meant freedom; it meant freedom from the stuffy atmosphere of Lancaster Gate, freedom from Aunt Emily's sharp tongue, and most important of all, freedom to pursue her personal ideals of happiness side by side with the husband she worshipped. Oscar to the world at large was brilliant and compelling; but Oscar in love, in the intimate atmosphere of their own ménage, was marvellous beyond description. He was gentle, chivalrous and attentive. He adored his shy young bride with her radiant beauty and slim form; he was proud of her, took infinite interest in her clothes (a rare quality in a husband) and loved going with her to choose more. He was her ideal mentor in matters of culture and taste, her professor in the art of love. He was the centre of her universe, till death and no doubt beyond.

Oscar's boyish desire to show her off to his friends, his anxiety that they should like her, delighted Constance even when it made her nervous, and in the main she found his friends far less terrifying in the flesh than they had been in her imagination. One such friend was the 31-year-old sculptor John Donoghue, whom Oscar had 'discovered' in a Chicago attic in 1882 and who owed much of his subsequent success to Oscar's efforts to bring him to the attention of the public. Constance liked his handsome Roman face and blue Irish eyes, and greatly admired the simple bronze bas-relief of a nude boy playing a harp which he had sculpted for the annual Salon in Paris. Donoghue also produced a fine bronze bas-relief of the scene suggested by Wilde's early poem 'Requiescat', which he had written in memory of his sister Isola. Donoghue's subsequent history was sad. His magnum opus was a colossal winged statue called *The Spirit*, which he executed in Europe for the Chicago World's Fair of 1892 and shipped to Brooklyn. Unfortunately he ran into difficulties over the freight charges and could not raise the money to pay them, so that after some time in the dockyard at Brooklyn the statue was eventually dumped in the sea. This so unhinged the sculptor that he took to drink, and finally committed suicide by drowning in 1903.

Apart from Donoghue's work, the only items exhibited in the Salon that Constance thought worthy of notice were two paintings by Whistler, *Harmony in Grey and Green: Miss Cicely Alexander* and *Arrangement in Grey and Black, No.2: Thomas Carlyle*. She had seen and admired the latter as a print and was particularly interested in it because J. E. Boehm had based his life-sized statue of Carlyle for the Chelsea Embankment on this picture.

They went to see *Lili*, a light opera by Hervé, in which Anne Judic played the lead. But best of all they enjoyed Sarah Bernhardt's performance in *Macbeth* at the Théâtre Matin. Constance had decided views about the theatre and took an intelligent view of all that she saw. Later she was able to turn her powers of criticism to good account by writing reviews of current performances. Yet to visit the theatre in Oscar's company was a special privilege, for his understanding of stage techniques was exceptional and his intimate acquaintance with actors, managers and designers gave him an inside knowledge of all that went on.

On 4 June Constance gave her first dinner party. The guests were John Donoghue, the American artist John Singer Sargent, who was later their neighbour in Chelsea, the French novelist Paul Bourget, and a wealthy American friend of Whistler's called Henrietta Reubell. Bourget, who met her again three days later when they lunched at Sargent's home, took an immediate liking to Constance, of whom he said, *'J'aime cette femme – j'aime la femme annulée et tendre.'*[3] Miss Reubell, white-faced, red-haired, shrill-voiced like a parrot, was anything but beautiful. She had a salon in the Avenue Gabriel, had already entertained the couple to breakfast, and made up for her want of beauty by being good-natured and amusing. Constance's dresses generally caused a sensation in Paris, and one of

them so impressed Miss Reubell that she asked Constance to get
Mrs Nettleship, her dressmaker (who always made Ellen Terry's
stage costumes) to make her one exactly like it. Constance had no
option but to agree, though she privately felt the dress would be a
disaster for Miss Reubell. She seemed positively ancient to
Constance; she was thirty-five.

One of the first letters Constance received on her honeymoon
came from her new mother-in-law.

Dearest Constance,

You were a most charming little bride and Willie is going
to get you appointed Special Correspondent to one of the
leading weeklys [sic]. Miss Lloyd paid me a visit yesterday and
looked well and happy. We had a crowd all eager in enquiries
about the Bridal pair. Mrs Ashton Dilke was here. The *Queen*
has a nice account also the *Ladies' Pictorial*, and I got a Dutch
paper with a long account of the wedding. Your dress was
greatly admired. Miss Drake was at the church. She and Willie
are good friends but I see no further tendresse.

Your *first dinner* was very nice. I am glad you have begun
the social duties.[4]

The letter was signed 'La Madre devotissima', the form which
Speranza always used in her letters to Oscar.

It appears that the couple abandoned their tentative plan to go on
from Paris to Italy, spending a delightful week at Dieppe instead.
They arrived back in England on 24 June and were annoyed by the
treatment they received at the hands of the British customs officials.
Quite apart from rumaging through Constance's lovely clothes with
grubby hands they tried to make her pay duty for the silver fittings
of her dressing case. They also seized all the Continental paperback
editions of British authors that Oscar had bought, but had to return
them because they were not, after all, in copyright.

During their absence Oscar had learned that his old bachelor
quarters had been let, and had had to make hasty arrangements for
the removal of his chattels. Willie had been asked to find them
temporary accommodation, but London was crowded for the
Season, and there was virtually nothing available. In the end he had
taken rooms for them at the Brunswick, but at two guineas a night
this was scarcely suitable for their pocket. They accordingly went

and dined with Aunt Emily, explaining their difficulty and hoping to be asked to stay; but to their dismay she refused to take the hint. In the end Constance had no choice but to ask her outright, whereupon she compromised by saying they could stay for a few days until they could get lodgings. Aunt Emily had not approved of the marriage, and was now apparently determined to make them fend for themselves as best they could.

On the day after they got back from France, Constance and Oscar made up a theatre party with a Mme Gabrielli, who was currently much smitten with Willie. Constance was intrigued by the situation. 'It's a pity there is an ancient nonentity called Mr Gabrielli in the background somewhere,' she wrote to Otho. 'She sends Willie a horse every morning and they ride in the row together; she sends him wine, cigarettes, even *tonics*, I believe!'[5] She had also given Willie a bangle, of which he said, 'I wear it because it's the gift of the Gab.'[6]

On 18 July 1884 Constance's grandfather finally died peacefully at his home. The will was proved on 15 October by his nephew Horatio Lloyd, who was appointed executor/trustee, and by Aunt Emily. When all the legal business had been sorted out, Aunt Emily decided to give up the old home, and in 1886 moved to 20 Oxford Square, where she remained for the rest of her life.

Though she mourned her grandfather, Constance sensibly decided to carry on as normal. The night after he died she went ahead with her plan to accompany her new husband to the brilliantly successful opening of *Twelfth Night* at the Lyceum. 'Mr Oscar Wilde and his bride occupied two chairs close to the orchestra, the apostle of culture being greatly altered in appearance now that his ample locks are shorn and elaborately curled. Mrs Oscar Wilde was dressed in a charming gown of dark crimson and gold brocade, made with a Watteau back and large puffed sleeves,' reported the *Lady's Pictorial*. 'She wore a wide collar of falling lace, and her costume was altogether admirably suited to her picturesque and southern style of beauty.'[7] Ellen Terry, Rose Leclercq and Henry Irving starred in the performance, which was widely acclaimed.

The lease of the affordable house in Tite Street which the couple had identified in March had been secured with Constance's 'dowry' before the wedding, but it would be some time before it could be got ready. It is not clear whether the short tenure of Aunt Emily's hospitality or John Lloyd's sudden death precipitated the couple's removal from Lancaster Gate, but in a letter written the day after he died, Oscar gave his address as 7 Great College Street, Westminster. Soon after, he learned that his old bachelor quarters in 9 Charles Street, Grosvenor Square, were once more unexpectedly vacant. This meant that he and Constance were able to dispense permanently with Aunt Emily's grudging hospitality. Here they remained until they could move into Tite Street.

As a leader of the Aesthetic Movement and lecturer on 'The House Beautiful' Oscar was eager to put his theories into practice. It was only to be expected that his idea of a home would be something special. No doubt some of their friends expected Oscar to indulge his own tastes to the exclusion of Constance's. If so, they had failed to realize the extent to which their tastes coincided. True, Constance was a disciple; yet she had the supreme advantages of innate good taste and practical common sense.

Externally, the house at 16 Tite Street (now number thirty-four) was an unexceptional four-storey mid-terrace house with basement, but Oscar and Constance had elaborate plans for transforming it. Their first step was to engage the architect E. W. Godwin, who had designed The White House, Tite Street, for Jimmy Whistler, and Skeats House, Tite Street, for Frank Miles. 'Godwino' had lived with Oscar's friend Ellen Terry for some seven years and she had borne him two children. Initially the couple had been unable to marry because at the age of fifteen Ellen had married the artist G. F. Watts. Ellen's innocence at the time of her marriage had been total. Watts had kissed her, and in her ignorance she had assumed that she was now pregnant and obliged to marry. Though the marriage was a disaster from the outset, Watts refused to divorce her. In 1875 Godwin deserted Ellen Terry and married Beatrix Philip, daughter of the sculptor J. B. Philip, who is chiefly remembered for his frieze on the podium of the Albert Memorial. Besides being an architect of exceptional merit, Godwin was a leading authority on Shakespeare and designed theatrical costumes for all Henry Irving's productions at the Lyceum. He founded the Fine Arts Society and, like Oscar, was in the forefront of the Aesthetic Movement.

The couple's plans for their new home were not realized without difficulty. There were numerous meetings with Godwin on and off site, and copious correspondence passed between them. Whistler, too, was consulted about the decorations to the ground and first

'Speranza', Oscar's mother

Sir William Wilde, Oscar's father

St James's, Sussex Gardens, where Constance and Oscar were married

Constance and Cyril, about 1891

The House Beautiful

floor. Constance, besides joining in the planning at all stages, was wholly responsible for choosing the furniture and decorative theme for her own room. What made matters more difficult was that Oscar's lecture tours took him frequently out of London, so that Constance often had to assume day-to-day responsibility for the decisions that needed to be made. In the second half of 1884 he lectured in York, Bristol, Leeds and Edinburgh. In December 1884 he wrote to Constance from Edinburgh, where he lectured twice in the Queen Street Hall:

Dear and Beloved,
    Here am I, and you at the Antipodes. O execrable facts, that keep our lips from kissing, though our souls are one.
    What can I tell you by letter? Alas! nothing that I would tell you. The messages of the gods to each other travel not by pen and ink and indeed your bodily presence here would not make you more real: for I feel your fingers in my hair, and your cheek brushing mine. The air is full of the music of your voice, my soul and body seem no longer mine, but mingled in some sweet ecstasy with yours. I feel incomplete without you.

Ever and ever yours

Oscar[8]

Here I stay till Sunday.

A few days later he wrote to Godwin, 'The house *must* be a success: do just add the bloom of colour to it in curtains and cushions.'[9]

Despite Godwin's skill as an architect he had one major professional failing: a certain naïvety in his nature made him accept impracticably low estimates from the builders he employed. When disagreements arose, he tended to side with the builder rather than with the client. Oscar should have been alert to this tendency on account of the experience of his friend Jimmy Whistler, who had had to sell the White House in 1879 to avoid bankruptcy. The original contractor selected by Godwin to carry out the Wildes' alterations was a man called Green, who skimped some of the work, with the result that Oscar dismissed Green and declined to settle his account. Meanwhile he authorized Godwin to engage another contractor called Sharpe.

Green, the original contractor, reacted by serving Oscar with a writ claiming the amount outstanding on the first account. He also began seizing items of furniture as they arrived. Oscar and Constance were in near despair. Further unpleasant shocks were also in store for them. To their consternation, Sharpe's bills came to about £100 more than the original estimate. Sharpe had promised to keep his profit margin on the items for Constance's room at a modest level, but it now became apparent that he had made up for the deficiency by overcharging elsewhere. His charges were in the long run worse than Green's. The matter of Green's account looked as though it would end in a court battle, which was unfortunate, especially since Godwin, whose evidence was vital, had fallen seriously ill and required a lithotomy operation. In principle his supporting evidence was always available to Oscar, but it was difficult to see how he was ever to be got into the witness-box.

In the event, the matter was settled out of court, and the unfortunate Godwin, who died a few months later, did not have to appear. The whole business had, however, cost the couple about £250 more than they had expected.[10] This was Oscar's second unfortunate experience of litigation. It was not to be his last.

5

The House Beautiful

For you a House of Ivory,
(Roses are white in the rose bower!)

A narrow bed for me to lie,
(White, O white is the hemlock flower!)
'Chanson'

The beginning of 1885 saw the couple safely installed in their new home. There they celebrated Constance's twenty-seventh birthday together; but Oscar's lecturing engagements still led to irksome absences. On the 5th and 6th of January he lectured in Dublin, but though Constance would surely have welcomed the chance to see Mama Mary and the Hemphills, she was unable to accompany him. 'We have only just moved into our new house, and she is busy over embroideries and housemaids,'[1] Oscar explained. The Dublin lectures were not altogether successful. Prices were high, with boxes at a guinea, thirty shillings, and two guineas, and only about 500 people attended in consequence. The *Dublin University Review* commented, 'In spite of the fact that Mr Wilde, like the elephant Jumbo, with whose notoriety his popularity was contemporaneous, has ceased to attract the sympathy and the shillings of the public, we feel bound to express our belief of the talents of that gentleman, and our regret that they have not lately been more usefully employed.'[2] By now Oscar was becoming decidedly bored with lecturing, and would have been only too glad to give it up and spend his time at Tite Street with his wife if only he could have found some alternative form of employment.

The *Pall Mall Gazette* of 21 February contained Oscar's comments on Whistler's famous *Ten O'Clock Lecture*. 'That an artist will find beauty in ugliness, *le beau dans l'horrible*, is now a commonplace of the schools, the argot of the atelier, but I strongly

53

deny that charming people should be condemned to live with magenta ottomans and Albert blue curtains in their rooms in order that some painter may observe the side lights on the one and the values of the other,' Oscar wrote. Magenta and Albert blue were most noticeably absent from the house in Tite Street. Godwin's original specifications and some of his drawings have survived and these, together with the observations of people who visited the house and, later, the recollections of Vyvyan Wilde, give a very clear and accurate picture of Constance and Oscar's 'House Beautiful'. It was indeed strikingly different from other houses of the period. To appreciate fully the revolutionary nature of its design' it is necessary to understand that the traditional Victorian preference was for dark wood panelling and sombre colours.

The visitor's first glimpse of the interior of the House Beautiful revealed an entrance hall whose predominant effect was of startling lightness. The woodwork was white, there was a grey dado, and the staircase walls and ceilings were yellow. 'Very ordinary'[3] was the verdict of Constance's cousin, Adrian Hope; but then he and his fiancée, Laura Troubridge, were inclined to be hypercritical of all the Wildes' doings. Oscar's personal library was on the ground floor with windows on to Tite Street. Bookcases lined its yellow walls; besides the modern presentation copies from his literary friends, their contents reflected his preference for Greek and Latin literature. The pictures included a lovely Beardsley drawing of Mrs Patrick Campbell, and a cast of the *Hermes* of Praxiteles stood on a red column in the corner. Most evocative of all was the desk at which Oscar did most of his writing; this had once belonged to Carlyle, for whom he and Constance had a profound admiration.

To the rear was a dining-room with bow windows overlooking the garden. Its decorative theme was white blended with delicate tints of blue and yellow. For this room Godwin had designed a unique white suite and a sideboard which stood on a special raised platform. The chairs, in various Grecian styles, were also white, with white plush upholstery. 'Each chair is a sonnet in ivory,'[4] Oscar wrote of them. His ancestral silver and other items were displayed in a glass-fronted cabinet. But most ingenious innovation of all, and striking in its simplicity, was a white shelf at wainscot height, used for buffet-style entertaining. The great advantage of this arrangement, which left the central area free for guests to circulate, could only be appreciated by those accustomed to attending the traditional 'crushes', where the conventional disposition of central table laden with food led to overcrowding and discomfort.

The drawing-room on the first floor was pleasantly aspected, looking out over the gardens of the Victoria Hospital. Buttercup walls were the perfect foil for pictures: opposite the fireplace was a full-length painting of Oscar by the American artist Harper Pennington; and several of Whistler's Venetian studies, which he had presented to the couple as a wedding gift, and some drawings by Burne-Jones were arranged to form a frieze. Also prominently displayed above the fireplace was Donoghue's lovely bas-relief inspired by Oscar's poem 'Requiescat'. Two low triangular divans fitted into the corners on either side of the fireplace and there were more chairs and a small Chippendale table finished in white lacquer. Constance's painted grand piano occupied a place of honour, but the real *pièce de résistance* was the ceiling, designed by Whistler, which featured two gold dragons and had two real peacock's feathers let into it. The ceiling margin was of leather specially provided by Oscar.

At the rear was the smoking room, always rather dimly lit. A sordid view over a slum called Paradise Street had been cleverly concealed by a wooden grating based on a Cairo pattern. The décor here was altogether decidedly North African, with ottomans, beaded curtains and Moorish lanterns. Originally its walls were distempered green, with ceilings in a darker shade, but later on dark red and gold Lincrusta wallpaper was added.

Oscar's second-floor dressing-room, which doubled as a guest room, was very simply furnished. In contrast, Constance's bedroom on the same floor provided the key to her personal preferences. The door opened into an archway formed by a fitted wardrobe range on one side and a bookcase and knee-hole writing desk on the other. All these were painted white. They were perfect companions to the draperies, lace curtains and embroidered chair covers, all of which Constance, who was a skilled needlewoman, made herself. The curtains were of blue and white, and the counterpane was white silk embroidered in gold. Beside the bed with its soft, romantic drapes was a little collapsible wooden bookshelf reserved for her special books, including her much-loved volume of Keats. When she travelled she always took this bookshelf with her to house those books from which she felt she could not be parted.

The attic rooms on the floor above had been knocked into one, with vermilion woodwork and a rich dado of gold leaves on vermilion. A bathroom, too, had been added. Below stairs in the basement was the servants' domain. Marvellous baking smells of home-made bread and cakes emanated from the kitchen, which was located at the rear and connected by a service lift with the dining-room. The female staff occupied the large basement front bedroom and Arthur, the butler, slept in an alcove upstairs.

At precisely 10.45 p.m. on Friday 5 June 1885, Constance gave birth to their first child, a boy whom they decided to call Cyril, and whose christening mug soon joined his father's in the dining-room. Oscar reported to friends that Constance was making capital progress and was in excellent spirits. As for Cyril, he was pronounced a positive genius, for he already had a bridge to his nose. He was said to exercise his voice regularly in essentially Wagnerian style. Aunt Emily consented to be godmother, and their explorer friend Walter Harris, who probably had something to do with the Moorish influence on the smoking room décor, was godfather. He had led an exciting life, exploring many countries, and had lived for a time in Tangier, where he spoke Arabic and passed as a Moor. Once he had even risked death by making a pilgrimage to Mecca and entering the Kaaba. But the story that really brought a *frisson* of delight to his godson in later years was of a cannibal feast where he had unwittingly eaten human flesh, which he said was delicately flavoured, like a sucking pig.

The comments of Adrian Hope and Laura Troubridge about the arrival of Constance's baby were predictably scathing. Both felt that Cyril was rather to be pitied. 'Will it be swathed in artistic baby clothes? Sage green bibs and tuckers, I suppose, and a peacock blue robe,'[5] Laura wrote. Most friends were kinder, and genuine in their messages of congratulation. Among those who sent their congratulations was Edward Heron-Allen, a London solicitor who dabbled in Persian literature, scientific romances and asparagus culture. He had recently sent Oscar a copy of his book, *Violin-making*, and was said to be in love with Constance,[6] who of course had eyes for nobody but Oscar. Heron-Allen's interests also included astrology, and at Constance's express wish Oscar wrote and asked him to cast Cyril's horoscope. It would have been interesting to see his predictions for Cyril, and indeed for Constance and Oscar too, both of whom took astrology very seriously, but no record has survived.

After the successful outcome of her pregnancy, Constance was free to throw herself wholeheartedly into the role of society hostess. Her feelings in regard to this were slightly mixed. She had been taught from childhood how to run her household, deal with the servants and entertain guests as befitted any young woman of her social class, and she entered into the part she was now to play with enthusiasm and determination. For her own sake and that of her guests she wanted to be a success. Above all, she wanted to please Oscar, to live up to his expectations of her, and to make him proud of her. Guided by her knowledge of his tastes and opinions, she designed her costumes with care, for she knew that the clothes worn by Mrs Oscar Wilde were bound to make news. The fare for her guests was chosen and prepared with equal pains. Many London hostesses had more cash to lavish on entertaining, yet the Wildes' hospitality was something extra special. Constance's at-homes soon became a byword, and invitations were greatly prized.

Oscar always made a point of being at his wife's parties, and Speranza was also a frequent attender. Whistler, before he fell out with Oscar, was often there; other distinguished guests were John Singer Sargent, Sir William Richmond, Edward Burne-Jones and many of his fellow Pre-Raphaelites; Sarah Bernhardt, Ellen Terry, Lillie Langtry, Herbert Beerbohm Tree; Swinburne, Browning, Ruskin, Robert Sherard; Lady Sandford, Lady de Grey, John Bright, and Arthur Balfour.

Constance kept an autograph book with a cover which she made herself, in which she asked her guests to sign their names. Some of them also added messages. G. F. Watts, who had refused to divorce poor Ellen Terry, wrote, 'Our greatest happiness should be found in the happiness of others.'[7] Walter Crane wrote:

> From your book I take a leaf,
> By your leave to leave and take;
> Art is long if life be brief,
> Yet on this page my mark I'll make.[8]

Swinburne contributed his lines on childhood, George Meredith his poem 'Love Is Winged for Two'.[9] Yet quite the most apt and beautiful entry was from Oscar, who wrote the first verse of his poem 'To My Wife, with a Copy of My Poems':

I can write no stately poem
　　As a prelude to my lay;
From a poet to a poem
　　I would dare to say.

For if of these fallen petals
　　One to you seem fair,
Love will waft it till it settles
　　On your hair.

And when wind and winter harden
　　All the loveless land,
It will whisper of the garden,
　　You will understand. [10]

Outwardly Constance was a success as a hostess; yet she was always overshadowed by her husband, and if he was absent boredom sometimes crept in. Katherine Bradley and Edith Cooper summed this up in *Works and Days*: 'Received by Mrs Wilde in turquoise blue, white frills and amber stockings. The afternoon goes on in a dull fashion till Oscar enters. He wears a lilac shirt and heliotrope tie . . .' [11]

What Constance never quite mastered was the art of supreme self-assurance which would have enabled her to relax and enjoy herself with her guests. Always just below the surface was a lack of confidence, a hint of insecurity, a fear that she might fail to please. There was a degree of pathos in her desire to live up to her husband's ambitions for them. In marrying him she had, in a sense, shaken off conventionality, yet vestiges of it remained and left her vaguely ill at ease in Bohemia. Even her gaiety had a hint of sadness about it.

Of course, these areas of timidity in Constance's personality had a special appeal of their own, especially when combined with her beauty, charm and sincerity – she was much loved, and had a wide circle of friends who had the highest regard for her. Her hesitancy had, indeed, been a facet of her make-up that had always appealed to Oscar himself. Yet to some extent it inevitably made her fall short of the target she had set for herself.

Many first-hand accounts of the Wildes at home have survived. One of the most interesting is by Anna, Comtesse de Brémont, who described her first meeting with Constance:

The next thing that arrested my gaze was a young woman arrayed in an exquisite Greek costume of cowslip yellow and apple-leaf green. Her hair, a thick mass of ruddy brown, was wonderfully set off by the bands of yellow ribbon, supporting the knot of hair low on the nape of the neck, and crossing the wavy masses above the brow. The whole arrangement was exceedingly becoming to the youthful, almost boyish face with its clear colouring and full, dark eyes. There was an air of shy self-consciousness and restraint about the wearer of that fantastic yet lovely costume that gave me the impression of what is called stage fright, and I jumped to the conclusion that she was a young actress dressed up for a recital, and somewhat nervous before all the society folk present. Imagine my surprise when she was introduced to me as the hostess.

'My wife,' said Oscar Wilde, as we paused before her. Then he whispered, but not too low for me to hear:

'You are looking lovely, Constance not a bit too tired with all these people.'

I saw her sweet face light up, and all the shyness and nervousness melt out of her eyes under the words of approval from her husband and teacher. She received me with that gentle cordiality that marked her bearing, but I could not overcome the first impression made upon me, and I was not quite at my ease in the consciousness of the secret weariness and effort that I knew lay under her smiling face and graceful bearing. I felt that she was bored and overwrought by the part she was playing before all those people and the aesthetic pose that she was not fitted to take. Perhaps something of this passed through the mind of Oscar Wilde, for he began to speak, and soon everyone was silent, and listening eagerly to all the beautiful things about art and life that he told us. [12]

Another writer who described Constance's delicate, youthful beauty and the anomaly between her private self and the part she was called on to play was Marie Belloc Lowndes, sister of Hilaire Belloc:

Constance Wilde was exceedingly pretty in a delicate English way. When I first knew her she must have been about thirty, even a little more, yet she looked like a girl. She had beautiful hair of chestnut brown and, when at home, dressed simply and in the type of frock which was beginning to be known as a teagown. But when she accompanied her husband to functions such as private views, which then played a very great role in London, she would appear in what were regarded as very peculiar and eccentric clothes. She did this to please Oscar and not to please herself.

I recall seeing her at a private view at the Grosvenor Galleries when she wore a green and black costume reminiscent of an 18th century highwayman. It made a considerable sensation, and instead of looking at the pictures on the walls, a great many people were asking each other if they had seen Mrs Oscar Wilde. I think she very much shrank from that sort of publicity, but undoubtedly Oscar enjoyed it.[13]

Soon Constance's reign as a hostess was interrupted once more by the imminent arrival of another baby. Though she was proud to be the mother of Oscar's children, neither she nor Oscar enjoyed her pregnancies. She was constantly unwell and often confined to her bedroom. So far from having that special bloom commonly associated with pregnancy, Constance's skin developed blotches and spots. That slim figure almost like a boy's that had promised to be the ideal model for Oscar's notions of female dress became gross and ugly. But at least the couple hoped that their desire for a daughter would be fulfilled with the arrival of a new little Isola, a kind of emotional replacement for the dead sister whom Oscar had loved so dearly.

On a bleak November day in 1886 Constance went into labour for the second time. The family doctor, Charles Lacy de Lacy, who was fetched from his home in Grosvenor Street, had difficulty in getting to Tite Street on account of the thick fog that smothered the city. Eventually the baby arrived. To their great disappointment it turned out to be another boy.

The proud couple had recorded not merely the date of their first son's birth, but the day and time also, even to the exact minute. In sharp contrast they forgot to register their second son's birth until several weeks had gone by. When they eventually got round to it, they could not even remember his date of birth, beyond that it was during the first five days of November. As a compromise the birth was registered as 3 November 1886; but Constance's brother Otho

Lloyd eventually told his nephew that he had in fact been born on the fifth, and that this was hushed up in order that the Aesthetic Movement should not be associated with Guy Fawkes Day. The baby was called Vyvyan Oscar Beresford Wilde.

Constance wrote and invited their friend John Ruskin to be godfather to their new son, but he declined because he felt that he was too old to take on the responsibility. Instead, the artist Mortimer Menpes allowed himself to be pressed into service, donating a set of his own etchings in lieu of the conventional christening mug. Though Menpes was highly regarded in the eighteen-eighties, his reputation declined until, some twenty-one years later, a small committee from the Royal Academy descended on him and challenged him to work in their presence. His refusal to comply strengthened allegations that he was unable to paint or draw and had paid someone else to produce 'his' works.

It is said that Oscar and Constance never resumed normal sexual relations after Vyvyan's birth. This may well have been true, for in an age unsophisticated in terms of contraception this demonstrably fertile young couple produced no more babies. There is no evidence to suggest that Constance resented this in any way. Victorian matrons were not expected to enjoy sex, merely to submit dutifully to their husbands' animal appetites. In an age of high mortality in childbirth, many women were only too glad to be relieved of further child-bearing, and there is no reason to suppose that Constance felt otherwise.

The reasons for the change in the Wildes' physical relationship are more controversial. Oscar's close friend Robert Sherard suggested that Oscar had contracted syphilis at Oxford and that this broke out again, and prevented him from resuming normal relations with Constance after the birth of their second child.[14] Modern medical knowledge suggests that this cannot have been the case, and there is no evidence whatsoever to support his theory.

In many ways the explanation offered by Frank Harris, also intimately acquainted with Oscar, seems more satisfactory. He describes a conversation which he claims to have had with Oscar after his release from prison.

'When I married, my wife was a beautiful girl, white and slim as a lily, with dancing eyes and gay rippling laughter like music. In a year or so the flower-like grace had all vanished; she became heavy, shapeless, deformed: she dragged herself about the house in uncouth misery with drawn blotched face and hideous body, sick at heart because of our love. It was dreadful. I tried to be kind to her; forced myself to touch and kiss her; but she was sick always, and – oh! I cannot recall it, it is all loathsome . . . Oh, nature is disgusting; it takes beauty and defiles it: it defaces the ivory-white body we have adored, with the vile cicatrices of maternity: it befouls the altar of the soul.

'How can you talk of such intimacy as love? How can you idealize it? Love is not possible to the artist unless it is sterile.'

'All her suffering did not endear her to you?' I asked in amazement; 'did not call forth that pity in you which you used to speak of as divine?'

'Pity, Frank!' he exclaimed impatiently; 'pity has nothing to do with love. How can one desire what is shapeless, deformed, ugly? Desire is killed by maternity; passion buried in conception,' and he flung away from the table.

At length I understood his dominant motive: *trahit sua quemque voluptas*, his Greek love of form, his intolerant cult of physical beauty, could take no heed of the happiness or well-being of the beloved.[15]

Frank Harris' books contain many statements which are demonstrably untrue, and allowance has to be made for his exaggerated style of reporting conversations. He habitually imputed the worst possible motives to Oscar and the best to himself. It has been proved, moreover, that at the time of the alleged conversation Harris was many miles away. Nevertheless, the basics of the explanation have a ring of truth about them. Oscar may well have said something resembling this to Harris at some time or another. He was, after all, the apostle of beauty, and may well have regarded Constance's pregnancies as a 'spoiling' of her slim and dainty figure. Certainly they disqualified her temporarily from being a mannequin to display his notions of beautiful and rational dress. Outwardly he was tenderly solicitous towards Constance during her pregnancies; but he was more intolerant than most of ill-health and her continual sickness was undoubtedly irksome to him. Marriage, he began to realize, was something of an anticlimax.

6

The Modern Woman

There is nothing in the whole world so unbecoming to a
woman as a Nonconformist conscience.
                                        Lady Windermere's Fan

Vyvyan's birth thus marked a kind of watershed in the marriage.
During the last few months of Constance's pregnancy Oscar ceased
to be romantically and passionately in love with her. That he loved
her still in a different fashion and one that was equally valid; more
tenderly than perhaps most of his friends realized, is equally
apparent. Constance, on the other hand, was probably as much in
love with her husband on the day of her death as she had been on
their wedding day. Whatever the tragedies and torments she was
ultimately to suffer, however her concept of his character and
qualities had to be modified in the terrible events that were to
overtake them, however those events tormented her and even made
her deny it, it is obvious that she loved him to the last.

It would appear that in some irrational, subconscious way both
Constance and Oscar blamed the new addition to the family for the
change in their relationship. Though Vyvyan always knew that his
mother and father loved him, he was from the first aware that they
preferred Cyril to himself. That preference was not imagined. It
shows through all the surviving correspondence. Though Oscar
speaks of Cyril, and collectively of his children, he never once
mentions Vyvyan by name. In later years Vyvyan put this down to a
natural tendency to favour their first-born, and certainly never
resented it, presumably because he felt wholly secure in those early
Tite Street days. Yet it is certainly arguable whether such a general
tendency exists, and the causes were almost certainly deeper rooted.
Early photographs of the boys suggest that Cyril resembled his
father more closely than Vyvyan; yet it was Vyvyan who appears to

63

have been the better-looking child. He was also probably the more intelligent, and certainly the more academically gifted of the two. On the face of it, these should all have been powerful attractions for Constance and Oscar, both of whom idealized physical perfection and academic distinction. Perhaps Vyvyan's early childish ailments made him a problem initially. When he was less than two years old he suffered an illness from which the couple feared he would never recover. So great was their anxiety at that time that Oscar could devote his mind to nothing else. Two years later it was Cyril's turn to strike terror into the hearts of Constance and Oscar, to the extent that all engagements had to be cancelled. Indeed, by the time he was nine years old, it was Cyril who had become the invalid, despite his active, practical nature.

The Wildes' preference for Cyril was, however, very reminiscent of Speranza's for the elder of her two sons. In 1889 Constance wrote to a friend,

> The children look very blooming, and Cyril is sweeter than ever . . . He told me that he was the goodest boy in the world . . . He chatters all day long and amuses me so much. The next time he goes into the country, he is going to fish, which he says you do by getting a net and putting a worm at the end of it, and then the worm catches the fish for you. [1]

One major problem in the Wildes' marriage was Oscar's social life, from which Constance was by now to some extent excluded. Frank Harris, who subscribed to the opinion that Oscar had married for money, describes what happened:

> As soon as the dreadful load of poverty was removed, Oscar began to go about a great deal, and his wife would certainly have been invited with him if he had refused invitations addressed to himself alone; but from the beginning he accepted them and consequently after the first few months of marriage his wife went out but little, and later children came and kept her at home. [2]

It should not be imagined that Oscar and Constance had altogether ceased to appear together in public; far from it. The *Lady's Pictorial* of 8 January 1887 describes a private view at the Grosvenor Gallery:

Mr and Mrs Oscar Wilde, intentionally or otherwise, formed a very effective harmony in green. The coat of the apostle of culture was of Lincoln Green cloth heavily trimmed with fur, while Mrs Oscar had a very pretty and graceful velvet gown of exactly the same shade of colour. Round her shoulders she had a small scarf mantle of green velvet embroidered with irridescent beads, and her little flat cap of velvet suited her admirably.

Yet something, undoubtedly, had been lost from their apparently united relationship.

Constance may well have been disappointed at this state of affairs, but she gave little sign of it. Gradually she filled her own social calendar; yet she never ceased to miss Oscar and to long for his company. In all her efforts to occupy her time to the advantage of herself and her family Constance had one staunch ally: her mother-in-law. The bond between the two women was exceptionally strong, and founded on genuine affection and sympathy. To Speranza Constance offered that companionship that she might have had from her daughter Isola if she had lived; Constance was roughly the same age as Isola would have been, and regarded Speranza with true daughterly affection. She revered Speranza almost as much as she reverenced her husband, and was greatly influenced by her. Despite the crowds of famous people who thronged Speranza's salon, despite the presence of Willie between marriages and social engagements, despite Oscar's frequent majestic visits, Speranza remained a somewhat lonely figure. Like Oscar and Constance, Speranza worshipped youth and beauty, and tried to cheat time by maintaining dim lighting in her salon and employing aids to retain her fading looks. Her majestic presence commanded admiration. As Anna, Comtesse de Brémont commented,

What mattered the old-fashioned gown, the towering head-dress of velvet, the long gold ear-rings or the yellow lace fichu crossed on her breast and fastened with innumerable enormous brooches – the huge bracelets of turquoise and gold, the rings on every finger! Her faded splendour was more striking than the most fashionable attire for she wore that ancient finery with a grace and dignity that robbed it of its grotesqueness.[3]

She and Constance were very companionable together. They visited each other, patronized each other's salons, went out to the Holborn silk shop together, took drives, and generally kept each other company. Constance appreciated Speranza's great intellectual gifts, and Speranza looked to her daughter-in-law for all things, even down to cashing her cheques for her. Perhaps significantly, she looked on Constance as someone who could be trained to read Oscar's proofs, rather than as someone capable of literary creativity in her own right. In this her judgement was absolutely sound. Though Constance was cultured and well-informed, and fully able to turn out the occasional prose piece of reasonable standard, she lacked true creative literary talent, and could not progress beyond the competent magazine article. She was a reader at the British Museum, where she spent many pleasurable afternoons, and when she contributed historically based articles to magazines she carried out her researches in an efficient fashion. On the history of dress she was a positive expert, consulting texts and drawings not only for her columns in the newspapers but also in order to design her own elaborate costumes. In short, she had a considerable range of skills which she exercised to the full with more than average success yet without really excelling in any of them.

So far Constance's notions of turning her talents to financial advantage had come to very little. Going on the stage had at one point seemed like an inviting prospect. Oscar's great friend Lillie Langtry had achieved remarkable stage success without any previous experience; but being the Prince of Wales' mistress had had a lot to do with it. Constance had taken part in *Helen in Troas*, a lavish production for which E. W. Godwin had designed the set; but her lack of true dramatic talent and her two pregnancies effectively put an end to any ambitions she may have had in that direction. Alternative ideas included becoming correspondent to a newspaper or writing a novel. She thought of modelling her writing on Victor Hugo, who was her idea of the perfect novelist, but nothing ever came of her grand design.

In one sphere at least, however, Constance achieved noteworthy success: that of drama critic. She was admirably suited to work in this area, for she loved the theatre and as Oscar's wife had the entrée to the world of the stage. Many notable theatre personalities were among their personal friends, and from them she was able to glean fascinating inside information. Unfortunately her articles were usually unsigned and cannot now be traced; but it is known that she

contributed to the *Lady's Pictorial*. One unsigned article known to
have come from her pen appeared in that journal on 23 July 1887.
It describes the Irving benefit at the Lyceum, which she and Oscar
both attended. After the performance the couple were present at a
special supper party on stage. The article runs as follows:

The season is at an end, the curtain has fallen upon the familiar
last scene of *The Merchant of Venice*, the last bouquets of the season
have been showered across the footlights, and that popular
speaker, Mr Henry Irving, has delivered his valedictory address.
The stalls and boxes were full of familiar faces, the pit and gallery
were crowded with old friends and hearty admirers, and a
tremendous burst of applause naturally greeted the appearance of
the popular actor-manager who, having exchanged the Jewish
gaberdine of Shylock for evening dress of the Victorian era, came
before the curtain to receive the parting congratulations of the
assembled audience. The speech was a characteristic one –
playful, yet earnest, and enlivened with many touches of quaint
satiric humour. He spoke of the phenomenal success which had
attended the run of *Faust* which, produced in 1885, had
continued its career with undiminished éclat until the close of the
present season of 1887. The devil's own luck, some people might
call it, said Mr Irving; but for his own part he preferred that
'Needs must, when the devil drives'. Invitations to represent
Faust in many of the great European capitals had reached the
managerial headquarters, and the successful production of the
play had been specially gratifying to all real lovers of Goethe, in
that it had been the means of multiplying his English readers by
tens of thousands, and of increasing the foreign sales of his work
to an extraordinary extent. Enterprising advertisers also had
availed themselves of the popular enthusiasm for *Faust* to impress
upon the blank spaces between the pages of the play recom-
mendatory paragraphs recounting their wares, and chaste designs
illustrative of the Margaret shoe, the Mephistopholes hat, and
other appropriately-named articles. Even Beecham, the immortal
inventor of the pill that bore his name, had endeavoured to turn
the thoughts of the many readers of the play from poetry to
prosaic medicine, by informing them that the price of the
infallible remedy was one and three half-pence a box, and that it
could only be purchased under a government stamp, and from a

licensed vendor. He then spoke of *Werner* and *The Amber Heart*, both of which would again be presented at the Lyceum stage on the return of the company to England, and, with a gracefully expressed compliment to Madame Sarah Bernhardt and a hearty wish of success to Miss Anderson, whose season at the Lyceum commences in September next, ended by bidding all his friends in front, in the names of himself, of Miss Ellen Terry, and the whole of the company, not farewell but au revoir.

In addition to the truly marvellous production of *The Merchant of Venice*, a most charming supper party was given afterwards on the stage, where there were assembled a great number of pretty and interesting people. Miss Ellen Terry appeared first in her terra-cotta Venetian dress, and afterwards in a soft white woollen costume embroidered in Oriental colourings. Her daughter, an interesting-looking girl, though absolutely unlike her mother, wore dark coral pink. Mrs Bram Stoker wore white satin. Mrs Savile Clarke wore dark bronze cotton crêpe embroidered with a surface pattern of gold, while her two younger children wore their 'Alice in Wonderland' dresses, and looked very pretty. The palm of beauty was perhaps borne off by Mrs Weldon, radiant and young-looking as ever . . .

Georgina Weldon, the singer, was so delighted at this compliment that she made it her business to write a note of thanks. Some confusion arose, however, over the authorship, and her note was addressed to Oscar. When Constance learned how much Mrs Weldon liked the article, she was very flattered.

In the end it was Oscar who, after years of hack-work often not even written under his own name, finally landed a secure and regular job. In 1887 the publishing house of Cassell, anxious to improve the quality of a magazine called *The Lady's World*, approached Oscar and invited him to be its editor. He duly accepted, but asked that the title might be changed. Thus *Woman's World* was launched. As soon as Oscar was editor, he successfully canvassed a most impressive list of contributors. They included Marie Corelli, Mrs Craik, Ouida, Nellie Sickert, the Queen of Rumania, and many others. Speranza, too, produced both prose and verse for her son's new project.

Constance's job was now to invite to her at-homes the notables from whom Oscar sought contributions. The Press regarded these as newsworthy events. On 13 July 1887 Constance and Oscar gave a particularly successful party which the *Lady's Pictorial* described as 'one of the pleasantest afternoons of the season'. As usual there was an account of the House Beautiful, and the reporter added,

Roses were the only flowers used for decoration, and although so many people were present, the house was kept delightfully cool and shady. The hostess looked most picturesque in a lovely gown made with a bodice and train of dark green and gold silk gauze, and with a high Medici collar lined with dark green silk and outlined with small gold beads; long hanging sleeves from the shoulder lined with dark green, and worn over tightly-fitting sleeves of gold gauze, completed this very charming and picturesque attire.[4]

Constance's mother was there, with Aunt Mary Napier and Speranza. Titled ladies were much in evidence: Lady Ardilaun, Lady Dorothy Nevill, Lady Monckton, and others. The drama was represented by Mrs Kendal, Mr and Mrs George Alexander, Alma Murray and Mr and Mrs Bram Stoker. Walter Crane and Waldo Story were also present.

At Oscar's suggestion Constance also became a contributor to *Woman's World*. Her first article was called 'Children's Dress in This Century', and was illustrated with line drawings based on books in the British Museum. It was a well-thought-out article, in which Constance argued for an essentially practical approach to children's clothing, with the emphasis on warmth, comfort, health and freedom of movement. She felt that fabric should be durable and styles simple, following the natural lines of the body. Her text reads like a commentary on the pictures in which she points out to the reader the best and worst features of the designs.

A year later Constance's second article, called 'Muffs', appeared. On the face of it, this subject would appear to offer little scope; yet Constance's article clearly indicates that there is more in their history than might be imagined. She guides the reader through their earliest recorded appearances, pointing to the various changes in size and shape, and showing how the muff can be an indicator of social class. Unfortunately for Constance, this outlet for her articles shortly disappeared. Though Oscar had initially thrown himself into the editorship with enthusiasm, he soon grew tired of continually presenting himself at the office. His visits became briefer and more infrequent, and he left more and more of the work to Arthur Fish, his assistant editor. In July 1889, little more than two years after he started, Oscar resigned the editorship of *Woman's World*. The journal limped on for a while under Arthur Fish, but without Oscar's influence it foundered and finally became defunct in the following year. From the point of view of Oscar's own development as a writer he never made a wiser move. When in creative mood he could work with incredible speed. He could not, however, churn out reviews to order with the same satisfaction, and cajoling others to write for him was a sheer waste of his own genius.

Significantly, the subject of both Constance's articles in *Woman's World* had been dress. This was no mere coincidence. Her interest in her personal wardrobe was considerable, but it should not be confused with the ordinary interest of the woman who simply wishes to look as attractive as possible and follow the fashion of the day. She had begun as Oscar's disciple and as a living exhibit of his ideas of the clothes that women ought to wear. As time went on Oscar's interest became somewhat more casual, and he turned increasingly to new pursuits. Constance, on the other hand, now emerged as a natural leader in the realm of women's and children's clothing, and automatically took her place among the leaders of the Rational Dress Society. By 1888 she had begun editing the newly formed *Rational Dress Society's Gazette*, the quarterly organ of the Society. The aims of the Society were clearly set out in the introduction to each edition of the *Gazette*:

> The Rational Dress Society protests against the introduction of any fashion in dress that either deforms the figure, impedes the movements of the body, or in any way tends to injure the health.
>
> It protests against the wearing of tightly-fitting corsets; of high-heeled or narrow-toed boots and shoes; of heavily-weighted skirts, as rendering healthy exercise almost impossible; and of all tie-down cloaks or other garments impeding the movements of the arms.
>
> It protests against crinolines or crinolettes of any kind as ugly and deforming . . .
>
> The maximum weight of clothing (without shoes) approved of by the Rational Dress Society, does not exceed seven pounds.[5]

Constance was a somewhat reluctant editor, and initially made it clear that she was merely seeing the first issue through the press. But nobody else came forward and she therefore continued as editor of the first eight numbers, which covered the years 1888 and 1889. The *Gazette* faced a number of problems, not least of which was the reluctance of the membership to submit articles of suitable quality and to allow their names to be published. Though Constance was convinced that women were interested in the movement, the membership was disappointingly small. Through an initial organizational failure the Society failed to include the cost of the *Gazette* in the membership fee. This Constance found to be a serious tactical fault, for some members of the Society failed to subscribe to the *Gazette*. Constance was continually urged to increase revenue by attracting new advertising, but could not do this without first increasing the circulation. Besides handling the literary side of things, she also had to manage all the business arrangements. She entrusted the publishing to Mr Hatchard, whom Oscar knew well because he was a frequent customer at his bookshop. Many letters passed between them, but sadly Constance's letters to Mr Hatchard, like many others from his famous customers and friends, have disappeared without trace.

Constance found it time-consuming work. The Society had no regular meeting place, but they did have their own depot at 11 Sloane Street, Chelsea, where members and their friends could go along to inspect and purchase garments approved by the Society or paper patterns from which they could make their own rational dress. One lady, Mrs Humphrey, who was invited by Constance to submit a 500-word article to the *Gazette* for a fee of one guinea, was also asked to call at the depot to inspect 'rational bodices', which Constance said were 'certainly worth seeing'.[6] When the Society wanted to convene meetings they had to rely on members to offer hospitality in their own homes. Lady Harberton, née Frances Pomeroy, who in 1885 had written a controversial book called *Reasons for Reform in Dress*, frequently obliged, as did Mrs Stopes (mother of Marie) at her home in Cintra Park, Upper Norwood. Mrs Stopes was one of the most active of the Society's members; she corresponded frequently with Constance about her various contributions to the *Gazette*, and invited her to speak at a meeting at her home on 10 December 1888. By now Constance was frequently in demand as a speaker, and often had to decline through sheer pressure of her many commitments. At meetings she was often asked to give an opinion, and her voice was regarded as authoritative. Fund-raising activities sometimes claimed her attention too, as in June 1888 when a concert was held which netted a profit of £80 for the Society, a by no means inconsiderable sum in those days.

On 6 November 1888 the Rational Dress Society attempted to reach a wider audience by booking the Somerville Club for a lecture, for ladies only, delivered by Constance. The title was 'Clothed in Our Right Minds'; Constance made no apology for its slightly biblical flavour. The *Gazette* reported:

> After referring to the more extended sphere opening for women in the future owing to the growing love of liberty, Mrs Wilde asked if women fully realised how they would be hampered by this most irrational and uncomfortable dress that they are doomed to wear? She reminded the audience that heavy clothing did not imply warmth, as warmth depended on the material. For those who would find wool irritating she suggested a trial of the material called 'Cellular Cloth', and also recommended divided skirts instead of petticoats. She denied there was any connection between this and a desire to dress like men, and deprecated any suggestion of indecency in a dual dress. 'Indecency!' said the lecturer, 'When you look unblushingly on young girls with arms and necks bare, a mere strap across the shoulder to prevent the bodice from slipping completely down, a bodice worn with nothing but a corset under it next to the skin, so that there may be nothing to increase the size of the body; when you see and suffer stout elderly matrons to go about even more unclothed than their young daughters, looking infinitely more so, because the expanse uncovered is much larger – indecency because we say, 'God has made us with two legs and not one, and we wish for freedom to use those two legs'. Believe me, there is no indecency here! If we did not so hide our legs that the lower part of our body looks like a large barrel rather than anything human, we should perhaps not see so much indecency as we do see in our ball-rooms.[7]

Not everyone appreciated Constance's performance on the lecture platform. Marie Corelli, who described Constance as 'a very pretty woman . . . in a Directoire costume, with a tall Cavalier hat and plume, and a great crutch stick',[8] wrote,

> Like her mother-in-law, Mrs Oscar also took a special interest in feminine garb. About this date she was persuaded to give a lecture on 'Rational Dress for Women' at the Somerville Club. An acid criticism by one of the company declared; Mrs Oscar Wilde is utterly devoid of the correct demeanor that should be observed on the lecture platform; she giggles at her own witticisms, and explodes in a titter of laughter when she says something that she thinks especially smart.[9]

Nevertheless Constance continued to be asked to speak and to preside at meetings. Her personal charm and delightful appearance had quite a lot to do with it. One newspaper columnist who saw her at an art gallery wearing a particularly attractive dress wrote, 'She would have won all hearts to "rational" dress, had she appeared in this very pretty gown upon the platform. Tan gloves and a muff of green velvet made up quite a charming picture.'[10] A later comment reads:

> At the conference of the Rational Dress Society in Queen's Gate last week, held under the presidency of Mrs Oscar Wilde, a letter was read to the gathering from some ladies in America who wished to co-operate in the movement. The room was crowded to overflowing, and great interest was exhibited in the subject discussed. No practical result, however, was reached by any of the speakers.[11]

When compiling her copy for the *Rational Dress Society's Gazette* Constance usually included accounts of some of the many women whose clothing had caused them death or serious injury. The following report is typical:

> A domestic servant, 24, named Elizabeth Ann Germany, residing at 120 King Edward's Road, Hackney, was standing on a windowsill on the first floor cleaning the windows. A gust of wind caught her petticoats, and while endeavouring to hold them down she missed her balance and fell backward on to the stone step. She died a quarter of an hour afterwards from fracture of the skull.[12]

But perhaps most heart-rending to Constance were the many accounts of women whose dresses had caught alight; for she must surely have heard from Oscar of the terrible death of his illegitimate half-sisters, Emily and Mary Wilde. Issue number six reported the story of 55-year-old Eliza Dixon, who was 'in the front room in the basement at the time when some linen on a clothes horse began to burn. In her endeavour to extinguish the flames her dress caught fire.' Mrs Dixon survived; she was more fortunate than Rosina Williams, whose clothes were set alight by a spark from the grate. 'Her screams attracted assistance, but she was found burned in a terrible manner.'[13] She died in hospital three hours later. From these examples and many others Constance developed a true crusading spirit and approached the question of rational dress with a strong sense of mission.

Speranza shared Constance's interest in dress, though her pronouncements on the subject tended to be more dramatic than those of her daughter-in-law. She thought that women ought to avoid black. 'Black is unlovely and unbecoming to everyone, especially to English women, with the delicate half-tints of their colouring, and the murky grey of the atmosphere. Besides it absorbs the light and spoils the effect of rooms, making it difficult to light them,'[14] she wrote, and, 'Dress ought to express a moral ideal; it symbolises the intellect and disposition of a native. I should like to reform women's garments.'[15] She also had notions about what women writers should wear:

As for the literary dress, it should be free, untrammelled and unswathed, as simple and as easily adjusted as Greek drapery, and fastened only with a girdle or brooch; no stiff corselet should depress the full impulses of a passionate heart; there should be no *false* coils or frizzy fringe on the brow to heat the temples and mar the cool logic of thought; and the fewer frills, cuffs, cascades of lace, the better, for in moments of divine frenzy or feverish excitement the authoress is prone to overturn her ink-bottle. No inspiration could have come to Pythia had she worn a corset or hoop . . . A woman should study her own personality, and consider well what she means to be and can be; either a superb Juno, a seductive Aphrodite, or a Hebe blooming and coquette, or a Pallas Athene; and when the style is discovered that best suits her — it may be for homage or for love — let her keep to it.

As the symbol of her higher self, unchanged by frivolous mutations of fashion, dress then attains a moral significance, and becomes the esoteric expression of the spiritual nature. [16]

After two years and eight issues Constance gave up the editorship of the *Rational Dress Society's Gazette*, and both it and the Society foundered, much as *Woman's World* collapsed soon after Oscar's resignation. It was not until 1898 when Lady Harberton and others resuscitated the Society under the slightly modified title of the Rational Dress League, mainly to further the campaign for cycling bloomers, that a new gazette was issued.

Constance had other campaigns to occupy her. Speranza had always hoped that Oscar would go into politics and indeed he had himself vaguely toyed with the idea. Oddly enough, though, it was Constance, not Oscar, who espoused a political cause. Her grandfather's commitment to the Liberal Party had undoubtedly had some influence on her, but her questing intellect would never have accepted blindly a set of values that she had not personally subjected to searching analysis. How she first met Margaret, Dowager Baroness Sandhurst, a Tory by birth but a Liberal by choice, is not clear; but Lady Sandhurst was an active member of the Women's Liberal Federation. She rapidly established herself as a major influence on Constance's life and soon the two women were almost inseparable. Constance was a member of the Chelsea Women's Liberal Association and was a leading light among the mainly working women who thronged its ranks. Lady Sandhurst was thirty years older than her protégée, and lived at 18 Portland Place. She had a home for poor incurables and cripples in the Marylebone Road, spending all her time and money on its occupants, and performing cures that were little short of miraculous on patients rejected by the hospitals. Under her influence Constance organized bazaars and joined in other fund-raising activities, spending much of her time in charitable works. The two women were constantly in each other's company and the great gap in their ages seems to have made no difference at all, for they were united by the cause of the poor and needy. Perhaps, too, Constance was more at home in a relationship in which she was a mixture of daughter and disciple.

Women did not, of course, have the franchise in those days. They had been eligible to sit on the School Board for London since 1870, and such colourful personalities as Annie Besant and Elizabeth Garrett Anderson had been among the early members. They were not eligible to stand for Parliament, though many of the more ambitious had been casting their eyes in that direction for years. When the Local Government Act was passed in 1888, many women saw this as an ideal way of getting female representation in an important sphere of influence, the London County Council. The first elections were due to be held on 17 January 1889. 'Lady Sandhurst was one of the devoted pair of ladies who stepped into the breach, remarking gaily that she regarded herself "simply as bones to be fought over",'[17] the *Pall Mall Gazette* reported.

Mrs Stopes, whose husband was also standing as a Liberal candidate, wrote and asked Constance whether any of the Chelsea Women's Liberal Association members could help him in his campaign. Constance replied that the Chelsea Committee had refused, both as a body and individually. She explained that as most of the women went out to work they could afford neither the time nor the money to work in Norwood, where the Stopes family lived. Mrs Stopes also indicated to Constance her willingness to help Lady Sandhurst, but Constance replied that she felt she ought instead to help her husband. 'Lady Sandhurst was told that if her nomination was accepted, (and this, I see, is settled) she would be returned by a large majority!'[18] she confided to Mrs Stopes. She was now spending every single moment that she could spare in helping Lady Sandhurst with her campaign. The name of Mrs Oscar Wilde really counted for something now in women's political circles.

The prophecy about Lady Sandhurst's prospects was indeed true. She stood as a candidate for Brixton, where she was opposed by Mr C. Beresford Hope, son of a former Member of Parliament for Cambridge, who was a member of the legal profession. Lady Sandhurst won the seat by an overwhelming majority. She was one of three women who had stood, all of them as Progressive candidates, which was the name then given to Liberals in a local government context. Two of the three were elected, the other successful candidate being Jane Cobden, daughter of the famous politician and businessman, Richard Cobden. They were joined by Emma Cons, famous proprietor of the Old Vic Theatre, who had been active in the problems of housing for the working classes, and who was now made an alderman. Of Lady Sandhurst's success the *Pall Mall Gazette Extra* said,

The Brixton Liberals had the good luck to secure her as a candidate, and thus to gain both seats in a Tory division where they only hoped for one. Lady Sandhurst looks every inch a dowager, but she is a most lovely and ingenious lady, and a capital speaker. Lord Hobhouse supported her on the platform at Brixton, and but for the incurable aversion of the Progressives to an Alderman from inside, she would probably have been chosen an Alderman.[19]

There was considerable rejoicing among women Liberals everywhere at Lady Sandhurst's success, and Constance was delighted. Their elation was premature, however, for there were difficulties ahead that none of them had foreseen. Lady Sandhurst duly took her seat; but Mr C. Beresford Hope, the Moderate Party candidate whom she had defeated at Brixton, immediately petitioned the Queen's Bench Division of the High Court to unseat her on the grounds of ineligibility. The situation, which was a complicated one, has been summarized by Alan R. Neate:

The 1888 Act used masculine terminology throughout but then, ever since Lord Brougham's Act of 1850, this was standard drafting practice in order to avoid an endless repetition of the dual forms, 'he or she', 'his or her', etc. In the beautifully picturesque language of the law courts, 'the male embraces the female' — except, that is, where the context or the subject matter militates against the inclusion of the latter. The 1888 Act stated quite simply that county councils were to be constituted in like manner as the council of a borough under the Municipal Corporations Act, 1882 and so the crucial thing was what the Act had to say. In fact, it is said that the right to stand rested with 'fit persons' eligible to be enrolled as a burgess, i.e., a person eligible to vote, and women had undoubtedly been eligible to vote in borough elections since the eighteen-sixties if they satisfied the relevant requirements in their own right and not that of their husbands. There had, however, never been a case of a woman having been elected to sit on a municipal corporation — so all hinged on the phrase 'fit person'.

The real stumbling block was Section 63 of the 1882 Act, which provided that 'For all purposes connected with the right to vote at municipal elections, words in the Act importing the masculine gender shall include women.' If Parliament had thus gone out of its way to make this specific provision in relation to the right to vote, it had doubtless intended it to be confined to the right to vote and not to the right to sit. Otherwise, it would have made a similar specific provision. So the court held.[20]

This decision caused widespread consternation among women interested in politics. At a London County Council meeting held prior to that decision the Council had resolved 'That the consideration of the motion for a reference to the Parliamentary Committee to consider and report what steps, if any, should be taken by the Council to place beyond dispute the right of women when duly elected to serve upon the Council, be deferred.'[21] Lady Sandhurst now decided to appeal against the court decision. On 30 April 1889 the Chairman of the Committee on the Housing of the Working Classes said, 'The Committee expresses a hope that Lady Sandhurst will be successful in her appeal against the decision given in the Law Courts on the thirteenth instant, as this Committee has had experience of the advantage of the assistance of Lady Members in carrying out its work in connection with the Housing of the Working Classes.'[22]

The result of the appeal was dramatically announced by the Chairman at the Council Meeting of 21 May 1889.

The Chairman stated that there had just been handed to him by the Clerk copies of orders of the Court of Appeal and of the Queen's Bench Division of the High Court of Justice, in the case of Hope versus Sandhurst, signed by two judges of the Supreme Court, as required by the Local Government Act, 1888, to the effect that Lady Sandhurst was not a person fit and qualified to be elected a Councillor, that the votes given to her were thrown away, and that the petitioner, Charles Thomas Beresford Hope, was, on 17th January 1889, duly elected a County Councillor for the Brixton Division.

Mr Beresford Hope having made the declaration in the form prescribed by the 8th Schedule to the Municipal Corporations Act, 1882, thereupon took his seat as the Councillor representing the Brixton Division.[23]

Thus the hopes of Lady Sandhurst and her supporters were dashed.

Not least galling to Constance and her friends was the decision to declare the rival candidate duly elected without even giving the electorate the chance of going again to the poll. The inference was that Lady Sandhurst's supporters were well aware that she was a woman and therefore ineligible, and that in voting for her they were deliberately invalidating their ballot papers.

Neither Miss Cobden nor Miss Cons could be unseated in the same fashion, since election petitions had to be submitted within a specified period, which had already elapsed. However, the Act provided for a penalty of £50 every time a person acted as a councillor or alderman without being qualified, and any informant could have brought an action against them. Counsel therefore advised them to attend meetings and committees but not to vote. For a time they went along with this, but eventually in frustration began actively to participate, with the inevitable result that Sir Walter de Souza, Councillor for Westminster, took action against them. At the next election, in 1892, no woman offered herself as prospective candidate. The law was changed in 1907, but the first opportunity for women to stand did not come until 1910. Mr Beresford Hope stood for Brixton at the 1892 election and was heavily defeated. However, he had a further opportunity to serve when a seat fell vacant in Kensington and a by-election was held. This was a Moderate Party stronghold and he was duly elected. It was his last term of office as a Member of the London County Council.

No doubt Constance was shattered by what happened to her friend; but her social and reforming zeal was in no way diminished. On 1 September 1889 she dragged an unwilling Oscar to a demonstration in Hyde Park connected with a series of dock strikes which had rocked the East End of London. Her pity for the plight of the working classes was considerable, and with true missionary zeal she did all that she could to further their cause. All the same, although she enjoyed the carnival-style demonstrations, she confided to her friend Emily Thursfield two strong impressions: 'One was that the people were very much in earnest, the other that they were very *unsavoury*, and I was glad to get out of the midst of them. They were very unwashed and smoked the most vile tobacco.'[24] Even so, she was conscious of being in the presence of a powerful force.

Her enthusiasm for politics overcame the traditional instinct of the Englishwoman not to speak to strangers on trains. On 28 October 1889 she wrote to her friend Emily Thursfield,

On my way here, a political discussion took place in the train, and the pity of one of the passengers was moved towards the unfortunate lady who was going to Windlesham and would not hear until Monday morning about the result of the election, and he undertook to telegraph to *her*, upon which an exchange of cards took place, and I finding that he was Dr Ginsberg claimed acquaintance on the grounds of our common friendship with you. The result of the election was in the paper on Saturday morning, all the same the telegram arrived![25]

Constance was on her way to stay with a much-loved relative, Cornelia Cochrane, 'Aunt Nelia' to Cyril and Vyvyan. She had married Vice-Admiral Basil Cochrane in 1873. Their home was Windlesham House, near Bagshot in Surrey. It was through Nelia that Constance got to know one of her most important friends, Lady Margaret Brooke, the Ranee of Sarawak.

Constance had always been of a religious turn of mind, and at some period during the 1880s she began to turn to spiritualism. Probably her friend Lady Sandhurst was a major influence in this sphere. Lady Sandhurst had been interested in the subject for four years when whe wrote to Gladstone and invited him to call secretly at her home in North Audley Street for a meeting with a lady who had 'most wonderful trances, in which very valuable communications are constantly made'.[26] After some further correspondence, Gladstone duly came and heard for himself. On 27 November she wrote saying that she had been asked to give him a message: 'It was said, in that same manner, "Write to Mr Gladstone, and tell him that the Navy ought to be looked after, and that quickly. Tell him also that it is thought to be a very blessed thing that he has taken this temperate way of dealing with these two questions and of meeting the views of the other side as much as possible." '[27] On 7 December she wrote again: 'This great revelation came to me without an effort on my part to meddle with anything like spiritualism. Four years ago, after you had entered on your present work, in times of such extraordinary difficulty, I was assured, "Jesus will support and guide Mr Gladstone." [28]

Lady Sandhurst saw religion and politics as inextricably bound up together, and as far as can be ascertained Constance shared this view. As a Christian she saw it as her duty to examine all avenues in an attempt to discover universal truths. When the theosophist Madam Blavatsky came to London and took the fashionable world by storm, Constance was one of those who flocked to see her. She decided to join the 'Order', and went along to the special initiation ceremony with Anna, Comtesse de Brémont, who described what happened:

> I passed the ordeal quite composedly, but not so my companion, Constance Wilde. I felt her tremble, and the hand that held mine was icy cold. Her voice faltered over the formula of admission that we recited together – a most formidable declaration which threatened dire calamity to those who disclosed the secret studies or proceedings of the Order. My sense of humour was secretly tried on that occasion and I felt more inclined to laugh, although Constance Wilde's beautiful eyes were full of tears. When it was known, later, that Constance Wilde had faithfully reported the ceremony and all details to her husband, many of the members attributed the tragic events that befell her family to the breaking of her pledged word. [29]

The Comtesse's accounts of what happened are often highly dramatic and have to be looked at with a certain amount of caution. Basically her memoirs were, however, founded on fact, and what clearly emerges is that although Constance may not have been as timid in her approach as the Comtesse suggests, she did join the order and made a serious effort to inform herself as fully as possible on the subject.

In 1888 Constance had been saddened by the death of her grandmother, 'Mama Mary' Atkinson, in Dublin. Mama Mary's great age should have prepared her family for her death, but she had seemed like an institution to Constance and the rest of the family, who could hardly believe that the spirited old lady was no longer there to preside over their home in Ely Place. Perhaps it was Mary

Atkinson's death that prompted Constance to write, as a kind of epitaph, a little book called *There was Once — Grandma's Stories* with fifteen pages of text and nine coloured illustrations by John Lawson. The book was published in 1889. The illustrations were in full colour and the cover design was delightful. The stories included 'Little Red Riding Hood', 'Puss in Boots', 'Cinderella', 'The Three Bears' and 'Jack the Giant-Killer'. There were poems about Little Bo-Peep, Old Mother Hubbard, the Babes in the Wood, and Three Little Kittens. This was followed three years later by another, similar collection of children's tales called *A Long Time Ago*, equally charming, though in no way up to the standard of Oscar's children's stories. Though he encouraged Constance to exercise her own talents and to produce work in those spheres which interested her, it is clear that he never interfered with her projects or imposed his own ideas on her. Likewise, during Oscar's editorship of *Woman's World* Constance was approached by writers who hoped that she would use her influence with her husband to get him to publish their work, but this she resolutely refused to do.

There were other family problems on Constance's horizon in 1888. Her mother's second marriage had never been happy, and relations between her second husband and Constance and Otho had not been good. But in November 1888, after a decade of marriage, George Swinburn King decided to call it a day and went to live with his daughter Eliza Mary at St Leonards-on-Sea. He made a new will at the same time, leaving everything to his daughter, 'everything' in his case, when he died in 1916, being in total only £485. 12s. 6d.

Oscar's brother Willie, on the other hand, after various amours finally decided to marry Mrs Frank Leslie, a wealthy American widow. She was a mulatto, some twenty years older than Willie, and had been married four times. On the death of her husband she had found herself proprietor of seven periodicals, and this had a certain appeal for Willie, who had for some time been a leader-writer for the *Daily Telegraph*. She moved in the same social circles as Constance, and sometimes attended her at-homes. She was usually to be seen at the most publicized functions, surrounded by friends and heavily laden with diamonds. Her outfits were usually described in detail by the Press. What she wore to a garden party at the Welcome Club was not untypical. It was 'a handsome toilette of black faille, profusely trimmed with gold embroidery, and a becoming bonnet of gold tinsel lace, with her famous emerald earrings set in diamonds'.[30] Oscar was not at all happy about the proposed alliance, particularly in view of the fact that there was no proper financial settlement. Mrs Leslie offered to make an allowance to Speranza of £400 a year, which she declined as being too much, though she was happy to accept £100 a year in order to keep a home for the couple in London until such time as they should wish to use it. That, however, was a separate issue. What Oscar feared was that Mrs Leslie would soon weary of Willie and discard him without a financial settlement of any kind. The wedding duly went ahead in September 1889 but it appears that Oscar was not at the wedding, for he left London and was absent for some time, leaving Constance feeling rather lonely. Perhaps his absence was diplomatic, for he was beginning to be irritated by his brother's behaviour. The wedding was in any event a rather quiet affair as Lord Addington, the Napiers' uncle, had just died and the family were still in mourning.

Oscar's fears were well founded, for Mrs Leslie did not detain Willie long. Hesketh Pearson summed up the situation:

In the rush and excitement of the moment it did not occur to either of them to question the other's intentions, and it became very clear, soon after their arrival on the other side of the Atlantic, that they held different views on the obligations of the married state. She wanted him to be not only an attentive husband to herself, but a valuable accession to the periodical she had inherited. He, on the other hand, preferred jolly evenings at the Century Club and occasional outings with girls . . . The question was debated at length between them, she urging the necessity of hard work and early hours, he retaliating that far too many people were working and too much work was done in America, where one sadly felt the need of a leisured class, which he proposed to supply.[31]

It soon became clear to Speranza that all was not well. 'The news from America is depressing,' she wrote to Constance. 'I don't know how it will all end.'[32] Within a couple of years Willie's marital problems hit the headlines under the title 'Tired of Willie', which did not go down at all well with Oscar. 'He was of no use to me either by day or night,'[33] his wife told reporters. 'As she ran through several husbands without finding satisfaction,' commented Hesketh Pearson, 'it is reasonable to suppose that she demanded more in the sex department than Willie was prepared or able to provide.'[34] Oscar's worst fears were realized. She left Willie without a penny.

7

Family Life

Men marry because they are tired; women because they
are curious. Both are disappointed.

A Woman of No Importance

W. B. Yeats first met Oscar at the home of the poet W. E. Henley
in 1888. Yeats was then twenty-three years old. 'The basis of
literary friendship is mixing the poisoned bowl,'[1] Oscar
remarked to him. At Christmas Yeats, who was at a loose end in
London, was invited to Tite Street. He later recalled the occasion:

> I remembered vaguely a white drawing-room with Whistler
> etchings 'let into' white panels, and a dining-room all white,
> chairs, walls, mantel-pieces, carpets, except for a diamond-
> shaped piece of red-cloth in the middle of the table under a
> terra-cotta statuette, and, I think, a red-shaded lamp hanging
> from the ceiling to a little above the statuette. It was, perhaps,
> too perfect in its unity. His past of a few years before had gone
> too completely, and I remember thinking that the perfect
> harmony of his life, with his beautiful wife and his two young
> children, suggested some deliberate composition.[2]

There was indeed something terrifyingly perfect in the happiness
that Constance found with her husband and children. Surely it was
too good to last. Constance's feelings for her husband were as strong
as ever. She was also passionately fond of her two little boys and
devoted immense thought to their welfare and upbringing. Young
Cyril and Vyvyan occupied a singularly privileged position in the
household. Most Victorian children were expected to be seen but
not heard. Not so the little Wilde children. They were not banished
to the nursery or kitchen when visitors, however distinguished,

came to call. Instead they were exhibited, lovingly and with pride, and allowed to stay and listen to the conversation of the most gifted and cultured men and women of their day.

Marie Belloc Lowndes was one of the distinguished people who commented on the Wilde household, and the children in particular:

My mother's acquaintance with Sir William and Lady Wilde in Dublin in the mid-sixties formed a very real link between myself and their son Oscar, and I was encouraged both by him and by his wife Constance – of whom I quickly became very fond – to come to her Sunday At Homes. The house was filled with a medley of agreeable people of all kinds. Oscar, unlike many notable wits, was just as amusing and delightful at home as he was in other people's houses, and it was natural to find those who journeyed to Chelsea to be drawn to No. 16 Tite Street by the host's brilliance and exuberant charm. He was also extraordinarily kind, always eager to do anyone a good turn. Constance was most courteous and pleasant and would take trouble to introduce those whom she thought shy or friendless, to some agreeable person.

I remember receiving from her a note asking me to come early, because she was expecting two Irish girls who knew no one in London, and she was anxious I should make friends with them and help them in any way I could. The two little boys, Cyril and Vyvyan, were often present at these Sunday gatherings. This was unusual as in those days it was the English custom to keep children in the nursery when their parents entertained. As I remember them, they were pleasant little boys with good manners.[3]

Considering the perfection of the House Beautiful, Constance allowed the children a surprising degree of freedom. Even the dining-room with its sacred white carpet was fully available to them. The only room they were not allowed to enter unaccompanied was Oscar's study on the ground floor, which was regarded as sacrosanct. To be invited into that room with its exciting smell of fine cigars and its waste-basket full of little treasures was a special privilege. The boys tended to avoid the drawing-room by choice, partly because there were too many fragile objects which might be knocked over, and partly because some of their parents' guests were a little too solemn for their liking. On the whole both Constance and Oscar were very understanding about the children's clothes, and realized that boys needed practical, warm costumes which would stand up to the rough and tumble of active games. There were occasional exceptions, though, as on one notable occasion when Cyril and Vyvyan were invited to a fancy-dress party. Being particularly proud of Cyril's lovely curly hair, Oscar suggested that Cyril should represent Millais' famous picture of *Bubbles*, while Vyvyan was to represent Little Lord Fauntleroy. The costumes were duly ordered, to the disgust of the boys, who didn't care at all for such sentimental nonsense and wanted to go in sailor suits. The drawing-room was full of guests when Oscar suddenly remembered the costumes and asked for a preview. This was an ideal opportunity for him to show off his beautiful sons to the company, and they were duly sent up to the nursery where they were kitted out in the offending garments. In due course they descended and made their grand entrance. There was a gasp of horror from the assembled company. They were stark naked! They had made the only protest they could think of, and had cast off the fancy costumes in the smoking room on their way back. The guests, like Queen Victoria, were not amused; but Constance and Oscar were wise enough to take the hint, and hastily ordered sailor suits instead. Of course, these had to be perfect, and so they were made of real naval cloth and the lanyards had knives at the ends. In these outfits they were the envy of all the little unfortunates made to go to the fancy-dress party in sentimental costumes.

On the whole the Wildes' guests tended to be less popular with the children than the Chelsea Pensioners with whom they played in the gardens of the Royal Hospital near their home. These great old campaigners were never tired of telling stories of their military exploits in days gone by, and the boys listened with rapt attention. Their favourite was a near-centenarian who had been a drummer boy at the Battle of Waterloo and who could tell them first-hand experiences of the Duke of Wellington. Sometimes they were even invited inside to have tea with these splendid old characters. Constance encouraged these contacts. When they were a bit older they were allowed to take the bus from Sloane Square to Knightsbridge unaccompanied. This rated as a special adventure. The horse-drawn bus had no conductor, but the passengers placed halfpennies in the box without any supervision except from the other passengers. At the end of the journey they were free to wander at will in Hyde Park, amusing themselves with games of hide-and-seek and touch-wood, but of course playing only with other boys. Girls were an altogether different breed, only fit for hopscotch and skipping.

On wet days the children played indoors, cajoling the cook for little dainties. She was their special ally, who continually irritated their very strict nurse by spoiling them. Sometimes they escaped the nurse's eagle eye and got up to boyish mischief of some sort. The worst occasion was when they found their father's sword-stick and had a duel, Cyril armed with the sword and Vyvyan with the stick. Doubly handicapped by his youth and his decidedly inferior weapon, Vyvyan was quickly vanquished and turned to flee. Cyril, excited by his conquest, pressed home his advantage with the point of his sword, leaving his tiny foe bellowing with pain and bleeding profusely. Vyvyan rushed to the cook, who dressed the wound; but he carried the scar of this childish encounter on his behind for the rest of his life.

Constance and Oscar were fortunately absolutely united in their ideas of how the children should be brought up. Both idolized the children and were happy and relaxed in their company. Even in the earliest years the boys saw more of Constance than of Oscar. However busy she was, she always found time to be with them, to listen to their stories and join in their games, to educate them in everyday values and expand their horizons with new experiences. 'Throughout my early years there was one person who always made me happy, and that was my mother, whom I adored,'[4] wrote Vyvyan in later years.

As a parent Oscar was absolutely marvellous. He had never lost that special quality of childhood, that sense of wonder that most grown-ups shake off with adolescence. To him, anything was possible. When he was at home he haunted the nursery or the dining-room, where the greater array of chairs and tables lent themselves to childhood games and fantasies. Here Oscar the immaculate, without any regard at all for his apparel, went down on all fours to be a horse, a lion, a bear. There was a special sense of camaraderie between him and his sons which was quite different from the gentle, caring relationship between Constance and the boys. One day Oscar came home with a splendid toy milk-cart, where everything was a true replica of the real thing, down to the genuine horse-hair in the mane and tail and the churns which could be taken down and opened. As soon as Oscar realized this, he went to the kitchen and fetched a jug of milk to fill the churns; and so they careered about the room without regard to the milk they spilled in the process. Eventually the arrival of the stern and disapproving nurse put an end to the game, leaving the three conspirators somewhat shamefaced. When it came to mending toys, Oscar the elegant threw aside his dignity and fixed whatever needed mending. And although it was usually Constance who dealt with any minor squabbles and misdemeanors, like any other mother she sometimes called in her husband to arbitrate or reprove. Frank Harris retails one such occasion as Oscar described it to him:

The other night I was reading when my wife came and asked me to go upstairs and reprove the elder boy; Cyril, it appeared, would not say his prayers. He had quarrelled with Vyvyan, and beaten him, and when he was shaken and told he must say his prayers, he would not kneel down, or ask God to make him a good boy. Of course I had to go upstairs and see to it. I took the chubby little fellow on my knee, and told him in a grave way that he had been very naughty; naughty to hit his younger brother, and naughty because he had given his mother pain. He must kneel down at once, and ask God to forgive him and make him a good boy.

'I was not naughty,' he pouted, 'it was Vyvyan; he was naughty.'

I explained to him that his temper was naughty, and that he must do as he was told. With a little sigh he slipped off my knee, and knelt down and put his little hands together, as he had been taught, and began, 'Our Father'. When he had finished the Lord's Prayer, he looked up at me and said gravely, 'Now I'll pray to myself.'

He closed his eyes and his lips moved. When he had finished I took him in my arms and kissed him. 'That's right,' I said.

'You said you were sorry,' questioned his mother, leaning over him, 'and asked God to make you a good boy?'

'Yes, mother,' he nodded, 'I said I was sorry and asked God to make Vyvyan a good boy.'

I had to leave the room, Frank, or he would have seen me smiling. Wasn't it delightful of him! We are all willing to ask God to make others good.[5]

Often Oscar sang to the boys, old Irish folk-songs mostly, that he had learned from his father. He romanced about the family house at Moytura, and the great carp that he said lay always at the bottom of the lake, waiting to be called up from the depths by the songs of their grandfather whom they had never known. It was one of his special dreams to take the family there one day to see the old home, a dream that sadly was never to be fulfilled. And of course he told them stories. Richard Le Gallienne recalled what Oscar had once said to him on that subject:

'It is the duty of every father,' he said with great gravity, 'to write fairy-tales for his children. But the mind of a child is a great mystery. It is incalculable, and who shall divine it, or bring to it his own peculiar delights? You humbly spread before it the treasures of your imagination, and they are as dross. For example, a day or two ago, Cyril yonder came to me with the question, "Father, do you ever dream?" "Why of course, my darling. It is the first duty of a gentleman to dream." "And what do you dream of?" asked Cyril, with a child's disgusting appetite for facts. Then I, believing, of course, that something picturesque would be expected of me, spoke of magnificent things: "What do I dream of? Oh, I dream of dragons with gold and silver scales, and scarlet things coming out of their mouths, of eagles with eyes made of diamonds that can see over the whole world at once, of lions with yellow manes, and voices like thunder, of elephants with little houses on their backs, and tigers and zebras with barred and spotted coats . . ." So I laboured on with my fancy, till, observing that Cyril was entirely unimpressed, and indeed quite undisguisedly bored, I came to a humiliating stop, and, turning to my son there, I said: "But tell me, what do you dream of, Cyril?" His answer was like a divine revelation: "I dream of *pigs*," he said.'[6]

In 1888 Oscar duly fulfilled his duty as a father by writing a book of fairy-tales. Called *The Happy Prince and Other Tales*, it was published by David Nutt. There were two editions, an ordinary one and a large paper edition limited to seventy-five copies signed by both Oscar and the publisher. The copy from which Oscar and Constance read to the children was copy number two of the latter. Whenever Oscar told them the story of 'The Selfish Giant' his eyes would fill with tears. Cyril once asked him why this was so, to which he replied that beautiful things always made him cry. Two notable artists illustrated the book; Walter Crane, one of whose pictures adorned the walls at Tite Street, and Jacob Hood. Oscar took the keenest interest in the illustrations, and one of his letters to Hood has survived. It suggests a drawing of a Prince kissing the hand of a Princess, ermine-clad, surrounded by courtiers. Hood produced just such a drawing for 'The Remarkable Rocket'.[7]

Robert Sherard described the book as 'A volume which many of his admirers look upon as his best and most characteristic prose work. There are no fairy-stories in the English language to compare with them. The writing is quite masterly; the stories proceed from a rare and opulent imagination; and while the tales that are told interest the child no less than the man of the world there underlies the whole a subtle philosophy, an indictment of society, a plea for the disinherited.'[8] Ruskin and Gladstone were among those to whom Oscar sent a presentation copy. The writer and critic Walter Pater, one of the founders of the Aesthetic Movement, also liked the book, and wrote to Oscar:

> I am confined to my room with gout, but have been consoling myself with *The Happy Prince*, and feel it would be ungrateful not to send a line to tell you how delightful I have found him and his companions. I hardly know whether to admire more the wise wit of 'The Wonderful [sic] Rocket', or the beauty and tenderness of 'The Selfish Giant': the latter is certainly perfect in its kind. Your genuine 'little poems in prose', those at the tops of pages 10 and 14, for instance, are gems, and the whole, too brief, book abounds with delicate touches and pure English.[9]

Oscar and Constance, and indeed Speranza too, must have been elated at this high praise from the great man, whom they all venerated. Oscar also received a letter praising the book from Leonard Smithers, a publisher who later on was very closely associated with him, and to whom he ultimately gave the manuscript of 'The Happy Prince'. The Toynbee Settlement in East London, which had been established in memory of the distinguished social reformer Arnold Toynbee, also received a complimentary copy from Oscar. Arnold Toynbee had been a contemporary of Oscar's at Oxford, and had died five years earlier. It seems likely, though, that it was mainly to please Constance, who was greatly interested in the social work going on in the East End of London, that Oscar donated the volume.

Clearly at this period Oscar was still very much bound up in his family life, and continued to treat Constance with unfailing gentleness and gallantry. Anything that caused her distress brought Oscar rushing to her defence. Just such an event occurred in June 1889 when a journalist and author of travelogues called Herbert Vivian wrote to Oscar inviting him to contribute an introduction to his book of reminiscences. Oscar's reply probably offended him, though it was couched in the kindest of terms:

> 'Good wine needs no bush' – at least somebody in Shakespeare says so, and certainly good reminiscences require no preface. And did I really say I would write one? I don't think one at all necessary. As for indiscretions, pray be indiscreet. If I can help you by reviews I shall certainly do so. [10]

No doubt piqued by this tactful refusal, Vivian published the letter in the *Sun* on 17 November 1889, as part of his serialized biographical note 'The Reminiscences of a Short Life'. He also wrote,

> For my own part I prefer to contemplate the present and the future rather than brood over the past, and I should probably never have persevered in my undertaking but for the suggestions and encouragement afforded me by Mr Oscar Wilde. He is the fairy-godfather, who presided at the birth of this book – I had almost dubbed him the midwife of my memoirs – and to him much of the praise or blame of their production must attach.

This alone was sufficient to produce a somewhat hostile response from both Constance and Oscar; yet it is doubtful whether Oscar would have taken the matter up with Mr Vivian had it not been for an anecdote about Cyril, repeated in an inaccurate and unacceptable form, which upset Constance a great deal. He said that at a private view in May 1889 he and Oscar had discussed 'The Decay of Lying', which had recently been published:

> The two characters in the dialogue, Cyril and Vivian [*sic*] he told

me, were named after his own little boys, to their no small delight. 'I plaster the walls of their rooms,' he said, 'with texts about early rising and sluggishness, and so forth, and I tell them that, when they grow up, they must take their father as a warning, and occasionally have breakfast earlier than two in the afternoon.' The story of Cyril's altruism is also well imagined. That youth, not a lustrum old, bewildered his family one morning by announcing that he did not mean to say his prayers any more. It was pointed out to him that he must pray God to make him good, but he demurred . . . after a prolonged altercation, the young philosopher offered a compromise, and said that he wouldn't mind praying God to make baby good.

To the modern reader this story, which sounds very like a distortion of the one told by Frank Harris, seems harmless enough. But Constance, wise and understanding though she was, remained rooted in the Victorian era. Where matters of religion were concerned, she had strong views which she was prepared to defend, and the notion that Cyril, her sweet little companion, could have renounced God must have been deeply distressing to her. Though she asked for nothing on her own account, she was deeply protective of her children, and besought Oscar to take the matter up at once with the tactless young man. Oscar accordingly wrote an immediate brief letter of remonstrance, but the dispute was still going on in May of the following year. Further instalments had appeared in the *Sun*, and Vivian proposed subsequently to publish in book form. Constance, Oscar wrote, did not wish to see her children 'paraded for the amusement of the uncouth'[11] in a newspaper which she considered vulgar.

The extent of Oscar's feelings for Constance was often misunderstood by outsiders, even those fairly intimately acquainted with Oscar. Richard Le Gallienne was one such friend. He commemorated a visit he paid to the Wildes at home with a couple of verses in a volume of his poetry. Afterwards he described the occasion.

After we had talked for a while in his study, we went upstairs to the drawing-room where Mrs Wilde sat with their two boys. Mrs Wilde was a pretty young woman of the innocent Kate Greenaway type. They all seemed very happy together, though it was impossible not to predict suffering for a woman so simple and domesticated with a mind so searching and so perverse and a character so self-indulgent. It was hard to see where two such different natures could find a meeting-place, particularly as poor Mrs Wilde was entirely devoid of humour and evangelically religious. So sweet and pretty and good, how came she by her outrageously intellectual husband, to whose destructive wit little was sacred and all things comedy? When one thinks that Mrs Wilde's chief interest after her children was – missionaries and her bosom friend Lady Sandhurst, who was one of the pillars of British church work.

'Missionaries, my dear!' I remember Wilde once saying at a dinner party. 'Don't you realise that missionaries are the divinely provided food for destitute and under-fed cannibals? Whenever they are on the brink of starvation, Heaven, in its infinite mercy, sends them a nice plump missionary.'

To this Constance replied with a shocked expression, 'Oh, Oscar! You cannot surely be in earnest. You can only be joking.'[12]

This judgement of Constance was not unkindly meant, and yet it is hardly just. It was also written with hindsight. The woman did not exist who would not have suffered as a result of the later developments in Oscar's life, and Constance bore up under their troubles more patiently and bravely than most others could have done. 'Domesticated' was hardly the word for her. She loved the House Beautiful and lavished care and attention on it. She adored her children without ever becoming matriarchal. She went in for embroidery and other forms of needlework, but as an art rather than in a strictly utilitarian way. What she produced could be likened to the sophisticated designs worked by William Morris' daughter May, who was a friend of the Wildes. At the dinner table Constance was outshone by her husband but then so, usually, was everybody else. It has often been said of Oscar that he did not converse but carried on a monologue which left his auditors – Constance not excepted – speechless with admiration.

As for Constance's sense of humour, that 'missionary' joke has often been cited as evidence that she had none. The story, which overlooked the fact that there were occasional subjects which seemed to Constance too serious for humour, is often linked with another to the effect that Constance once interrupted Oscar's brilliant flow of table talk with the remark 'Oh, Oscar, *did* you remember to call for Cyril's boots?' As Vyvyan Wilde later aptly pointed out, the story is clearly apocryphal, for no lady would have saddled her husband in Victorian England with such a petty chore, particularly when there were servants to do the job for them.[13] It is inconceivable that a woman of Constance's imagination and intelligence did not appreciate Oscar's fine wit, along with every other single aspect of his glittering personality.

Arthur Ransome made an interesting comment on Constance's character though he, like Richard Le Gallienne, also clearly failed to appreciate the situation:

> She was sentimental, pretty, well-meaning and inefficient. She would have been very happy as the wife of an ornamental minor poet, and it is possible that in marrying Wilde she mistook him for such a character. It must be remembered that she married the author of *Poems* and the lecturer on the aesthetic movement. His development puzzled her, made her feel inadequate, and so increased her inadequacy. She became more a spectacle for Wilde than an influence upon him, and was without the strength that might have prevented the disasters that were to fall through him on herself. She had a passion for leaving things alone, broken only by moments of interference badly timed. She became one of those women whose Christian names their husbands, without malice, preface with the epithets 'poor dear'. Her married life was no less ineffectual than unhappy.[14]

Ransome, despite his flowing style, based this summary of her character on a few brief facts which were embroidered by his prolific imagination. At no time did Constance mistake Oscar for a minor poet. She was at all times convinced of his genius, as her later letters show. It was not the development of his genius that puzzled her, but the sudden realization of those socially unacceptable proclivities that brought about his downfall. As for alleged lack of strength, it is true that she was in no sense a nagging wife. Her 'passion for leaving things alone'[15] was really part of the tacit understanding which she had with Oscar whereby each trusted to the other's innate sense of love and loyalty.

Trust was in fact one of the great strengths of Constance's

married life, and though in the end she felt herself betrayed, her own conduct could not be faulted. An unknown girl, she had married a man who had publicly worshipped at the shrine of such notable society beauties as Lillie Langtry, Ellen Terry and Sarah Bernhardt, to all of whom he had offered his poetry and his pure devotion. On rare occasions Constance exhibited a little jealousy, though not entirely without cause. Oscar's frequent absences from home were accepted by her as part of the inevitable way of life. Once, it is said, she grew jealous of his many calls on a lady called Bibidie Leonard, whose father was a former Young Irelander and an exile in Paris, who had a house in York Terrace. She was well known to Speranza, who had written to Oscar during his editorship of *Woman's World* asking whether Bibidie could contribute articles about Paris to the journal. Whether Constance had any special grounds to be jealous concerning her husband's relationship with Miss Leonard, who was rich and reputedly very beautiful, is not clear, but certainly nothing serious came of the matter.

Constance and Oscar were united in their interest in religion; yet with Oscar this remained throughout most of his life a purely theoretical adherence to the Anglican Creed, with strong inclinations to High-Church practices and a positive urge at various stages to embrace Roman Catholicism. This he did not actually do until he was on his deathbed. The fact is that he was basically somewhat self-indulgent in the matter, and wanted to embrace the idea without any of the discipline. He was not a churchgoer, unlike Constance, who liked to attend service on Sundays and joined in parish activities. Perhaps if Oscar had spent more time at home she would have been less likely to concentrate her attention on 'safe' callers, like men of the cloth. Such visitors undoubtedly proved rather boring to Oscar, yet he was invariably civil. Marie Belloc Lowndes described one such occasion, when there were altogether six people to dinner at Tite Street and the guest of honour was the bride-to-be of the local parson. She felt that Oscar must surely have found the company dull, yet he gave no sign of it, and poured out a stream of paradoxical talk that delighted the guests. On another occasion Yeats found him 'closeted with a missionary, who did not mind his native parishioners running about nude on week-days but wished to see them clothed at divine worship on Sundays'.[16] Perhaps it was Constance who had persuaded him to advise the missionary which of the various coloured smocks that were strewn upon the floor in Tite Street would be most appropriate for Central Africa.

Oscar's unfailing politeness and his skill in disguising his ennui in company would not have deceived Constance. She understood perfectly well his positive need for intellectual stimulus yet she was not entirely able to meet it. As his great interest in clothes and the home declined he looked for new topics and new friends. His absences from home became more frequent, even though he realized that in this he was being unfair to Constance. Nellie Melba recalled hearing from him how he told his sons about naughty little boys who made their mother cry and of the dreadful things that happened to them. One of them then asked 'what punishment would be reserved for naughty Papas, who did not come home till the early morning, and made Mother cry far more?'[17]

Constance tried vainly to conceal her unhappiness. Had she, like Speranza, been gifted with the dramatic instinct, she could have taken refuge in the rôle of poseuse. But she was simply not fitted to play the part of a tragedy queen. Instead she went on bravely with her own quiet life, clinging all the while to her two little boys. They were, after all, the physical manifestation of her love for her remarkable husband.

8

The Decadent

I am so glad you like that strange coloured book of
mine: it contains much of me in it. Basil Hallward is
what I think I am; Lord Henry what the world thinks
me; Dorian what I would like to be — in other ages,
perhaps.

Wilde on *The Picture of Dorian Gray*

It was in the year 1886 that the 'Friend of Friends' stepped into
Oscar's life for the first time. Robert Baldwin Ross was a Canadian
of singularly distinguished stock. His maternal grandfather, Robert
Baldwin, was the first Premier of Upper Canada, and his father was
John Ross, who became Attorney-General in Baldwin's government. An Ulsterman by birth, John Ross had emigrated to Canada
as a child, but died shortly before the birth of his third son. By his
express wish his children were brought up in Europe, and 'Robbie'
was destined for Cambridge. He was living in Oxford when Oscar
first met him, and in the following year, while his mother was
wintering in the South of France, he spent two months as the guest
of Oscar and Constance in Tite Street. He was small, dark, neat and
boyish, with an engaging modesty and an easy, infectious laugh.
His intelligence was exceptional, but he was totally unassuming.
He had a special genius for bringing out the best in the highly
gifted circle of friends with whom he surrounded himself.

In 1888 'Robbie' Ross went up to King's College, Cambridge, to
read history. He was by no means unathletic, and indeed rowed in
the second college eight; but he was well known as an aesthete, and
this quickly brought him into difficulties with his fellow
undergraduates. He also made himself unpopular in certain quarters
by criticizing in undergraduate journals the method of electing
Fellows. In March 1889 he was ducked in the college fountain and
although he bore it like a man, it was too great a shock for a

sensitive soul like his and he contracted pneumonia. Some said that his illness was a violent brain attack, and that he was too ill to see any of his friends. It was feared that he might take his own life, but in the end he rallied and recovered. Despite the abject apologies of the perpetrators and the pleading of his many friends, he was unable to face up again to college life and instead became a literary journalist and art critic.

Robbie Ross was a practising homosexual. He was also the nicest fellow imaginable. It was said publicly and within his lifetime that it was he who initially introduced Oscar to homosexuality, and this he never saw fit to deny. Probably Constance was ignorant of this aspect of Robbie's nature, but even had she known of it, it is unlikely that she would have seen in it anything of a threat to herself or her marriage. As a happy wife she had had abundant proof of Oscar's 'normality'.

Nor, indeed, was there any threat to the relationship of Constance and the two boys with Oscar in the friendship of the two men, except in so far as it introduced him to a range of appetites which were to have dangerous consequences elsewhere. The two men were good for each other. They generated intellectual sparks that encouraged literary achievement on both sides. Robbie's conversation was always stimulating, and he was to a large extent responsible for Oscar developing 'The Portrait of Mr W. H.' which Oscar produced in 1889, and which was published in *Blackwood's Magazine* in July of that year. This essay, which sought to identify the elusive Mr W. H. to whom Shakespeare dedicated his sonnets, caused considerable interest. Oscar wrote to Robbie, however, saying that the story was half his, for without him it would never have been written.

In February 1890 Oscar made the acquaintance of the poet Lionel Johnson. Patrick Braybrooke wrote of him, 'That his work would never appeal to a really big audience follows naturally from the very nature of it . . . . Scholarship, that very gentle addition to inspirational genius, adorned all his work.'[1] It was also said of him:

Lionel was a delightful fellow, though exceedingly eccentric, and, alas, in his later years greatly addicted to potations, which his small and childlike frame could not withstand. He was not much over thirty when he died. He had a mania for not going to bed, and if he could get anyone to sit up with him he would discourse in the most brilliant way up till five o'clock in the morning. At other times of the day he was rather noticeably silent. He was a great scholar and undoubtedly a great poet, but the austerity and profundity of his work makes him one who is never likely to appeal to any but a very eclectic audience.[2]

Oscar had read and liked his poetry and went out of his way to meet the young man, who was still an undergraduate at Oxford. Johnson described their first meeting in a letter to a friend, Arthur Galton:

> On Saturday at mid-day, lying half asleep in bed, reading Green, I was roused by a pathetic and unexpected note from Oscar: he plaintively besought me to get up and see him. Which I did: and found him as delightful as Green is not. He discoursed, with infinite flippancy, of everyone; lauded the *Dial* : laughed at Pater, and consumed all my cigarettes. I am in love with him . . .[3]

Later in the year Johnson wrote a Latin poem in praise of Oscar Wilde and *The Picture of Dorian Gray*. The relationship was not of itself particularly significant in Oscar's life; yet Johnson was later to introduce him to someone else whose influence was destined from the outset to be catastrophic: Lord Alfred Douglas.

The Picture of Dorian Gray is Oscar's only novel. It was first serialized in *Lippincott's Monthly Magazine*, beginning in June 1890. It caused an immediate sensation, and many of the reviews were hostile. The *Daily Chronicle* said, 'It is a tale spawned from the leprous literature of the French *Décadents* – a poisonous book, the atmosphere of which is heavy with the mephitic odours of moral and spiritual putrefaction.'[4] Oscar responded, 'My story is an essay on decorative art. It reacts against the crude brutality of plain realism. It is poisonous if you like, but you cannot deny that it is also perfect, and perfection is what we artists aim at.'[5] A year later it appeared, enlarged and with a preface, in book form. It is said that Coulson Kernahan, who worked for the publishers of the book, had an eleventh-hour telegram from Oscar, who was in Paris:

'Terrible blunder in book. Coming back specially. Stop all proofs.'[6] When Oscar discovered that it was not too late, and that Kernahan had stopped the proofs, his relief was boundless. The so-called blunder was that of giving the name Ashton to one of his characters, a mere picture-framer. 'Ashton is a gentleman's name and – God forgive me – I've given it to a tradesman.'[7] The offending name was accordingly changed to Hubbard, which he felt positively smelt of the tradesman.

When he wrote *The Picture of Dorian Gray* Oscar had not met Lord Alfred Douglas, had indeed probably never even heard of him. The name was to have fearful implications for both Oscar and Constance. Yet it is impossible to read *Dorian Gray* without seeing in it some uncanny prescience of the tragedy that was to wreck Oscar, and Constance with him. To begin with, there is his physical appearance:

He was certainly wonderfully handsome, with his finely-curved scarlet lips, his frank blue eyes, his crisp gold hair. There was something in his face that made one trust him at once. All the candour of youth was there, as well as all youth's passionate purity. One felt that he had kept himself unspotted from the world.[8]

Then, too, there is the description of the artist Basil Hallward's relationship with him. He recalls their first meeting:

I turned half-way round, and saw Dorian Gray for the first time. When our eyes met, I felt that I was growing pale. A curious sensation of terror came over me. I knew that I had come face to face with some one whose mere personality was so fascinating that, if I allowed it to do so, it would absorb my whole nature, my whole soul, my very art itself. I did not want any external influence on my life. You know yourself, Harry, how independent I am by nature. I have always been my own master; had at least always been so, till I met Dorian Gray. Then – but I don't know how to explain it to you. Something seemed to tell me that I was on the verge of a terrible crisis in my life. I had a strange feeling that Fate had in store for me exquisite joys and exquisite sorrows. I grew afraid, and tried to quit the room. It was not conscience that made me do so; it was a sort of cowardice.[9]

Hallward goes on to describe their day-to-day relationship:

As a rule, he is charming to me, and we sit in the studio and talk of a thousand things. Now and then, however, he is horribly thoughtless, and seems to take a real delight in giving me pain. Then I feel, Harry, that I have given away my whole soul to someone who treats it as if it were a flower to put in his coat, a bit of decoration to charm his vanity, an ornament for a summer's day.[10]

Oscar made another of his characters, Lord Henry Wotton, claim that 'The one charm of marriage is that it makes a life of deception absolutely necesary for both parties.'[11] Biographers have tended to latch on to this as an exact indication of the state of affairs in Tite Street. What follows makes it clear that this is not to be taken seriously:

'I never know where my wife is, and my wife never knows what I am doing. When we meet – we do meet occasionally, when we dine out together, or go down to the Duke's – we tell each other the most absurd stories with the most serious faces. My wife is very good at it – much better, in fact, than I am. She never gets confused over her dates, and I always do. But when she does find me out, she makes no row at all. I sometimes wish she would; but she merely laughs at me.'

'I hate the way you talk about your married life, Harry,' said Basil Hallward, strolling towards the door that led into the garden. 'I believe that you are really a very good husband, but that you are thoroughly ashamed of your own virtues. You are an extraordinary fellow. You never say a moral thing, and you never do a wrong thing. Your cynicism is simply a pose.'[12]

This amused tolerance was in fact very like the relationship between Constance and Oscar. Though on Oscar's side the romance had gone, his marriage suited his needs very well, or at least it had up till now. But the time was approaching when areas of selfishness began to creep in. Oscar's allegiance to Constance was about to undergo a change.

Oscar was particularly busy at this time, for the period of his greatest creativity was now upon him. In July 1891 *Lord Arthur Savile's Crime and Other Stories* was published. Constance was so delighted with it that she sent a copy to their friend Edward

Heron-Allen. She herself received a presentation copy inscribed 'Constance from Oscar, July '91'. Three passages in the book are marked in pencil, presumably by Constance herself. It is impossible to tell whether she marked them before or after Oscar's ultimate disgrace. In either case they are curiously significant.

Actors are so fortunate. They can choose whether they will appear in tragedy or in comedy, whether they will suffer or make merry, laugh or shed tears. But in real life it is so different. Most men and women are forced to perform parts for which they have no qualifications. Our Guildensterns play Hamlet for us, and our Hamlet has to jest like Prince Hal. The world is a stage, but the play is badly cast. [13]

And yet it was not the mystery, but the comedy of suffering that struck him; its absolute uselessness, its grotesque want of meaning. How incoherent everything seemed! How lacking in all harmony! He was amazed at the discord between the shallow optimism of the day and the real facts of existence. He was still very young. [14]

The great piles of vegetables looked like masses of jade against the morning sky, like masses of green jade against the pink petals of some marvellous rose. Lord Arthur felt curiously affected, but could not tell why. There was something in the dawn's loveliness that seemed to him inexpressibly pathetic, and he thought of all the days that break in beauty and that set in storm. [15]

Robert Sherard described the stories as 'amusettes'. [16] Oscar had a genius for plots and was capable of inventing them by the dozen. His brother Willie often used to make use of this facility when he needed to write a story in a hurry. Before Oscar's marriage he used to turn up early in the morning, when Oscar was still in bed, in the certain knowledge that he would come away with something to work on. Oscar's new book, unlike *The Picture of Dorian Gray*, was favourably received by the critics. The *Athenaeum* reported, 'Mr Oscar Wilde's little book of stories is capital. They are delightfully humorous, witty, and fresh, sparkling with good things, full of vivacity and well put together.' [17]

They also demonstrate that there was no cow too sacred for the exercise of Oscar's wit. Both Constance and Oscar were very superstitious. They both took very seriously astrology, occultism and palmistry, and though Oscar tempted the fates by poking fun, he was as interested as Constance in all these subjects. Lady Windermere, who cannot live without her 'chiromantist', says, 'I would not dream of giving a party without him. He tells me that I have a pure psychic hand, and that if my thumb had been the least little bit shorter, I should have been a confirmed pessimist and gone into a convent.'[18] Lord Arthur Savile, however, ends up by killing the palmist who has predicted that he will commit a murder. Thus Oscar clearly demonstrates the principle that people are governed by the power of suggestion. Yet this ability to analyse did not prevent either him or Constance from being influenced by superstition even in the most important issues of their lives.

Of late, Oscar had begun to spend more and more time away from Constance. In part, ill-health of an unspecified nature and a sense of frustration brought on by adverse press notices were responsible. In August 1890 he spent several days at Springwood Park, Kelso, the seat of the minor poet Sir George Brisbane Scott-Douglas, who described Oscar's conversation as 'always more remarkable than his writing'.[19] From Kelso he moved on to stay with more friends in Perthshire, where he was glad to find himself in the midst of purple heather. 'I only like green in art,' he said. 'This is one of my many heresies.'[20] In October it was Constance's turn to go away for a fortnight, leaving Oscar behind in Tite Street.

In February 1891 he had complained of ill-health and overwork, and had gone to Paris for a rest, which in his case meant for a change of companionship and fresh mental stimulus. The visit certainly achieved that. On 3 March he wrote to Cyril telling him that he was much better, and describing his drives in the Bois de Boulogne and his visit to the poet Mallarmé. 'I hope you are taking great care of dear Mamma. Give her my love and kisses, and also love and kisses to Vyvyan and yourself.'[21] He returned to Paris again in May of the same year, and for about two months at the end of 1891. Having conceived the idea of writing his drama *Salome* in French, he felt that it was only in Paris that he could find inspiration.

On 3 November 1891, having just read Pater's late review of *The Picture of Dorian Gray* in the *Bookman*, Speranza wrote Oscar a long and enthusiastic letter, praising his style. The letter ends:

'Constance was here last evening. She is so nice always to me. I am very fond of her. *Do* come home. She is very lonely, and mourns for you.'[22] Less than a month later Speranza received her presentation copy of Oscar's latest book, *A House of Pomegranites*, a collection of four delightful stories. The book was dedicated to Constance, and each story to a society lady. To Constance's great friend Lady Brooke, the Ranee of Sarawak, he dedicated 'The Young King'; to Princess Alice of Monaco, 'The Fisherman and his Soul', to Mrs Grenfell, who afterwards became Lady Desborough, 'The Birthday of the Infanta', and to Margot Tennant, who later became wife of Asquith, the Liberal Prime Minister, he dedicated 'The Star-Child'. Speranza wrote again to Oscar praising the new book and its 'jewels of thought set in the fine gold of the most exquisite words' and adding, 'Constance is looking well and is much pleased at the dedication to her, and the other ladies are named prettily.'[23] In financial terms this was, however, the only one of Oscar's books that failed to sell well, probably because the plates were accidentally spoiled in the cleaning, leading to indistinctness in the illustrations.

In January 1892 *Lady Windermere's Fan* went into rehearsal at the St James's Theatre. Its real title was deliberately kept secret until a few days before it opened, and it was until that time provisionally known as *A Good Woman*. When news of its tentative title came to Speranza's ears she wrote at once to Oscar urging him to change it. In her view it was mawkish, and a good woman would interest nobody. Rumours of quarrels between Oscar and George Alexander, the producer, who had cast himself in the part of Lord Windermere, made Speranza distinctly uneasy. What she feared was that Oscar might try to absent himself from the first night. In a long letter full of wise comment she urged on him that it would be both practical and dignified for him to be at the first performance. 'It would be right and proper and Constance would like it. Do not leave her all alone . . . Above all remember that Constance would like you to be there. So do make up your mind to be present . . . I am very anxious about it, and for you, and for Constance, whose whole heart is in the success.'[24]

Oscar may or may not have been influenced by his mother's importunities, but he duly escorted Constance to the first night of his play. Constance lavished even more care than usual on her costume and decided to wear a blue brocade dress modelled on the styles of Charles I's time. It had a long tabbed bodice, slashed sleeves, and was decorated with pearls and antique lace. Many of their friends were there to witness Oscar's triumph, including Lillie Langtry, Richard Le Gallienne and his wife, and Robbie Ross. So too was Reggie Turner, the illegitimate son of Lord Burnham, and Lord Alfred Douglas. Though some of the critics proved hostile, the play was a runaway box-office success. After the performance Constance went back home while Oscar went on to dine with some of his male friends at Willie's, where they spent several hours in celebration. Constance was delighted with Oscar's success, and took some pleasure too in the prospect of financial reward. Oscar had turned down what looked like an advantageous cash settlement, preferring to gamble on taking a royalty, and in the end his instinct was proved correct, for the play brought him in some £7,000.

9

The Gilt-headed Youth

I couldn't help it. I can resist everything except
temptation.

Lady Windermere's Fan

The year 1892, which had begun so well for Constance and Oscar,
brought her sadness too. Her Aunt Emily had been in frail health
for some time past, so that Constance had occasionally found it
necessary to go and stay in order to look after her. On 17 March
1892 she died at St Leonards-on-Sea.

Aunt Emily was a very wealthy woman. She had inherited the
income on a quarter share of old John Lloyd's wealth but this does
not account for an estate which at her death stood at £42,000.
Constance's share of all this amounted to £3,000. Otho had received
only £1,350, but his sons Otho and Fabian each had bequests of
£1,000. In making this apportionment Aunt Emily seems to have
taken into account Constance's greater need of hard cash. There was
a bequest of £250 to be held in trust for Cyril, who was Aunt
Emily's godson, but Vyvyan received nothing.

About a year later Constance suffered another bereavement. Aunt
Carrie Kirkes died in the Far East, leaving Constance some £5,500,
making a total from the two bequests of £8,500. This is the capital
inheritance, always assumed to have been from her grandfather,
John Lloyd, which is often referred to as having come to Constance
in the eighteen-nineties. No record has been found to suggest any
major capital purchases on Constance's part. There were no major
alterations to the House Beautiful. Constance wrote to a friend on
14 September 1892, 'We are still at Tite Street, Chelsea, but in a
few months we shall probably move to another house in Tite Street,
rather larger as we are somewhat cramped in our present one.'[1]
Perhaps the first bequest had encouraged them to think in these
terms, but in the event nothing came of it.

Laura Troubridge, who had married Adrian Hope by this time, lived a few doors away from the Wildes in Tite Street. Laura was something of an artist, and in November 1891 wrote 'I am deep in a portrait of Cyril Wilde, who is awfully picturesque and nice to do'.[2] After this she did a portrait of her cousin Minnie Cochrane, who was lady-in-waiting to Princess Beatrice. Her grandmother, Lady Cochrane, had a residence on the Isle of Wight, and when the Royal Family were in residence at Osborne, Queen Victoria got to hear about the portrait. She accordingly asked to see a specimen of Laura's finished work, whereupon Laura promptly telegraphed to Constance to lend the portrait to Adrian, who took it with him to the island. 'The Queen liked my pastels so much she wanted me to do portraits of the Connaught children, Princess Beatrice and Princess Ena [later Queen of Spain],' she wrote in her diary. 'It was Cyril Wilde's picture that made them so keen about Princess Ena who, they say, is very pretty. She is to be done in the same style, as they all liked it so much.'[3] Shortly afterwards Adrian Hope wrote to his wife, 'Have just met Oscar who was killing about the picture of Cyril for which he said he expected a knighthood.'[4]

Lord Alfred Douglas, 'Bosie' to his intimates, had stepped into Oscar's life at some time in the summer of 1891. Lionel Johnson, who was also a homosexual, had met Bosie at Oxford. For that first meeting with Oscar, Johnson collected Bosie from his mother's house in Cadogan Place in a hansom cab, and took him to Tite Street. Here they spent some time with Oscar in his ground-floor study. It would appear that Bosie was somewhat in awe of Oscar, and, as a poet of some merit in his own right, he claimed the attention of the older man. From the outset Bosie adopted the rôle of disciple. He possessed sufficient talent to produce work of major significance, but his idleness and love of luxury robbed him of his true potential. Probably Oscar was unaware of this at the time. The three men chatted amicably together for a while before going up to the drawing-room, where they had tea with Constance. Bosie later recorded his impressions of her:

> I liked her and she liked me. She told me, about a year after I first met her, that she liked me better than any of Oscar's other friends. She frequently came to my mother's house and was

present at a dance which my mother gave during the first year of my acquaintance with her husband. After the débâcle I never saw her again, and I do not doubt that Ross and others succeeded in poisoning her mind against me, but up to the very last day of our acquaintance, we were the best of friends.[5]

Although Oscar later denied it, it is probably true that Constance liked Bosie initially. Both she and Oscar had a supreme admiration for youth, beauty and intellect. Other people they knew possessed these qualities in varying degrees but none had the same abundance of all three as the young Lord Alfred Douglas. Bosie was also descended from one of the noblest titled families in the country, and the Wildes were clay-footed enough to set a high regard by titles and wealth. At twenty-one he was intelligent, though indolent, and had the kind of looks that send an arrow through the toughest hearts. He was elegant and slim as a wand. His hair was fair, with a suspicion of curl about the temples. Candid blue eyes were the most striking feature of a face that was almost too perfect. His nose was finely chiselled, his lower lip slightly full and moist. Everything about his countenance indicated frankness, openess, clean living. His expression had all the innocence of a child. It was exactly the face to capture the imagination of the Wildes with their passion for beauty.

Perhaps Oscar felt a pang of envy as he looked upon that face. Probably if he could have chosen his own physical appearance he would have looked like this ideal young man. Oscar was thirty-seven and conscious of the passing of youth. As the apostle of beauty he had capitalized on every one of his physical assets, yet despite his many attractions few would have described him as handsome. Lord Alfred Douglas on the other hand was incomparable.

Unfortunately the character that lay behind that perfect exterior was neither frank, innocent nor childlike. In years he was young; in dissipation and experience of the world's vices, Lord Alfred Douglas was as old as the hills. He was spoilt, selfish, a reckless spendthrift and an idler of the worst kind. Rarely has there been a disposition with so little to commend it and so much to condemn. The best one could say of him is that to a degree his upbringing was to blame.

Bosie was the third son of the eighth Marquess of Queensberry. The Marquess was as ugly as his third son was beautiful. An 'ultra-hickory type' was how George Bernard Shaw described him. He was a sportsman, dedicated to his dogs and his horses, and without a single charitable thought for his wife and children. He often rode his own horses in the Grand National, for he was an excellent and fearless horseman. He also won the Amateur Light-weight Boxing Championship, and drew up the rules of boxing named after him. There were areas of aggression in his character that led to outbursts of violent rage, and his family were in terror of him.

Bosie's mother, also an aristocrat, was a very beautiful woman, and it was from her that Bosie had inherited those looks that were in reality more of a curse than a blessing. Throughout their marriage the Marquess tyrannized over his wife, and when eventually he brought his mistress into the house with the intention of setting up a *ménage à trois*, she could stand no more and divorced him. With his track record it came as no surprise to anyone when his second marriage was annulled after only six months. The Marquess was immensely wealthy, and had managed to squander £400,000 with no effort at all. There was still plenty of cash left in the kitty, though, and from this he was obliged by court order to make generous maintenance payments to his ex-wife. Such was his nature that he never paid over the money to her until he was threatened by legal proceedings.

The Marquess of Queensberry's eldest son, Lord Drumlanrig, was an excellent young man who had in his character every virtue that Bosie and his father lacked. When Lord Rosebery was Foreign Minister under Gladstone, Drumlanrig was his private secretary. In due course he was recommended for an English peerage. Queensberry himself as a Scottish peer was not automatically entitled to a seat in the House of Lords, but was chosen as one of the sixteen Scottish peers elected by their fellows to represent them. In time he rendered himself ineligible by refusing to take the oath, which he called 'Christian tomfoolery'. He was an atheist, and loudly proclaimed that fact on every conceivable occasion. So far from being pleased at the honour which was proposed for his heir, he was furious; and though he went ahead and wrote a letter to Gladstone expressing pleasure at his son's becoming Lord Kelhead, he soon began to write rude letters to Gladstone and Rosebery and even the Queen on the subject. He then followed Rosebery to Hamburg with the idea of horsewhipping him, and only gave up the plan when the Prince of Wales intervened.

Queensberry's second son, Lord Hawick, incurred his father's displeasure by marrying a clergyman's daughter. This incensed Queensberry the atheist, who refused to meet his son and his family. There were violent scenes between Queensberry and Hawick around the time of the Wilde débâcle, and when ultimately the young man visited him on his deathbed the Marquess spat at him.

Ever since his infancy, Bosie had hated his father. Life for him was one long running battle in which he hoped to see his father humiliated. Outwardly he always pretended to be his mother's champion, but in reality it was on his own account. Each saw wrongdoing in the other and claimed justification on those grounds. The fact is that it was a case of two evils in sharp conflict. Bosie, indolent and selfish, spendthrift and amoral, hated his father in a fierce and bitter way. He was incapable of love while hatred remained his strongest passion. Yet the world, recognizing his father for a madman, tended to take the part of the beautiful young man.

There was nothing specially dramatic about the first meeting between Oscar and Bosie. They chatted pleasurably, and each took to the other. As an ordinary courtesy Oscar invited the young man, who was already displaying poetic qualities that won Oscar's admiration, to dine with him at the Albemarle Club, to which both Oscar and Constance belonged.

The friendship took some time to develop, and they had met only four times, including the first night of *Lady Windermere's Fan*, when Oscar received a pathetic letter from Bosie begging his help because he was being blackmailed. It was an appeal that Oscar could not resist, and he got him out of the difficulty, though not without considerable inconvenience to himself. Bosie always claimed that it was Oscar who pursued him, but this seems unlikely. What seems to have prevented him from tormenting Oscar from the outset was that he was in North Africa with Lord Cromer, to whom he acted as private secretary. A sharp dispute with Lord Cromer brought Bosie back to England and left him unexpectedly at a loose end.

It was fashionable at the time of Oscar's trials to look upon him as the corrupter of the younger man. Bosie with his aristocratic birth, his slim, boyish physique and fair colouring looked like the cream of British manhood. He was, however, of full age and had been a practising homosexual for years before he met Oscar. Oscar the open-handed, the generous, with his pockets for the first time in his life overflowing with money; Oscar with his ready understanding of human frailties and his inherent love of the young and the beautiful, was easy game for this unscrupulous young man. In all respects except one Oscar's was the strong personality and Bosie's the weak. But Bosie's apparent weakness was that of the parasite whose strongest instinct is for self-preservation. Oscar, on the other hand, was by nature and upbringing the generous protector of the weak. Though he possessed wit in abundance, he was without guile.

By some unerring instinct Bosie realized that he could triumph over the strong man, and this drew him to Oscar like a magnet. He had already had limited first-hand experience of Oscar's generosity. On only their second meeting, when he dined with Oscar at the Albemarle Club, he had received from him an autographed copy of the Large Paper edition of *The Picture of Dorian Gray*. The inscription read: 'Alfred Douglas from his friend who wrote this book. July 91. Oscar.' He had also dined lavishly at Willis's on the opening night of *Lady Windermere's Fan*. It seems extraordinary that Bosie can have had the effrontery to beg help from a friend of so slight acquaintance in the matter of the blackmail; yet Oscar not only sorted the problem out, no doubt at some cost to himself, but even gave him a copy of the 'author's edition' of his *Poems* which came out at the same time.

An undated letter from Oscar to Robert Ross which seems to have been written at this time indicates how completely Oscar had already fallen under the spell of the young man. It is written from the Royal Palace Hotel in Kensington, where Bosie had insisted on stopping for a sandwich, and reads: 'He is quite like a narcissus – so white and gold . . . Bosie is so tired: he lies like a hyacinth on the sofa, and I worship him.'[6]

In June 1892 Oscar met his old friend Sarah Bernhardt at a party given by Henry Irving. To his great delight she undertook to play the lead in his new play, *Salome*. Rehearsals, with an all French cast, began almost immediately, and Oscar's friend W. Graham Robertson designed the costumes. Unfortunately the production was doomed. When the text was submitted routinely to the Lord Chancellor's office for licensing it was banned. The reason was lamentably weak: three hundred years earlier, during the Reformation, plays in which biblical characters were represented had been banned, with the object of stamping out the old Roman Catholic

Mystery Plays which had had such extraordinary public appeal. Oscar's health was already giving cause for some concern at this time and news of the ban made matters even worse. He smarted under a sense of bitter injustice. The licence had been refused by a commonplace official called Pigot, described by George Bernard Shaw as 'a walking compendium of vulgar insular prejudice',[7] a man accustomed to license vulgar farce and melodrama yet prepared to ban the publication and performance of a superb work of art.

Lord Alfred Douglas was on the point of travelling to Hamburg with his maternal grandfather, and suggested that Oscar should travel with them to take the cure. They accordingly left England and took rooms at 51 Kaiser-Friedrich Promenade, Hamburg, where Oscar placed himself under the supervision of five doctors. In a letter to her brother Constance described his regime as 'getting up at 7.30, going to bed at 10.30, smoking hardly any cigars and being massaged, and of course drinking waters. I only wish I was there to see it.'[8]

Under this treatment Oscar's health did in fact improve, and he was also gratified by the publication in the *Pall Mall Gazette* on 1 July of a letter by the dramatist William Archer, who wrote:

Ever since Mr Oscar Wilde told me, a fortnight ago, that his *Salome* had been accepted by Madame Sarah Bernhardt, I have been looking forward, with a certain malign glee, to the inevitable suppression of the play by the Great Irresponsible. Quaint as have been the exploits of that gentleman and his predecessors in the past, the record of the Censorship presents nothing quainter than the present conjuncture. A serious work of art, accepted, studied, and rehearsed by the greatest actress of our time, is peremptorily suppressed, at the very moment when the personality of its author is being held up to ridicule, night after night, on the public stage, with the full sanction and approval of statutory Infallibility. But is is surely unworthy of Mr Wilde's lineage to turn tail and run away from a petty tyranny which lives upon the disunion and apathy of English dramatic authors . . . Mr Wilde's talent is unique. We require it and we appreciate it — those of us, at any rate, who are capable of any sort of artistic appreciation.

Archer's letter may well have been a factor which persuaded Oscar to abandon his first impulse to throw over his own nationality and take out French citizenship. In France, he felt, his work would be better appreciated. Archer's reference to the ridicule on the London stage every night referred to a travesty of *Lady Windermere's Fan* by Charles Brookfield, an actor, with music by Glover, called *The Poet and the Puppets*. The poet was called Oscar, and the play was a vicious attack. Oscar appealed to the Lord Chamberlain about the play, but when it was read to him he asked only that the name Oscar be altered. 'O'Flahertie' was substituted, and to this he did not object.

Constance, meanwhile, had remained behind in England with the boys. Oscar rejoined them in August at Tite Street, but then moved on to a farmhouse he had rented near Cromer in Norfolk. As for Constance, she had been invited to Babbacombe, near Torquay. Her great friend, the politician Lady Sandhurst, had died in January of that year, but Constance had an even more powerful political friend, Lady Mount-Temple, to whom she was distantly related and with whom she had stayed, apparently, for the first time in the autumn of 1889. At that time Lady Mount-Temple had recently been widowed, and as she was childless she had found herself rather lonely. She herself came from a distinguished family. Her father was a Vice-Admiral and her mother was a daughter of the third Earl of Aldeburgh. Her husband had been very rich, having inherited through his mother the estates of both Lord Melbourne and Lord Palmerston, including Broadlands, where he was buried.

Lady Mount-Temple was a patron of the Pre-Raphaelites, and the great, rambling house at Babbacombe Cliff to which she retired after her husband's death had been designed and decorated for her by William Morris and Edward Burne-Jones. She had a fine collection of paintings, notably by Burne-Jones and Dante Gabriel Rossetti, which were later bequeathed to the Tate Gallery. The most notable room in the house, which had the sun all day, was called 'Wonderland' because it was decorated with scenes from *Alice's Adventures in Wonderland*. The large rooms and exposed site made it a cold house in winter, even though it boasted the first central-heating system in a private house in England. But the grounds, with their wooded slopes which went down to the cliff edge, were ideal for the children.

Anxious to get away from London with the children during the summer months, and hoping that Oscar could be persuaded to join

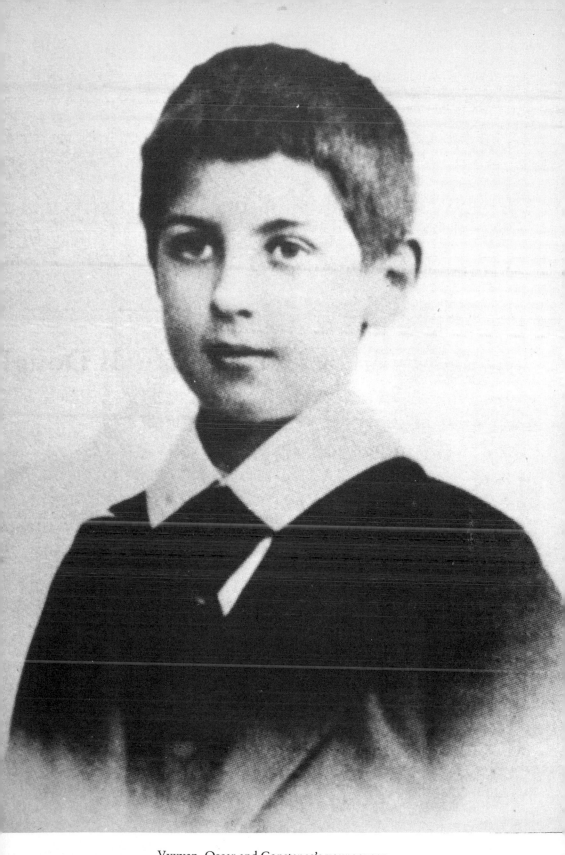

Vyvyan, Oscar and Constance's younger son

Ellen Terry

Robert Ross *(left)* and Reginald
Turner, Oscar's two loyal friends

Lady Sandhurst, Constance's friend
and mentor

Lord Alfred Douglas, aged twenty-three, at the time he met Oscar

Oscar in 1894

them, Constance needed no further incentive to close up the house in Tite Street, pay off the servants, and move into Lady Mount-Temple's lovely home. As for the latter, she planned to spend several months abroad, and allowed them the rare privilege of occupying the whole house until March 1893.

In Cromer Oscar was intending to work on the script for his new play, which he provisionally called *Mrs Arbuthnot*, but which was ultimately entitled *A Woman of No Importance*. Before long, Bosie joined him there, and stayed for ten days. They spent a lot of time on the golf course, Oscar having taken to the game with an enthusiasm that amused Constance. But after he had been there a few days, Bosie fell ill. When Constance heard of it, she wrote her husband a letter full of sympathy:

Dearest Oscar,
I am so sorry about Lord Alfred Douglas and wish I was at Cromer to look after him. If you think I could be any good, do telegraph for me, because I can get easily over to you.[9]

It is clear from the tone of her letter that she saw nothing unusual in Oscar's relationship with the young man; and it also tends to support Lord Alfred's contention that, initially, Constance liked him. It is impossible that she could have continued to like him for long, however, as subsequent events will show.

Constance had plenty of company at Babbacombe, despite Lady Mount-Temple's absence, 'I am not alone here, and I think I shall hardly be alone again,'[10] she wrote to Oscar. There were occasional overnight visitors, and some wealthy people called the Van Rualtas who had a fine yacht, to which they invited Constance, and a little launch in which they took her round Torquay harbour. There was also Miss Phipps, an American whose family had leased Knebworth. Constance took to her immediately, and described her as a 'beautiful girl, with a bright, enthusiastic face, and very little American'.[11]

While Oscar was at Cromer he managed to complete more than two-thirds of *A Woman of No Importance*, and got the first two acts typed up. But none of the work was done while Bosie was in the house, for he demanded constant attention. At the end of September Oscar went up to Glasgow to see Herbert Beerbohm Tree and discuss the play, staying at the Central Station Hotel. At around this time, probably just after the start of the academic year, he spent a long weekend with Bosie in Oxford. In early October he visited Bosie's mother at Bracknell. He later recalled the occasion in *De Profundis*, the bitter account of their relationship which he wrote in prison, in the form of a letter to Douglas.

> I remember one morning in the early October of '92 sitting in the yellowing woods at Bracknell with your mother. At that time I knew very little of your real nature . . . The conversation turned on you, and your mother began to speak to me about your character. She told me of your two chief faults, your vanity, and your being, as she termed it, 'all wrong about money'. I have a distinct recollection of how I laughed. I had no idea that the first would bring me to prison, and the second to bankruptcy. I thought vanity a sort of graceful flower for a young man to wear; as for extravagance – for I thought she meant no more than extravagance – the virtues of prudence and thrift were not in my own nature or my own race. But before our friendship was one month older I began to see what your mother really meant. Your insistence on a life of reckless profusion: your incessant demands for money: your claim that all your pleasures should be paid for by me whether I was with you or not: brought me after some time into serious monetary difficulties, and what made the extravagances to me at any rate so monotonously uninteresting, as your persistent grasp on my life grew stronger and stronger, was that the money was really spent on little more than the pleasures of eating, drinking and the like. Now and then it is a joy to have one's table red with wine and roses, but you outstripped all taste and temperance. You demanded without grace and received without thanks. [12]

Shortly afterwards Oscar went to stay for a few days in the Royal Hotel, Bournemouth, for his health was still giving him cause for concern. From there he went to Paris, and it was not until November that he joined Constance at Babbacombe Cliff, where she and the children had been enjoying their prolonged holiday. Oscar was determined to work hard, and indeed during his stay there, which lasted into March, he finished *A Woman of No Importance* and most of *A Florentine Tragedy*, a play in blank-verse. He also started to put together another play, to be called *La Sainte Courtisane*.

On 4 December Constance wrote to Robbie Ross and invited him to come and stay with them at Babbacombe Cliff for as long as he liked. Her letter was formal, though gracious. Over the next few months she was to become much closer to her husband's friend. Perhaps both of them had begun to feel that they were being squeezed out of Oscar's life by his new friend and his new-found success. Just to have Oscar with her and the boys for such a stretch must have seemed like heaven to Constance after his long absence.

The weather was far from clement, but Oscar found time to relax with the boys, and no doubt there were occasions when they all went down to the beach together. Oscar was at his best at the seaside. The athletic side of his nature often tends to be overlooked, but in fact he was a very strong swimmer, and loved sailing and fishing too. Sometimes he took the family out boating with him. This delighted Cyril, though Vyvyan had his reservations. He was not too keen on the idea of catching fish, for whom he felt too much sympathy. What he really enjoyed was building sand-castles. Oscar excelled at this, producing elaborate fairy-tale castles, usually with toy soldiers to add further realism. Despite Constance's advanced views on dress, she and Oscar insisted on a degree of cover-up for the children on the beach that would astonish modern parents. There was a permanent fear of chills or sunstroke, perhaps understandable in an era when the antibiotic had not been invented. Usually Constance dressed the boys like their father for the beach. He used to wear knickerbockers and a Norfolk jacket, and a large hat. When they got on to the sand he used to take off his socks and shoes just like the boys.

During their visit, Oscar supervised the rehearsals of an amateur production of *Lady Windermere's Fan*, which opened at the Theatre Royal in Torquay on 2 January 1893. Mrs Splatt, the Mayoress, starred as Mrs Erlynne, but a professional actor called Nutcombe Gould took the part of Lord Darlington. Unfortunately Oscar missed the opening night because of a bad cold.

Shortly after this Bosie, who was in London, sent Oscar a sonnet of his own composition which he called 'In Sarum Close'. Oscar was delighted, and wrote:

My Own Boy,

Your sonnet is quite lovely, and it is a marvel that those red rose-leaf lips of yours should have been made no less for music of song than for madness of kisses. Your slim gilt soul walks between passion and poetry. I know Hyacinthus, whom Apollo loved so madly, was you in Greek days.

Why are you alone in London, and when do you go to Salisbury? Do go there to cool your hands in the grey twilight of Gothic things, and come here whenever you like. It is a lovely place – it only lacks you; but go to Salisbury first.

Always, with undying love, yours Oscar[13]

In late January or early February Oscar had some business in Paris connected with the French edition of *Salome*, which was published on 22 February 1893. Constance, meanwhile, had been planning a European tour of her own with her Aunt Mary, and had arranged with Oscar that on his return to Babbacombe he would stay and look after the boys in her absence. She had occasionally left the children with friends in the past, but on the whole she preferred that they should be with either Oscar or herself. Oscar had not the slightest objection; in fact he welcomed it, for as Constance knew well, he worshipped the two boys. She recognized that certain elements of childhood that most people mislay somewhere between adolescence and maturity were still present within him and were part of the essence of his remarkable genius.

Always dutiful in the matter of letter-writing, Constance wrote many enthusiastic letters home, mostly extolling the beauties of Florence, which to her artistic temperament was something of an ideal city. She had always enjoyed the company of her Aunt Mary, with whom she shared many interests. Though grey-haired, Aunt Mary carried her years well and had retained her slim figure. Like Constance she was keenly concerned with fashion, and her outfits were occasionally described on the fashion and social pages of women's magazines. Constance greatly influenced her aunt's choice of clothes, and her gowns tended to be simpler than those of most other women of fashion as a result. There was much to occupy Constance and Aunt Mary in Italy, and this helped them to get over the sadness of their recent bereavements. They even began to think of extending their stay. But while Constance was enjoying her well-deserved holiday, Oscar and the boys were not alone at Babbacombe Cliff. Bosie was with them.

In early February Lady Queensberry had engaged as tutor for

Bosie the notable scholar Campbell Dodgson, who was summoned to her house in the Cathedral Close at Salisbury to await his new pupil. Bosie, who had done badly in his examinations, arrived characteristically late, spent the whole evening on his neglected correspondence, and then announced that they were off to stay with Oscar Wilde. Bosie was without books, cigarettes, or money, but none of this seemed to trouble him. A few minutes before the train was due to leave, the little pony chaise was overloaded with a vast quantity of trunks. Dodgson recalled, 'I was charged with a fox terrier and a scarlet morocco dispatch-box, a gorgeous and beautiful gift from Oscar. After hurried farewells to the ladies, we started on a wild career, Bosie driving. I expected only to drag my shattered limbs to the Salisbury Infirmary, but we arrived whole at the station.'[14] Once on the train, Bosie recollected that he had forgotten to tell Oscar that they were coming, so he sent a vast telegram to Oscar from Exeter. They arrived in time for a most luxurious dinner.

To Lionel Johnson Dodgson wrote 'Our life is lazy and luxurious; our moral principles are lax . . . Bosie is beautiful and fascinating, but quite wicked . . . We do no logic, no history, but play with pigeons and children and drive by the sea.'[15] Oscar drew up rules for 'Babbacombe School':

> Headmaster – Mr Oscar Wilde
> Second Master – Mr Campbell Dodgson
> Boys – Lord Alfred Douglas[16]

The rules were not exactly onerous, and included such items as five o'clock tea for the headmaster and second master; brandy and sodas (not more than seven) for the boys; compulsory hide-and-seek, for the headmaster, and écarté, limited to five-guinea points. To Lady Mount-Temple Oscar wrote that Babbacombe Cliff had become a kind of College, with Cyril studying French in the nursery, Oscar himself working on his new play in 'Wonderland', and Lord Alfred Douglas studying Plato with his tutor. He added that with the latter in the house he was not lonely in the evenings.

Campbell Dodgson had to leave Babbacombe sooner than he had hoped. Of Oscar he wrote:

I think him perfectly delightful with the firmest conviction that his morals are detestable. He professes to have discovered that mine are as bad. His command of language is extraordinary, so at least it seems to me who am inarticulate, and worship Irishmen who are not. I am going back on Saturday. I shall probably leave all that remains of my religion and morals behind me.[17]

When Campbell Dodgson left them, Oscar gave him a paper-knife as a permanent souvenir of the visit, and wrote that he thought that he had succeeded in combining the advantages of a public school with those of a lunatic asylum.

Constance, meanwhile, had moved on from Florence and was now in Rome. Her plans had now become firmer, and she wrote to Speranza saying that she and Aunt Mary had resolved to go on to Switzerland after their Italian tour had ended. Speranza at this time was becoming increasingly worried about Willie's divorce. He had arranged to go to the American Consulate about it, but was firmly against any notion of a reconciliation. Though it seems rather unreasonable to have expected Oscar to travel up from Torquay specially, Speranza was clearly feeling a little neglected. 'You really *must* come to your *mother's* receptions, you won't have me long, and you might give me some time now . . . I trust the dear children are well. Cyril must be quite a companion now,'[18] she wrote.

Had Constance had the slightest inkling of the true relationship which was daily taking an even greater stranglehold on her husband, she would have returned home immediately. Nothing, however, occurred to give her the least suspicion that all was not well. Her days were unclouded and full of the delights of travel and new friends. The boys were safe with their father, and there were no worries to rob her of her sleep.

What was happening now at the house at Babbacombe in her absence went much deeper than any question of mere homo-sexuality. There was nothing rare or new about the physical relationship that, unbeknown to Constance, had sprung up between her husband and the gilt-haired young lord. Men have been making love to men since time began. The young were recruited to its secret mysteries in the public schools of England. Such a life for grown men who moved in society was a series of calculated gambles, like a game of Monopoly, but with rules that changed from time to time. The man who had established himself in Park Lane or Mayfair might seem unassailable, but a wrong throw of the dice could send a player directly to jail, without even the chance to pick up his cash *en route*. The player who suddenly finds that he is expected to play by the Queensberry rules is understandably confused.

Though she herself remained in ignorance of it, Oscar had now abandoned all notions of physical fidelity to Constance. He had also formed a private relationship which, under a law imposed only a few years previously, turned a sin of the flesh into a major crime for which imprisonment was the only fitting punishment. Even so, the risk of police action would normally have been minimal for persons of rank and position in what was still a society governed by privilege. In the marital context, Oscar's conduct was a serious breach; yet many marriages have survived as much, and even more. Oscar deceived Constance not out of fear of the consequences but because he did not want to make her suffer or disturb the harmony of their relationship. The real danger lay in the fact that Oscar had allowed himself to fall under the dominion of an evil young man who did not release him until he had brought down the house of Wilde.

Constance was still abroad when their tenure of Lady Mount-Temple's house came to an end. Before he left Babbacombe Bosie made a scene so terrible that Oscar vowed never to speak to him again. These vile rages, which alternated with fits of sulking silence, were truly terrifying, seeming almost epileptic in their violence. It was this which ultimately provoked sympathy and forgiveness, for Oscar always managed to convince himself that the condition was medical rather than social, and that Bosie was unable, therefore, to accept responsibility for his actions. Campbell Dodgson, who had returned to Babbacombe after his examination at the British Museum was over, seemed to be of the same opinion: 'Your tutor, who had stayed behind, told me that he thought that at times you were quite irresponsible for what you said and did, and that most, if not all, of the men at Magdalen were of the same opinion,'[19] Oscar wrote afterwards.

Had Oscar kept to his resolution and refused to see him again, the tragedy that later befell him and his family would have been averted; but Bosie had not the smallest intention of relaxing his hold on his golden goose. Instead he bombarded him with letters and telegrams, until Oscar the tender-hearted could not help but forgive him. Oscar took rooms at the Savoy, where he stayed until the end of March, and once installed there he wrote to Bosie.

Dearest of all Boys,
Your letter was delightful, red and yellow wine to me; but I am
sad and out of sorts. Bosie, you must not make scenes with me.
They kill me, they wreck the loveliness of life. I cannot see you,
so Greek and gracious, distorted with passion. I cannot listen to
your curved lips saying hideous things to me. I would sooner be
blackmailed by every renter [male prostitute] in London than
have you bitter, unjust, hating. I must see you soon. You are the
divine thing I want, the thing of grace and beauty; but I don't
know how to do it. Shall I come to Salisbury? My bill here is £49
for a week. I have also got a new sitting-room over the Thames.
Why are you not here, my dear, my wonderful boy? I fear I must
leave; no money, no credit, and a heart of lead.

Your Own Oscar[20]

Having won the forgiveness he had always known he could extract
from Oscar, Bosie begged him to accommodate him in the Savoy.
In a sense Oscar had only himself to blame, for though he had
hinted at his financial problems, he had painted an attractive
picture of his rooms, and had clearly indicated that he wanted to
share them with Bosie. He gave in all too easily, but later
commented, 'That was indeed a visit fatal to me.'[21]

Before Constance and Aunt Mary Napier got back from the
Continent, Oscar went to stay for a few days with their friends the
Walter Palmers at Frognal in North London, taking Cyril and Vyvyan
with him. The Palmers were strict about Sabbath observance, and the
boys found Sundays at Frognal, when they were not allowed to play
games or run about, particularly dull. Most of the time they simply sat
on chairs in the nursery in their Sunday best, with no books except the
Bible and, curiously, *Gulliver's Travels*. The letters which Constance
received from Vyvyan were full of descriptions of Shetland ponies and
the flowers of which he was so fond, and of the goldfish in an artificial
lake in the splendid gardens.

During the visit Oscar met the novelist George Meredith for the
first time. Other guests were Henry Irving's son, H. B. Irving;
Johnston Forbes-Robertson, an actor-manager; and the artist Louise
Jopling. A professional photographer turned up to take a photograph of the group, who had listened with emotion to Oscar reading
the last act of *A Woman of No Importance*, which was already in
rehearsal; at the last moment Jopling flung her arms about Oscar's

neck for another photograph. On some unspecified future occasion Constance was shown the picture, and Jopling later claimed that after looking at it for about a minute Constance said, 'Poor Oscar'.[22]

Almost immediately after her return from her continental tour Constance went to stay with friends at Banacle Edge, Witley, in Surrey. The house in Tite Street had been closed up for some eight months, and there was much to be done there before the family could settle in again properly. Usually during their absences from home Constance put the servants on board wages, but on this occasion in view of her prolonged absence she had not kept on a full staff. On 7 April she returned there and occupied herself with household matters; but she found time to write a letter to Robert Ross:

> I am going to ask if you will do a great kindness for me and get your friend to lend the Simeon Solomon picture to a small Dante [Gabriel Rossetti] exhibition that Mr Wicksteed is having next week in University Hall. I will make myself responsible for its safety and would convey it back and forward if allowed.[23]

She added that she had arranged to take a number of other items over for the exhibition on the following Saturday, and would very much like to take the picture with her. Robbie Ross and his friend duly obliged, and about a week later Constance wrote to Robbie again:

> Mr Wicksteed told me yesterday that he considered your picture the gem of his collection; and I cannot tell you how delighted he has been with it. The exhibition is open tomorrow and after that I will fetch the picture as soon as I possibly can. Shall I bring it to you or may I have it here for a day or two? I want so much to show it to Lady Mount-Temple if I may.[24]

On 13 May Constance wrote to Robbie again, telling him that the picture was ready for collection and confessing that she would like to steal it. 'I took it to show Lady Mount-Temple who was as pleased with it as I expected her to be,'[25] she added.

She and Robbie had begun to draw closer together at this period. Perhaps they were both beginning to feel somewhat neglected by Oscar, though Constance was far too loyal to admit the fact.

Naturally, as Robbie also led a double life, he was only too well aware of the real nature of that neglect, and was under no illusion about the relationship between his friend and Bosie Douglas. Whether he fully realized the extent of Bosie's hold over his friend, is not clear, but it is unlikely that even he, whose eyes were fully opened to the true state of affairs, could have anticipated the extent of the misfortune which later overtook the Wildes. One important interest that Constance and Robbie had in common was Roman Catholicism. Constance, like Oscar, had often felt attracted to the Catholic Church without ever having taken the plunge. Laziness was almost the whole of the answer in Oscar's case, and he paid no more than lip-service to religion at that time. Constance, on the other hand, was a regular churchgoer with a strong interest in parish affairs. Perhaps her holiday in Italy and Switzerland, both primarily Roman Catholic, had tended to increase her Catholic sympathies. She bought herself a rosary, and another as a little present for Robbie, who was a practising Roman Catholic. In return he sent her a charming little book explaining how to use the rosary properly. 'I hope that when the play comes out and Oscar is to be seen you will come and dine with me,'[26] she wrote in her letter of thanks. On 13 May she wrote and asked him when he was going to come and see her. She suggested that Robbie might come to her Wednesday at-home, before the arrival of the other guests, or call alternatively one evening at six-thirty.

After his visit to Oscar at the Savoy Bosie went to Germany, but before departing for the Continent he gave away one of his suits to an unemployed man called Wood. In the pocket of the suit was a bundle of Oscar's letters to him. Most of them could be regarded as highly incriminating, and it is frankly difficult to imagine that this was an accident. One letter, even two, might conceivably have been the result of carelessness; but a whole set of them can hardly have come into Wood's possession by mistake. The inference is clear: Lord Alfred Douglas gave them to Wood deliberately, either in one of those moments of malicious rage to which he was subject or, as is more likely, as part of a deliberate plan to extort money from Oscar, with a cut of the proceeds for himself.

Wood now formed a conspiracy with two professional black-mailers called Clibborn and Allen. Together they made copies of the most incriminating of the letters and wrote to Beerbohm Tree, who was at that time busy with rehearsals for *A Woman of No Importance*. The letter chosen was the one written from Babbacombe acknowledging Bosie's sonnet, and including the famous words, 'Your slim gilt soul walks between passion and poetry.'

Beerbohm Tree immediately showed Oscar the letter, and asked for his comments. Nonchalantly Oscar dismissed it as a 'prose poem', worthy of inclusion in Palgrave's *Golden Treasury*. Shortly afterwards Wood approached Oscar with demands for money, which he said he needed to start a new life in America. Perhaps when Oscar handed over £35 to him for the letters, he thought of Mary Travers and her extortion of money for her passage to Australia from his father. Wood, unlike Mary, actually went to his stated destination, though he did not stay there for very long. Only afterwards did Oscar realize that the letter of which a copy had been sent to Tree was not in the bundle.

Soon afterwards Allen turned up at Tite Street and asked to see Oscar. When he said that he had come about a letter, Oscar realized the situation at once. 'If you had not been so foolish as to send a copy of it to Mr Beerbohm Tree, I would gladly have paid you a very large sum of money for the letter, as I consider it to be a work of art,'[27] Oscar said. The man claimed to have been offered £60 for it, whereupon Oscar told him that he would be well advised to go back to the man and accept the offer. Allen replied that the man was out of town, and owned to being in serious financial difficulties. Oscar gave him half a sovereign, and told him that the letter was a prose poem which was about to be published in sonnet form in a literary magazine.

Only a few moments later Oscar had yet another caller. By now Oscar's patience was wearing a little thin; yet he answered the third blackmailer with characteristic courtesy. Somewhat to Oscar's surprise, Clibborn, the third blackmailer, pulled out the original letter and handed it over without making any demand for money. When Oscar asked why he had brought it, Clibborn explained to him that Allen had told him to return it, partly because Oscar merely laughed at them and partly because Oscar had been kind to him. Oscar accordingly gave him a half sovereign for his trouble and there the matter would probably have ended, except for one vital fact. A copy of the letter had already found its way into the possession of the Marquess of Queensberry.

10

Deception

I treated art as the supreme reality, and life as a mere
mode of fiction.

De Profundis

A Woman of No Importance opened at the Haymarket Theatre on 19
April 1893. Its cast was impressive, and included Herbert
Beerbohm Tree and Mrs Tree, Mrs Bernard Beere, Fred Terry, and
Julia Neilson. Oscar had taken forty of the best seats in the house
for his own friends, and as always bore the cost of this himself. In
the front row of the dress circle, occupying what Oscar regarded as
the finest seat of all, was John Lane, soon to begin publishing *The
Yellow Book*, whose ticket was sent by special messenger and marked
'Important'. Next to him was the young French poet Pierre Louÿs,
to whom Oscar had dedicated his recently published *Salome*. Louÿs'
brief telegram on the publication of *Salome* had offended Oscar by its
apparent curtness, but clearly he was now forgiven. Indeed it would
appear that Oscar, who never really liked Lane, but who drew his
attention in advance to the presence at his side of his gifted young
friend, was making a calculated effort to do Louÿs some good.

Oscar sat in his box throughout the performance looking rather
splendid in a white waistcoat and with a bunch of tiny lilies in his
buttonhole. Though the audience called for the author at the end of
the performance, he stood up in his box and said loudly, 'Ladies and
Gentlemen, I regret to inform you that Mr Oscar Wilde is not in
the house.'[1] He then descended briefly to make a bow before the
curtain and went backstage to congratulate Tree on a fine
performance.

Afterwards, Oscar went to dinner at the home of a society
hostess, Blanche Roosevelt. The palmist, Cheiro, whom she had
engaged to read her guests' hands through a curtain, later recalled
his meeting with Oscar Wilde:

He had produced that very night *The Woman of No Importance* (sic) but I little thought when his rather fat hands were passed through the holes in the curtain that such hands could belong to the most talked of man in London at that moment. I was however so struck with the difference in the markings of the left and right hands, that from behind my curtain I explained that the left always denoted the hereditary tendencies, while the right showed the developed or attained characteristics, and that when we use the left side of the brain the nerves cross and go to the right hand, so that it consequently shows the true nature and development of the individual. I pointed this case out as an example where the left had promised the most unusual destiny of brilliancy and uninterrupted success, which was completely broken and ruined at a certain date in the right. Almost forgetting myself for a moment, I summed up all by saying, 'the left hand is the hand of a king, but the right is that of a king who will send himself into exile'.

The owner of the hands did not laugh. 'At what date?' he asked rather quietly.

'A few years from now,' I answered, 'between your 41st and 42nd year.' Of course everyone laughed. 'What a joke!' they said, but in the most dramatic manner, Wilde turned towards them and repeated gravely, 'The left is the hand of a king, but the right is the hand of a king who will send himself into exile,' and without another word he left.

That was the end of the evening. Blanche was rather annoyed (at least as much as she could be over anything) that I had sent the lion of her party away. She told me I was too realistic for drawing-room entertainments, so my curtains were taken down and supper was served instead of science.

I did not meet Oscar again until shortly before he commenced the case that was to end so fatally for him. He came to see 'if the breach was still there'. I told him it was, but that surely his Destiny could not be broken. He was very, very quiet, but in a far-off way he said: 'My good friend, you know well Fate does not keep road-menders on her highways.'[2]

On the second night of the new play the Prince of Wales was in the Royal Box, which, but for his arrival, would have been occupied by Lillie Langtry. Rumour had it that she had offered to occupy it with the Prince, but that he declined. After the performance Oscar dined at the Albemarle with Lord Alfred Douglas, Beerbohm Tree, and his young half-brother Max Beerbohm who was still an undergraduate (he had just written his first published article, on the subject of Oscar Wilde). For once the critics were kind; yet their notices mattered little these days, for Oscar's plays were immensely popular at the box-office. Max Beerbohm reported, however, that Oscar had met an insignificant journalist who regularly attacked him in the papers; to Oscar's surprise the man greeted him cordially. Oscar met the man's gaze with a blank stare. 'You will pardon me: I remember your name but I can't recall your face.'[3]

Oscar did not come home to Constance in Tite Street at this time. Instead he preferred to take a room in a hotel, ostensibly to be nearer the theatre. At the time of the opening of *A Woman of No Importance* he and Lord Alfred Douglas were staying together at the Albemarle Hotel. A week after the opening Bosie went back to Oxford for the summer term. Oscar moved with him into his lodgings at 34 The High. They socialized a great deal, and Max Beerbohm and Trelawney Backhouse, an undergraduate with homosexual proclivities who later became a famous Chinese scholar, were their most regular companions. For some time Bosie had been editor of an Oxford magazine called *The Spirit Lamp*, and during the month of May a French sonnet based on Oscar's 'slim gilt soul' letter, composed by Pierre Louÿs, was published in it.

Another companion of those Oxford days was Will Rothenstein, who produced several drawings of Bosie during the course of Oscar's visit. Often Oscar had urged Bosie to sit for a portrait in oils, and had even suggested the artist Prince Pierre Troubetzkoy, a Russian American who had recently painted a portrait of the first Lord Battersea, a former Liberal M. P. and a distinguished patron of the arts. Oscar had already spoken tentatively to Troubetzkoy, but he was committed until the autumn. In the absence of a suitable oil painting or ivory statue, which Oscar also wanted, he bought one of Rothenstein's drawings of Bosie. It was called 'The Editor of *The Spirit Lamp* at Work', and was a profile of Bosie lolling in an armchair. Oscar was delighted with the picture, and ordered it to be mounted in a black and white frame with no margins. Here was Dorian Gray personified; but the portrait never changed.

Bosie left Oxford for good at the end of the term. The general assumption was that he had done badly in the examinations and was too lazy to continue with his studies; but later it emerged that there were other circumstances surrounding his departure. It seems that he was being blackmailed again for his homosexual activities. It was not until some time after the event that the Marquess of Queensberry got to hear of it. 'It is a horrible story,' Queensberry wrote, 'nothing to do with Oscar Wilde, and as it has been told me by a personal friend, an eminent lawyer who himself supplied the money, £100, to hush up the scandal, there can be no doubt of the truth of it . . .'[4]

Meanwhile, Constance had moved down to a cottage at Goring in the month of June. The children were with her, and doubtless she now hoped to see more of Oscar. But when Oscar arrived, Bosie was with him. Perhaps it is significant that, within only a few days of their arrival, Constance took the children and moved on to Dinard.

Constance was at the time still totally ignorant of the homosexual relationship between Oscar and Bosie, but though she had liked the young man at first, other aspects of his friendship with Oscar had surely begun to disturb her. She had been to a ball given by Lady Queensberry, with whom she was a favourite, and it may well be that Bosie's mother had confided to her all her worries about Bosie's recklessness and extravagance. By now she must have noticed that Oscar's personal expenditure, which was always high, had risen under the young man's influence to astronomic proportions. Constance rarely reproached her husband but, understandably, she could not conceal an attitude of faint disapproval. This irritated Oscar, doubtless the more so because his conscience was not easy in regard to her. Hesketh Pearson wrote of their relationship at this period:

Wilde and his wife were on affectionate terms, but there was something wistful and a little sad about Constance. She seems to have been rather sorry for her husband, in the way a mother is sorry for a wayward son. She could not understand why he should resent her mild censure when he had indulged in some extravagance of thought or behaviour; but the very gentleness of her reproofs made them more diffucult to bear than if they had been accompanied by crockery.[5]

Goring must have seemed like an ideal place for two little boys whose father loved messing about in boats. Oscar had got hold of a

Canadian canoe in which he paddled about on the river and explored its innumerable backwaters. Perhaps Cyril and Vyvyan were dissappointed when their holiday with their papa was cut short in this way, but Constance was no doubt wise to put the Channel between herself and her husband's unsavoury house-guest. She was becoming increasingly disenchanted with Bosie Douglas.

The 'official' reason given for Constance's hurried departure was her husband's need of peace and quiet so that he could work on his next play, *An Ideal Husband*. Bosie, too, was said to require peaceful surroundings so that he could work on his translation of Oscar's play *Salome* from French into English. Oscar also wanted to read the proofs of his poem *The Sphinx*, which he had decided to lengthen, and look over the setting for *Lady Windermere's Fan*, which was finally published by Elkin Mathews and John Lane in November 1893. But in practice very little work was done. When the local vicar called, no doubt hoping to see Constance, he was said to be shocked to find Oscar and Bosie lying in the garden clad only in bath-towels, having turned the hosepipe on each other.

Though Constance probably remained in ignorance of the fact, Oscar and Bosie managed to go through £1,340 of Oscar's money during those three months at Goring. Nor were all their days calm and happy, though they mostly tended to discourage visitors. Willie Wilde asked to come and stay, but Oscar put him off with a feeble excuse. Bosie did work at the *Salome* translation, but Oscar was very dissatisfied with the standard of his work, which had many childish errors. At one stage some of Bosie's Oxford friends descended on them for a long weekend and disrupted the calm which Oscar needed for his work.

Later, in *De Profundis*, Oscar explained what happened:

Some of your Oxford friends come to stay from a Saturday to a Monday. The morning of the day they went away you made a scene so dreadful, so distressing that I told you that we must part. I remember quite well, as we stood on the level croquet-ground with the pretty lawn all round us, pointing out to you that we were spoiling each other's lives, that you were absolutely ruining mine and that I evidently was not making you really happy, and that an irrevocable parting, a complete separation, was the one wise and philosophic thing to do. You went sullenly after luncheon, leaving one of your most offensive letters with the butler to be handed to me after your departure. Before three days had elapsed you were telegraphing from London to beg to be forgiven and allowed to return. I had taken the place to please you. I had engaged your own servants at your request. I was always terribly sorry for the hideous temper to which you were really a prey. I was fond of you. So I let you come back and forgave you. Three months later still, in September, new scenes occurred, the occasion of them being my pointing out to you the schoolboy faults of your attempted translation of *Salome*. You must by this time be a fair enough French scholar to know that the translation was unworthy of you, as an ordinary Oxonian, as it was of the work it sought to render. You did not of course know it then, and in one of the violent letters you wrote to me on the point you said that you were under '*no intellectual obligation of any kind*' to me, I remember that when I read that statement, I felt that it was the one really true thing you had written to me in the whole course of our friendship. I saw that a less cultivated nature would really have suited you much better. I am not saying this in bitterness at all, but simply as a fact of companionship. Ultimately the bond of all companionship, whether in marriage or in friendship, is conversation, and conversation must have a common basis, and between two people of widely different culture the only common basis possible is the lowest level. The trivial in thought and action is charming. I had made it the keystone of a very brilliant philosophy expressed in plays and paradoxes. But the froth and folly of our life grew often very wearisome to me: it was only in the mire that we met: and fascinating, terribly fascinating though the one topic round which your talk invariably centered was, still at the end it became quite monotonous to me.[6]

Oscar was indeed bored by Bosie's appetite for Bacchanalian feasting and drinking, which never seemed satisfied, and by his constant visits to music-halls and the like. Oscar tagged along with him, outwardly patient for the most part, and always indulgent; but there were many times when he felt that he could no longer go on with this way of life.

When the breach over *Salome* came Bosie left and Oscar again took rooms at the Albemarle Hotel. His intention was to join Constance and the boys as soon as he had cleared up business matters. As usual he was bombarded by letters from Bosie, initially berating him and then begging forgiveness. He was exceedingly angry with Oscar for refusing to take him to Dinard. Constance's hope of a holiday with her husband was realized, for finally Oscar did arrive in France for a stay of a fortnight unaccompanied by his friend.

No correspondence survives to indicate just how Constance and her husband fared during those two weeks they spent together. Oscar was weighted down with money problems which he probably chose to conceal from Constance. On the other hand, he was relieved, though only briefly as it turned out, to have shaken off Bosie, and this alone may have been enough to lift his spirits. Whatever his state of mind, it is likely that he relaxed in the company of his wife and the boys, and made full use of their opportunities for family fun on the beach and in the neighbour-hood.

Constance and the children were obliged to travel back to England without Oscar, who elected to return via Jersey, in order to see the local first night performance there of *A Woman of No Importance*. As Constance and the boys were not yet back at Tite Street when he got to London, he put up at the Albemarle Hotel again. Here he received a telegram from Bosie, whom he had forgiven against all his instincts. Oscar now had to settle up the matter of the cottage at Goring, and pay the bills, and advised Bosie to spend some time with his family, whom he had neglected for a whole season. In reality, Oscar could not now bear to have him near him. 'I required rest and freedom from the terrible strain of your companionship. It was necessary for me to be a little by myself,'[7] he wrote later.

Constance and the boys joined Oscar at Goring in mid-September, shortly before the lease expired. Here Oscar did what he could to straighten out his tangled financial affairs; but though he seemed to have creditors at every turn, he still found enough money to bail Speranza out of her financial troubles. These in the main were connected with repairs to her house, which necessitated moving home into the bargain. She was immensely grateful for Oscar's help, but it was obvious that she was lonely. 'I shall be glad when Constance returns, and then we will have some drives together. There is no news of anyone. All is quiet as the grave,'[8] she wrote.

All the family were at this time concerned about Willie, who seemed to have gone to pieces since the failure of his marriage to his American newspaper heiress. Hesketh Pearson succinctly sums up the situation:

> He went to America a clever if sluggish journalist; he came back a nervous wreck. He had always been fond of the bottle; he was now a confirmed toper. He never recovered his position, and though his second marriage was a happy one his ability as a journalist had deserted him. His appearance deteriorated; he borrowed right and left; and he was sober only when penniless.[9]

Willie's amours had always been something of a problem, and now that he found himself once more on the marriage market he began to think in terms of a replacement for his ex-wife. A letter from Speranza dated 8 October is thought to have been written in 1893. In this she reports on the sources of information for rumours concerning Willie and a mysterious lady to whom she refers as 'Miss L.' It would seem from her account of matters that half the world had already got to hear of the liaison, of which she wrote,

> I am not at all miserable about the affair, for *I don't believe it*, and Miss L. acknowledged to Willie that she had told *an untruth*, and never consulted the Dr as she had said on a certain point. I believe Miss L. got up the whole story just to try and force on the marriage, which will *never be* now. Willie was very angry with her, and she will not come to this house again.[10]

As always, Speranza did her best to reconcile her two sons, partly because it distressed her to see them at odds with each other, and partly because she genuinely believed in Oscar's power to reason with Willie. The name of Willie's second bride was Miss Sophie ('Lily') Lees, but the fact that her surname began with 'L' may have been sheer coincidence. She bore him one daughter.

From October 1893 until the end of March 1894 Oscar took rooms at 10 and 11 St James's Place, chiefly because, despite the ordered atmosphere at Tite Street, he needed greater peace in which to work than he could find in his own home with two young children in it. Constance believed that his genius required this, and though she never liked his absences, she accepted the situation. What she did not realize was that Oscar also made use of these rooms to entertain Bosie Douglas and other homosexuals. He still made efforts to free himself of Bosie, but could never resist him for long. In November 1893 he even went so far as to write to Lady Queensberry, ostensibly for Bosie's benefit but really because he was desperate to finish the association. To her he confided all his fears about Bosie's sleeplessness and bouts of hysteria, his neurotic behaviour and total loss of interest in intellectual matters. Bosie had now become completely idle, having done nothing at all since he had worked on the translation of *Salome* in the summer. Unless some form of direction could be introduced into his life, Oscar forsaw the gravest consequences for the young aristocrat, and urged her to try and get him to go abroad. He suggested that she should try to arrange for him to go to Lord Cromer (for whom he had worked before) in Egypt for four or five months, in the hope that the change of atmosphere might encourage him to recover. He did not add that, unless he and Bosie were separated by many miles, he did not know how he could ever rid himself of him. To Oscar's great relief, Lady Queensberry took his advice, and Bosie set sail for Egypt, though not before he had made his peace with Oscar.

Before his departure, Oscar had been finding life absolutely intolerable. During his first week alone in St James's Square he had got through a whole act of *An Ideal Husband*. Thereafter Bosie's constant demands on his time made it impossible for him to carry on with his work. Constance continued to receive them both for dinner at Tite Street on those occasions when Bosie did not elect to be taken to Willis's instead. Once matters got so desperate after Bosie came to his rooms one Monday night with a couple of his friends and made a revolting scene that Oscar decided the only thing he could do was to flee the country. At this point his morale had reached rock-bottom, and all because of his inability to break with his gilt-haired *bête noire*.

Constance must have been thoroughly bewildered when Oscar came to her and said that he had to go away, making up an excuse for his absence and giving a false destination. He realized as he sat in the railway carriage *en route* for Paris what an impossibly wrong state his life had got into. If only he could have enlisted Constance's help he might have managed it; but she was, of course, the very last person he could confide in.

Still in ignorance of the nature of things, Constance continued to run their home and family life virtually unassisted, and even managed to find time to care for Speranza, of whom she was so deeply fond. That Constance could still be unaware of Oscar's activities seemed to many people impossible at the time; yet wives are usually the last to find out about their husbands' mistresses. How much more are they likely to remain unaware that their husband has taken a male lover. Constance had two fine healthy sons to prove the 'normality' of her husband's sexual instincts. Homosexuality was the last thing in the world of which she was likely to suspect him.

Oscar's skill in covering his tracks was consummate. He was not a natural deceiver, and indeed in most things he was transparently honest. But given that he had something he wished to hide at all costs, he was uniquely able to do it. His normal standards of fair dealing naturally predisposed Constance to trust him, and she did so without fear or hesitation. Perhaps it was naïve on her part; and yet trust has never been regarded as a vice. Perhaps she might have taken a firmer line in regard to their joint finances; but given the climate of opinion in Victorian England where, whatever recent acts of parliament might declare, a woman's property was automatically deemed to be vested in her husband, it is difficult to see how she could have opposed her husband's will. It was never part of Constance's nature to adopt the role of nagging wife, and she can hardly be blamed for that.

Once in Egypt, Bosie bombarded Oscar with letters. He also wrote many letters to his mother, urging the absolute need he felt of continuing his association with Oscar, and doing all he could to enlist her aid. A typical letter ran:

I am passionately fond of him, and he of me . . . There is nothing I would not do for him and if he dies before I do I shall not care to live any longer. Surely there is nothing but what is fine and beautiful in such a love as that of two people for one another, the love of the disciple and the philosopher . . . There is no good in saying any more, except that while I perhaps have no right to say that Oscar Wilde is a good man, neither you nor anyone else has the right to say that he is a bad man. A really bad man I might admire intellectually but I could never love, and what is still more he could never love anyone faithfully, loyally, devotedly, unselfishly and purely as Oscar loves me.[11]

His mother realized that Bosie was the only one of her children to be burdened with the fatal Queensberry temperament. It was her considered opinion that his friendship with Oscar had intensified his already colossal vanity to the point where it had led him into wilder recklessness than ever before. He had recently gone to Belgium with a friend introduced to him by Oscar, and his mother was inclined to blame Oscar for their behaviour since but for him the friendship would not have occurred. She was still corresponding with Oscar, however, and he finally told her how her son had originally come to him on the slightest acquaintance for help in the matter of his being blackmailed for homosexuality at Oxford. It was a revelation to her that Bosie had been set on the path of homosexuality long before Oscar had met him, and that there was no question of his having seduced the young man. He begged her to use her influence to get Bosie a post as an honorary attaché abroad, or at least to keep him out of the country to learn modern languages, so that their paths might not cross again for a few years.

Lady Queensberry took the hint, and to oblige her, Lord Cromer arranged for him to stay in Cairo. Afterwards, through the combined influence of his grandfather, Alfred Montgomery, and Lord Cromer, Bosie was offered an appointment as an attaché in Constantinople. Nevertheless, though he accepted the appointment, he went first to stay with a friend, E.F. Benson, in Athens. From Athens he continued to besiege Oscar with importunate letters. All of these Oscar resisted. But with the weakness that characterized her, Lady Queensberry finally yielded to her son's pleadings and wrote to Oscar, sending him Bosie's address and begging him to contact him. Still Oscar remained firm.

One day in March 1894 Constance received a long telegram from Bosie beseeching her to use her influence with Oscar to persuade him to consent to see him. At this juncture Constance ought, for the sake of Oscar and the children, and for her own protection also, to have urged Oscar to stand firm. But she was ignorant of those special factors which made a break with Bosie imperative. Her tender susceptibilities were roused, with the result that she actually begged Oscar to relent. He recalled, in De Profundis,

Our friendship had always been a source of distress to her, not merely because she had never liked you personally, but because she saw how your continual companionship had altered me, and not for the better: still, just as she had always been gracious and hospitable to you, so she could not bear the idea of my being in any way unkind – for so it seemed to her – to any of my friends. She thought, knew indeed, that it was a thing alien to my character. At her request I did communicate with you. I remember the wording of my telegram quite well. I said that time healed every wound but that for many months to come I would neither write to you nor see you. [12]

Bosie started for Paris right away. He sent telegrams on the way begging Oscar to meet him. When he arrived at his Paris hotel he found a brief letter from Oscar declining to see him.

He was now desperate. As a final resort he sent Oscar a telegram some ten pages long imploring him to relent and threatening to kill himself if Oscar refused. This was finally too much for Oscar. He hastened to Paris, where a sentimental reunion took place between them. Bosie behaved like a penitent child throughout, crying perpetually and clinging pathetically to his hand. Oscar's capitulation was complete.

They returned to London together. Two days later, Bosie's father saw them lunching together at the Café Royal. His initial reaction was hostile, but Oscar invited him to their table and temporarily won him over.

Oscar's success with the mad Marquess was short-lived. Shortly afterwards Queensberry began his first attack.

11

The First Attack

A man cannot be too careful in the choice of his enemies
The Picture of Dorian Gray

When Constance, compassionate as always, had urged Oscar to be kind to Bosie, she had had misgivings. Renewed association between the two men could only result in new extravagances of behaviour and hard cash. Inevitably it would fall to Oscar to settle the bill. What she did not realize was that the nature of Oscar's association with Bosie, and indeed with other young men of lower social class, was causing widespread scandal. Oscar's name was now on everyone's lips, and it was not always because of his plays. He had returned to London £150 lighter in pocket after a stay of eight days at the Hôtel des Deux Mondes in the Avenue de l'Opéra and, more importantly, the Marquess's resolve to bring him to ruin had hardened. Shortly after their meeting at the Café Royal, Bosie received the following letter from his father:

Alfred,
It is extremely painful for me to have to write to you in the strain I must; but please understand that I decline to receive any answers from you in writing in return. After your recent hysterical impertinent ones I refuse to be annoyed with such, and I decline to read any more letters. If you have anything to say do come here and say it in person. Firstly, am I to understand that, having left Oxford as you did, with discredit to yourself, the reasons of which were fully explained to me by your tutor, you now intend to loaf and loll about and do nothing? All the time you were wasting at Oxford I was put off with the assurance that you were eventually to go into the Civil Service or to the Foreign Office, and then I was put off with an assurance that you were going to the Bar. It appears to me that you intend to do nothing.

I utterly decline, however, to just supply you with sufficient funds to enable you to loaf about. You are preparing a wretched future for yourself, and it would be most cruel and wrong for me to encourage you in this. Secondly, I come to the more painful part of this letter – your intimacy with this man Wilde. It must either cease or I will disown you and stop all money supplies. I am not going to try and analyse this intimacy, and I make no charge; but to my mind to pose as a thing is as bad as to be it. With my own eyes I saw you both in the most loathsome and disgusting relationship as expressed by your manner and expression. Never in my experience have I ever seen such a sight as that in your horrible features. No wonder people are talking as they are. Also I now hear on good authority, but this may be false, that his wife is petitioning to divorce him for sodomy and other crimes. Is this true, or do you know of it? If I thought the actual thing was true, and it became public property, I should be quite justified in shooting him at sight. These Christian English cowards and men, as they call themselves, want waking up.

Your disgusted so-called father,

Queensberry[1]

Bosie's only response to this letter was to send him a telegram which read simply: 'What a funny little man you are! Alfred Douglas.'[2]

This reply did not help matters at all. It was calculated to drive Queensberry into a paroxysm of rage, and in this it succeeded. These little games that Bosie insisted on playing out with his father had little effect on the idle young man except to afford him the opportunity of sharpening his wits at his father's expense. Nothing that his father might do caused him any serious inconvenience. He simply enjoyed seeing his father's anger roused. Even the taunts that he was illegitimate, which Queensberry had often resorted to in the past in his exchanges with his ex-wife meant nothing to Alfred Douglas. He was well used to receiving missives from the Marquess signed 'your so-called father' and this had now no power to wound him. It may dimly have flitted across Oscar's consciousness that the person really at risk in this situation was himself. Whether he paused to consider that Constance and the children might also fall victim to the Marquess of Queensberry's vindictiveness is debatable.

There was no truth at all in Queensberry's suggestion that

Constance was considering taking divorce action against Oscar. Her only cause of complaint against her husband at that time was that he left her too much alone. She did not enjoy this, but she had accepted it from the outset of their marriage. His level of personal expenditure may have given her cause for concern, but she had money of her own now fully adequate for a life of moderate luxury, and in terms of personal needs she wanted for nothing. It may have crossed her mind from time to time that there were, perhaps, other women in Oscar's life. It is said that on one occasion when Oscar was describing in an unusually detailed way the grounds of a mansion where he claimed to be staying, Constance said, 'And did she act well, Oscar?'[3] Yet these were rare occasions, for Constance had never really doubted her husband's love for her.

Queensberry's letter undoubtedly came as an unpleasant if not unexpected shock to Oscar. Given the man's record of bullying and offensive behaviour towards his entire family, something of the sort was almost bound to occur sooner or later. What would have concerned Oscar most were the allegations about Constance's proposal to divorce him. Oscar knew his wife too well to imagine that she had any such intention; yet he would not have wished ugly gossip about the nature of his association with Alfred Douglas to come to her ears. He would not have doubted his ability to handle Constance. He knew that she was saddled with blind faith in him and that, whatever the outward circumstances, she would believe anything he chose to tell her. She was a thoroughly good woman incapable of thinking evil of anyone, least of all her beloved Oscar. What he shrank from at all times was offending her delicate susceptibilities, for he would no more have wished to wound her than one of his own little children. That there was something childlike in Constance's gentle nature he had always realized. His instincts towards her were highly protective. They made a life of deception absolutely necessary.

Other family matters were troubling the Wildes at that time. Willie had apparently been obtaining money from Speranza, and Oscar knew that she had little enough to live on. He had always given money to her liberally, and it was galling to find his brother accepting cash from her in this way. He and Willie were now openly at loggerheads, and Speranza began to bombard Oscar with letters, urging him to be more understanding and to bury his differences with Willie:

It is commonly said that *you hate* your Brother. Now this does *not* make me happy: nor to find that you will not come here for fear of meeting him . . . He is reckless and extravagant, *preach to him* but do it *kindly*. Willie has some good points, and do try and help him to be better. *I am miserable* at the present position of my two sons, and at the general belief that you *hate your brother* . . . I pity Willie in that he does not get a sixpence from Moytura and so I am content to give him what I can . . . If he has taken help from me in money, why, that *does not injure you* and I don't want you to hate Willie on my account . . . Let the present bitterness die, otherwise, *I shall die* in despair   You will have to meet by my coffin, and I want you to meet before that in friendly feeling.[4]

That Oscar should be in dispute with Willie over matters of this kind is ironic. With vulture creditors flapping their wings about his ears while he continued spending money with reckless abandon, Oscar now accused Willie of extravagance. Willie's continual toping irritated him; yet he consumed large quantities of alcohol himself, although he never actually became drunk. He objected to Willie's gourmandising; yet in the house in Tite Street he said wearily of the roast chicken placed before him, 'Constance, why do you give me these . . . pedestrians . . . to eat',[5] and forsook the family dinner table in favour of Willis's or Kettner's, or any one of a number of fashionable but expensive eating-houses. His brother's increasing carelessness in regard to his appearance disgusted him; yet though Oscar's clothes were always immaculate, he had begun to lose his struggles against flab. His appearance suffered as a direct result of his own intemperance. He objected to Willie's various amours, while dining in public places with Lord Alfred Douglas in circumstances which had inevitably given rise to gossip and speculation. A more obvious case of pot and kettle had never existed. Constance's exact views on this particular issue are not known. She probably sympathized with Oscar's feelings; but she was always in favour of peaceful coexistence, and she would not have liked to see Speranza unhappy. She would almost certainly have supported any moves on the part of her mother-in-law to re-establish cordial relations between Oscar and Willie.

In May 1894 Constance and Oscar decided to send the children away to boarding school. Their reasoning on this particular point is a little difficult to fathom. It was normal for boys in well-to-do families to go to a boarding school but Vyvyan, at seven, was unusually young, and the only reason in normal circumstances for such an early start would have been to enable the boys to be kept together. Cyril and Vyvyan, however, were sent to different establishments. The school in Haywards Heath chosen for Cyril was principally for boys who wanted to go into the Navy. It was a little early, since he was only nine years old, to anticipate his future career. Maybe the Napiers and the Cochranes had something to do with it, hoping for another admiral in the family; or perhaps they were all just a little carried away by those charming little sailor suits. The school was very spartan in outlook, with the boys having to do all those chores that were usually carried out by the indoor non-teaching staff. Despite the rigours of school life, Cyril appeared to like it. Vyvyan was sent to Hildersham House, a small preparatory school for fifty boys. It was at Broadstairs, well known for its healthful climate. The headmaster, Mr Snowden, was a kindly man and Vyvyan liked him. As he was by far the youngest boy in the school, however, he had great difficulty in keeping up with the other boys. His reading was excellent, but he was deficient when it came to handwriting, and had extreme difficulty in keeping up with dictation. Although he could not join in the tough competitive games of the older boys he was happy at the school, after his inevitable feelings of initial homesickness had worn off.

The children's departure to preparatory school made a considerable difference to Constance's life. She was now much freer in term time to follow her own interests, and there were always the holidays to look forward to. But for the first time since the early days of her marriage she found herself frequently alone in the house in Tite Street except, of course, for Arthur the butler and the other servants.

With characteristic inconsistency of behaviour Lady Queensberry, who had encouraged Oscar to renew his association with her son, had now sent Bosie away to Florence in the hope that his absence would break up the affair. Her father, Alfred Montgomery, had been angered by Bosie's irresponsible behaviour. He and Lord Cromer had gone to considerable trouble to get Bosie appointed an attaché in Constantinople, but when Lord Currie, the British Ambassador in Constantinople, got to hear that Bosie had met Wilde in Paris, he cancelled his appointment. Despite his monetary problems, Oscar managed somehow to raise enough cash to join Bosie in Florence for a month, where for once they managed to get through a fair amount of work. Oscar was busy with *A Florentine Tragedy*, while Bosie was writing some of his best poems.

The Marquess of Queensberry was still fuming about Bosie's telegram, and continued to send him abusive letters. 'You miserable Creature'[6] was the way in which he addressed him. Begetting him had, he said, been verging on the criminal; but then he thought that he was not Alfred's father after all, so the blame could not be laid at his door. Inconvenience and disgrace were the least of the threats he used against him. He had already stopped his allowance of £250 a year. His threats now included physical violence.

The letter referring to Constance's so-called plans for divorce proceedings greatly disturbed Oscar. On his return, acting on Robbie Ross's advice, he consulted Charles Octavius Humphreys, the senior partner in the firm of C.O. Humphreys, Son and Kershaw. What he wanted to find out was whether Queensberry's letter referring to Constance was actionable, and whether he could be restrained from further threatening and abusive behaviour. George Wyndham, Bosie's cousin and a Member of Parliament, took a hand at this juncture and dissuaded Oscar from proceeding, as he felt that a family scandal ought to be avoided. It was agreed by all parties, however, that Oscar was entitled to an apology, and Humphreys accordingly wrote to Queensberry on Oscar's behalf to demand one.

It was presumably that letter which brought Queensberry, accompanied by a professional boxer, to Tite Street one afternoon in June 1894. Oscar saw them in the library.

'Sit down,' bawled the Marquess, by way of introduction.

'I do not allow anyone to talk like that to me in my house or anywhere else,' Oscar replied. 'I suppose you have come to apologise for the statement you made about my wife and myself in letters you wrote to your son. I should have the right any day I choose to prosecute you for writing such a letter.'

'The letter was privileged, as it was written to my son,' Queensberry countered.

'How dare you say such things about your son and me?'

'You were both kicked out of the Savoy Hotel at a moment's notice for your disgusting behaviour,' the Marquess insisted.

'That is a lie.'

'You have taken furnished rooms for him in Piccadilly.'

'Somebody has been telling you an absurd set of lies about your son and me,' replied Oscar. 'I have not done anything of the kind.'

'I hear you were thoroughly well blackmailed for a disgusting letter you wrote to my son.'

'The letter was a beautiful letter, and I never write except for publication. Lord Queensberry, do you seriously accuse me and your son of improper conduct?'

A note of caution crept into Queensberry's blustering tone. 'I do not say you are it,' he answered, 'but you look it, and you pose as it, which is just as bad. If I catch you and my son together in any public restaurant, I will thrash you.'

'I do not know what the Queensberry rules are,' Oscar replied, 'but the Oscar Wilde rule is to shoot on sight,' and with this he asked the Marquess to leave. When he refused, Oscar threatened to call the police to evict him.

'It's a disgusting scandal,' said the Marquess.

'If it is so, you are the author of the scandal and no one else.'[7]

As the Marquess and his companion left the house, Oscar pointed them out to the apprehensive Arthur. 'This is the Marquess of Queensberry, the most infamous brute in London,' he said. 'You are never to allow him to enter my house again.'[8]

It is not clear whether Constance was in the house when this disagreeable confrontation took place. If she was, she can hardly have helped but hear the unusual sound of raised, angry voices emanating from the usually tranquil library. Probably she was out, for she had a wide circle of friends and many interests. Luckily the boys were away at school, and were thus spared the sight and sound of their father's unwelcome visitor and his bodyguard.

The acrimonious correspondence between Bosie and his father continued. The Marquess had declared that he would not open any more letters from his son, whereupon Bosie wrote to him in the following terms:

As you return my letters unopened, I am obliged to write on a postcard. I write to inform you that I treat your absurd threats with absolute indifference. Ever since your exhibition at O.W.'s house, I have made a point of appearing with him at many public restaurants such as the Berkeley, Willis's Rooms, the Café Royal, etc., and I shall continue to go to any of these places whenever I choose and with whom I choose. I am of age and my own master. You have disowned me at least a dozen times, and have very meanly deprived me of money. You have therefore no right over me, either legal or moral. If O.W. was to prosecute you in the Central Criminal Court for libel, you would get seven years' penal servitude for your outrageous libels. Much as I detest you, I am anxious to avoid this for the sake of the family; but if you try to assault me, I shall defend myself with a loaded revolver, which I always carry; and if I shoot you or he shoots you, we shall be completely justified, as we shall be acting in self-defence against a violent and dangerous rough, and I think if you were dead many people would not miss you.[9]

Not content with attacking Oscar and his sons, the Marquess now carried the feud into the camp of his ex-wife and her father. He accused Lady Queensberry of supporting Alfred to defy him, and of pretending to believe that he wanted to make out a case against his own son. He now wrote to his ex-wife's father.

I have made out a case against Oscar Wilde and I have to his face accused him of it. If I was quite certain of the thing, I would shoot the fellow at sight, but I can only accuse him of posing. It now lies in the hands of the two whether they will further defy me. Your daughter appears now to be encouraging them, although she can hardly intend this. I don't believe Wilde will now dare defy me. He plainly showed the white feather the other day when I tackled him – damned cur and coward of the Rosebery type. As for this so-called son of mine, he is no son of mine, and I will have nothing to do with him. He may starve as far as I am concerned after his behaviour to me.[10]

In July Bosie was still abroad while Oscar, dogged by financial worries, stayed on in London. Several friends tried to persuade Oscar to go with them to Paris, where they wanted him to put on grey flannels and a straw hat and dine with them in the Bois; but he could not afford to go. 'Besides I want to see you,' he wrote to Bosie. 'It is really absurd *I can't live without you*.'[11] One thing consoled him. He had been to see a palmist, prosaically named Mrs Robinson, whom he referred to as 'the Sibyl of Mortimer Street', a woman whom Constance was known sometimes to consult. She had told him that in January of the following year he and Bosie would take a long voyage together, and that their lives would go hand in hand. Shortly afterwards, he made an appointment to consult her again, with two friends, but unfortunately the Goodwood Races proved a powerful counter-attraction and he cancelled the appointment.

In theory at least, Oscar detested the stormy nature of his relationship with Bosie. In reality, though, it was probably these emotional scenes that kept the relationship alive. It was a part of Oscar's essential make-up to require new and stimulating experiences, and the continual quarrels and dramatic reunions prevented the friendship from becoming dull. In Constance's case her reasonableness was her undoing. An occasional explosive response on her part might well have achieved what tolerance and understanding could not. Bosie by his impossible behaviour had achieved complete ascendancy over Oscar. Constance not only never achieved such ascendancy, but never even sought it. To her, Oscar's genius explained all.

Constance, meanwhile, had been looking around for a holiday home to rent for the summer, and had finally taken a small house on the Esplanade at Worthing. Oscar complained a little at the lack of a separate writing room for his use, but nevertheless he felt that anything was better than staying on in London. It was a great delight for Constance to have her boys about her again, and Oscar's arrival was an added pleasure. Queensberry had been on the rampage in London, and had been to the Café Royal to enquire for Oscar and Bosie again. Oscar now rather regretted not having had him bound over to keep the peace, for he found it intolerable to be dogged by the maniac. Only the thought of the scandal deterred him from taking action even now. He urged Bosie, who was apparently still abroad, to come and join him at Worthing, though he feared that he would find the meals tedious.

A few days later Oscar wrote to Bosie again. Constance had engaged an ugly Swiss governess to look after the boys, and Oscar had taken an immediate dislike to her. He found her quite insufferable. It was also fairly clear that, much as he loved his little boys, he found them decidedly tedious at mealtimes. He therefore decided that it would be better for Bosie not to join the family, and said that he would come to him instead. Bosie made three visits to Oscar during the course of that summer. The first two occasions passed without incident. The third time, however, Bosie turned up with a friend, presumably a male lover, and demanded to be given lodgings in the house. Here Oscar positively drew the line. He did offer him and his companion hospitality, but at a neighbouring hotel. Oscar was not jealous, but angry with Bosie for so indelicately flaunting a socially unacceptable relationship in front of his family. Bosie had failed to realize that his home, with Constance and the children, was a place apart which he did not wish to see violated, and Oscar resented this deeply.

When Bosie's friend returned to his own occupation on the following day, Bosie insisted on being taken to the Grand Hotel at Brighton. Oscar accordingly left Constance to her own devices yet again, in order to take him there. During the course of the day Bosie fell ill, and Oscar nursed him with devotion, showering him with fruit, books, flowers and presents and leaving his side only for a brief walk each morning and a short drive each afternoon. After about four days Bosie recovered sufficiently for Oscar to take lodgings nearby, and transfer Bosie with him. Here Oscar hoped to get a chance to work on *The Importance of Being Earnest*, to which he had devoted most of his time while in Worthing.

On the following day Oscar contracted influenza from Bosie. Though he felt exceedingly ill, Bosie went to London on business, promising faithfully to return that very afternoon. Once in London, Bosie met a friend and with typical selfishness decided not to return until late the next day. By this time Oscar was in a terrible fever, and had no servant or friend to attend to his needs. For two days Bosie utterly neglected him, and Oscar could not even get the milk which the doctor had told him he must have. This neglect on Bosie's part was deeply painful to Oscar, who had nursed him so patiently through his own influenza, and but for whom Oscar would not have contracted the illness. But worse was to follow.

One night, having been alone for several hours, Oscar begged the young man to dine with him and he somewhat ungraciously agreed. Oscar waited until eleven o'clock before leaving a note in Bosie's room, reminding him of his broken promise. At three in the morning, unable to sleep and parched with feverish thirst, Oscar went downstairs to the sitting-room in search of water. There he found his friend. If he felt remorse, Bosie showed no sign of it. Instead he launched into a tirade against Oscar, accusing Oscar of standing between him and his amusements and depriving him of his pleasures. Had he not needed to change out of his dress clothes, he admitted, he would not have come back at all; but when he found Oscar's note his sense of remorse robbed him of all desire to go out in search of further entertainment. For this he berated Oscar in a terrifying paroxysm of rage until Oscar wearily returned to his bedroom. Next morning the same scene was repeated with renewed emphasis until Oscar asked Bosie to leave the room. He pretended to do so, but when Oscar raised his head from the pillow he saw that he was still there. Suddenly Bosie came towards him, laughing in a brutal rage and hysteria. A sense of utter horror swept over Oscar, and he went downstairs, barefooted, and sought help from the owner of the house, who called the doctor immediately.

The doctor found Oscar in a state of nervous prostration, and more feverish than ever. After an hour, Bosie came silently into the room, took what money he could find on Oscar's dressing-table, collected his luggage from his own room, and left the house.

Oscar's state of mind in the days that followed was curiously calm. He had not known the exact nature of Bosie's intentions on that terrible occasion when he had felt compelled to flee. Physical fear was virtually unknown to Oscar, who when fit and well had enormous physical strength to match his stature. Bosie was, at most, some five feet nine inches in height and was slim and unathletic, so that he could have been no threat to Oscar unless armed. The threat was what had really counted, and the fear that some horrible deed was about to be committed, with dreadful consequences all round. He now saw that the association must end, come what may.

A few days later Oscar's health was much improved. It happened to be his birthday, and on the table among the many messages of congratulation was a letter in Bosie's handwriting. He slit open the letter, expecting to find the usual pathetic appeal for forgiveness. Instead he found a dramatic repetition of the two terrible scenes, told in mocking terms, and expressing satisfaction at having dined at the Grand Hotel at Oscar's expense on leaving him. Oscar described the letter in *De Profundis*:

You congratulated me on my prudence in leaving the sick bed, on my sudden flight downstairs. 'It was an ugly moment for you,' you said, 'uglier than you imagine.' Ah! I felt it but too well. What it had really meant I do not know; whether you had with you the pistol you had bought to try to frighten your father with, and that thinking it to be unloaded, you had once fired off in a public restaurant in my company; whether your hand was moving towards a common dinner knife that by chance was lying on the table between us; whether forgetting in your rage your low stature and inferior strength, you had thought of some special personal insult, or attack even, as I lay ill there; I could not tell. I do not know to the present moment. All I know is that a feeling of utter horror had come over me, and that I had felt that unless I left the room at once and got away, you would have done or tried to do something that would have been, even to you, a source of lifelong shame . . .[12]

Bosie's letter had ended, '*When you are not on your pedestal you are not interesting. The next time you are ill I will go away at once.*'[13] There was no apology, no remorse, only a bold and humiliating assumption that there would inevitably be a next time. When he read the coarse, unfeeling words Oscar felt that he had allowed himself to be polluted by associating with someone so utterly unworthy. He resolved to return to London on the following Friday and consult his friend the solicitor Sir George Lewis. His intention was to ask him to send a letter to the 'Scarlet Marquess' telling him that under no circumstances would he ever allow Lord Alfred Douglas to enter his home, or talk with him, or to be his companion at all.

At this point the affair of Oscar Wilde and Lord Alfred Douglas and the Scarlet Marquess ought to have come to an end. Had Oscar gone ahead with his plan and seen Sir George Lewis and had that letter sent, the whole terrible tragedy which wrecked Constance's life along with that of her husband would have been averted. But by some grim irony Fate took a hand at exactly this juncture.

On Friday morning, immediately prior to his departure for London, Oscar sat at the breakfast table idly turning the pages of the newspaper when his eye lighted on a Stop Press item. This gave news of a terrible tragedy which had overtaken Bosie's family. His eldest brother, the heir to all the Marquess of Queensberry's estates, had been found shot dead in a ditch with his own gun at his side.

Lord Drumlanrig had been a guest at a private shooting party in Somerset and his death seemed at the time 'stained with darker suggestion'.[14] A few days later the coroner returned a verdict of accidental death, it having been argued to his satisfaction that Drumlanrig's gun had gone off accidentally, killing him instantly. But there were, and are, good grounds for believing that he took his own life on account of a suppressed scandal. He had held a ministerial post in Gladstone's government, thanks to the influence of Lord Rosebery, whose private secretary he had been. It was reliably rumoured that he was implicated in a homosexual affair with Lord Rosebery, always the Scarlet Marquess's chief *bête noir* until Oscar came upon the scene. Drumlanrig had been universally loved and respected, and the family grief was terrible.

Oscar, with typical generosity, immediately forgave Bosie. That night he took him back to Tite Street, and never once referred to the incidents that had passed between them.

12

The Constant Wife

I will make her stand by her husband. That is the only
thing for any woman to do. It is the growth of the moral
sense in woman that makes marriage such a hopeless,
one-sided institution.

An Ideal Husband

It might have been imagined that Constance, neglected and
plunged into difficult financial straits by Oscar's wild extravagances, might now have bombarded him with grievances. Not so.
Loyally she held the family together, making sure that he was
undisturbed in his work and running the household as though
nothing had happened. She was certainly aware of his financial
difficulties, and now set to work to do what she could to alleviate
them.

While Oscar had been intermittently working at his new play,
she had devoted the summer months to a book of her own. Called
Oscariana, it was a selection of her husband's epigrams, chosen by
herself. This was a real labour of love, which Constance undertook
gladly, and ought to have given pause to her later critics who
claimed that she lacked wit and humour. One would have thought
that she had precious little to laugh at, yet she remained calm and
cheerful. Her selections show how well equipped she was intellectually to appreciate her husband's personal genius. If she allowed him
far more freedom than other wives gave to their husbands, it was
because she appreciated that his remarkable talent needed freedom
to develop. Oscar was singularly fortunate; not many women would
have accepted the situation so uncomplainingly. Lord Alfred
Douglas wrote of her, 'He was still fond of her, but he was often
impatient with her, and sometimes snubbed her, and he resented,
and showed that he resented, the attitude of slight disapproval
which she often adopted towards him.'[1] Yet few wives would

have displayed her patience and loyalty in the face of the eccentricities which Oscar displayed at that period.

Constance's publisher for *Oscariana* was Arthur L. Humphreys, well known to Constance and Oscar because he was for many years head of Hatchard's bookshop in Piccadilly. Mr Hatchard himself had been publisher of the *Rational Dress Society's Gazette* during Constance's editorship, and her decision to look in the same direction for publication of *Oscariana* rather than to Oscar's publishers is a clear indication of the fact that this was truly her personal project, and not just something 'ghosted' for her by her husband. Constance's relations with Humphreys, while excellent where business was concerned, were less happy at a personal level. Humphreys, who prided himself on his realistic approach to social and political matters, was diametrically opposed to Constance's enlightened attitude to social reform. Constance felt very deeply on matters which concerned the welfare of the working classes, and was appalled at the degree of proverty to be found in London at that time. In one letter of the period she pointed out to him that a quarter of all the adult population of London died in receipt of public charity. Unemployment had reached terrible proportions, and skilled artisans, she said, were forced to accept sixpence an hour. Clearly she felt that her outspoken analysis of the situation troubled him, but she was too frank and honest not to speak out on behalf of those who were unable to plead their own cause.

Oscariana came out in January 1895, in an edition of fifty copies. It proved an instant success, and within four months a further edition of two hundred copies was produced. This was the most important of Constance's literary works, and far outshone her previous pleasant but uninspired publications. Meanwhile her fame as a hostess continued undiminished. In November 1894 *Today*, which was then edited by Jerome K. Jerome, published a full-length feature called 'Mrs Oscar Wilde at Home'. It was one of a series of articles centred around the homes of famous women, and though somewhat artificial in style, gave a clear impression of the decor and furnishing at 16 Tite Street, plus a vignette of the distinguished lady of the house. Constance's views on colour and harmony in the home were reporter in detail. 'I am not one of those who believe that beauty can only be achieved at considerable cost,' she told the reported who interviewed her. 'A cottage parlour may be, and often is, more beautiful, with its unconsciously achieved

harmonies, and soft colouring, than a great reception room . . .'
The art works that lined the walls were commented on, including
the pen and ink drawing by Walter Crane which the Wildes greatly
prized, and an etching by Bastien-Lepage of Sarah Bernhardt, with
a few words inscribed on it by the great actress herself. Constance
spoke about the embroideries in which she specialized, and of her
views about flowers on the dinner table. She was not in favour of
large and elaborate centrepieces, and tended to a small and very
simple arrangement, rather more in the style of the Japanese, whose
economy of design was more to her taste. One fashion she disliked
intensely: 'I think that scattering cut blossoms on a table cloth is
both a foolish and cruel custom.' This gentle approach was typical
of something very special in the character of Constance Wilde,
whose tenderness was almost unequalled, except, curiously, by her
own husband. It was surely this quality above all others that had
first drawn him to her.

It is said that these simple qualities in his wife's nature
determined Oscar to call a proposed new play, the plot of which he
had tentatively worked on in Worthing, after her. Like most of his
plays, it had a provisional title, *Mr and Mrs Daventry*, but its real
title was to have been *Constance*. Though Oscar clearly intended it as
a compliment, the character of the wife in the plot is not altogether
sympathetic, for she switches her affections from her husband to
another man, and engineers her husband's suicide into the bargain.
It seems more likely that Oscar, pleased with the punning in
Earnest, saw similar possibilities in his wife's name, and decided to
make use of it.

Christmas 1894 was a rather lonely time for Constance. She had
her boys with her, of course, but Oscar was in the middle of
rehearsals for *An Ideal Husband*, which was due to open at the
Theatre Royal, Haymarket, on 3 January. The cast was a
distinguished one, including Lewis Waller, Charles Hawtrey and
Julia Neilson. Charles Brookfield, who had written the skit on *Lady
Windermere's Fan*, also had a minor role. The cast were decidedly
unenthusiastic when Oscar, instead of returning to the bosom of his
family on Christmas Day like any other husband and father, insisted
on spending the day in rehearsals.

Constance was a little consoled on Christmas Day when she
unexpectedly received a lovely bouquet of flowers from Robbie
Ross. Nor had he forgotten the boys. Throughout the year his

kindness and his thoughtful behaviour had impressed themselves more and more on Constance. She had finally abandoned formal modes of address when whe wrote to him, and now that he was no longer 'Mr Ross', but simply 'Robbie' she came to rely on his support and help. There was never any word of criticism of Oscar. Each was too loyal for that. Yet Robbie saw her loneliness and went out of his way to be kind. When Oscar was at home, she often asked him to dinner. 'No party, so don't come en grande tenue,'[2] she wrote on one such occasion. She even accepted an invitation to tea with him: 'I will come to tea with pleasure, and shall not notice the want of furniture in your delightful company and with all the charming bits of art that you always have round you'.[3]

When *An Ideal Husband* opened on 3 January 1895, the Prince of Wales was in the Royal Box. This in itself caused something of a sensation, for the Royal Family did not normally attend first-night performances. After the final curtain the Prince sent for Oscar and congratulated him on the success of the play. Oscar said that he felt some of the scenes should be cut, but the Prince replied that he ought not to take out a single word.

With her husband's name on everyone's lips Constance, too, lonely and neglected as she now was, seemed to have achieved the height of success. Money was now flooding into the Wildes' coffers, and their financial problems, in theory, were at an end. Whatever Constance did was likely to make news. At the beginning of January 1895 Constance went along to Cooper and Green of Regent Street and ordered a new dress. Her clothes had often been featured in magazines before, but this gown was particularly attractive. On the very day that the *Lady's Pictorial* ran an account of the first night of *An Ideal Husband*, it also carried an article about the new dress, with a picture.

It is composed of green chiné moiré arranged with green chiffon and black silk muslin, and trimmed with velvet roses and ribbon to match. The full skirt is of green chiné moiré with a black silk muslin round the hem, while the bodice is of green chiffon with sprays of roses and with long ends of ribbon reaching almost to the hem of the skirt. The sleeves are formed of two big puffs of black silk muslin, headed with green chiffon and moiré, while a garland of velvet roses may be seen on the shoulders.[4]

Though the dress seems elaborate from its description, it was in fact romantic and charming, and much simpler than those worn by most society beauties of her day. Many women would have read of Constance's new dress with envy, and would have wished to change places with the wife of Oscar Wilde; yet if they could have looked into the future and have foreseen the tragedy which was about to overtake her, not one of them would have stepped into Constance's shoes.

Oscar was staying mostly at the Albemarle at this time, and shortly after the first night of *An Ideal Husband* he was taken ill. By 8 January he reported that he was too ill to go out. But about a week later he and Bosie set off for Algeria.

At about this time, probably soon after the boys had returned to their respective schools, Constance tripped on a loose stair-carpet in the House Beautiful and fell from top to bottom of the long flight. It would appear that in trying to save herself she injured her arm rather badly; but worse still, other alarming health symptoms shortly developed. Initially their real significance was not realized. The actual severity of the symptoms in those early stages is not known, but her spine was affected and the prognosis was not good. Constance was an uncomplaining person; and though she immediately sought medical advice, the truth was either withheld from her or she chose not to divulge it.

Whether Oscar knew about the accident at all at this stage is doubtful. He had gone abroad without even notifying Constance of how she might get in touch with him. On 28 January Constance wrote to Robbie and asked him to get in touch with Oscar, as she was going to Torquay for a month and did not know how to reach him. She would not be at the first night of *The Importance of Being Earnest* in a fortnight's time, but wanted tickets for the performance sent to the Reverend A. L. Lilley and his wife, and felt that she could not rely on Oscar's memory in the matter. She was also £38 overdrawn at the bank, and hoped that Oscar would be able to replace some of this, and send her five pounds to Torquay to cover incidentals. She had been too ill on the previous day to attend to the hundred and one things that had to be done before leaving the house for a month, and had had to defer her journey for another day. She had decided in any event not to travel if there was a snowstorm, as she was terrified of being snowed up. She said that she would much appreciate being sent any notices about the play, as she felt she would have difficulty in getting hold of them in Torquay. 'I will send a letter to him on Thursday "chez vous" as I don't know where he will be,' she added. 'My servants will be on board wages, and if he wants to come home, he *must* let them have a day's notice.'⁵

As soon as he received this pathetic, uncomplaining appeal, Robbie acted. On 1 February Constance wrote to thank him for telegraphing Oscar's address to her.

> How very sweet and kind you are – a real friend, such as I knew you always to be! If I do want anything, I will let you know, and you shall let me have the £5, but at this moment I have no expenses, and can well wait until Oscar returns.
>
> And now, is there any chance of your being able to come here for a week? Lady Mount-Temple wants you so much to come next week when she will have a room for you. And I should be so glad to have you here, altho' at present it is so cold that it is quite unbearable.⁶

She had written to Oscar at the address Robbie had given her, but ended 'I shall like very much to know when Oscar returns.'

Oscar returned with Bosie from Algiers in February, shortly before the opening night of *The Importance of Being Earnest*, and booked into the Hotel Avondale in Piccadilly, where they stayed for ten days. To Oscar's indignation, Bosie insisted on bringing a friend also, so that both had to be paid for by Oscar. The bill came to £140.

The opening night of the new play was Oscar's greatest triumph. Oscar's great friend, Ada Leverson, whom he nicknamed the Sphinx, recalled the occasion thirty-five years later. According to her account, Constance attended the first night, though on the face of it this seems doubtful:

> On Valentine's day, the 14th February 1895, there was a snow-storm more severe than had been remembered in London for years. A black, bitter, threatening wind blew the drifting snow. On the dark, sinister winter's night, when the first representation of *The Immportance of Being Earnest* was produced at the St James's Theatre, it was with difficulty that we drove there at all . . . Outside, a frost, inside, the very breath of success; perfumed atmosphere of gaiety, fashion, and apparently, ever-

lasting popularity . . . The loudest cheers were for the author who was as well known as the Bank of England, as he got out of his carriage with his pretty wife, who afterwards joined friends when the author himself went behind the scenes.[7]

Never had London known a first night like it. Yet there was a reason why Oscar spent so little time in his box and so much behind the scenes. The Scarlet Marquess was on the rampage again, and the management feared trouble.

Oscar had got to know about the Marquess's intentions through a friend called Algernon Bourke, younger son of the Earl of Mayo. Queensberry had booked into Carter's Hotel in Albemarle Street, had purchased tickets for himself and his prize-fighter friend, and had let it be known among his acquaintances that he intended to cause trouble. Oscar accordingly arranged for the Marquess's money to be returned to him with a message that the seat had already been sold. Notwithstanding this, Queensberry turned up at the theatre, which was surrounded by police. For several hours he prowled outside, trying to gain admittance. Finally he left a grotesque bouquet of vegetables at the stage door for the author, and retired in frustration.

Four days later he called at the Albemarle Club, of which both Oscar and Constance were members, and left his card with the porter on duty, instructing him to give it to Oscar Wilde. The porter looked at the card and the message on it in some perplexity. He did not altogether understand the words the Marquess had written there, but he put his card into an envelope, unsealed, and kept it by him until such time as the dramatist should come into the club again.

Some time passed before Oscar visited his club. Bosie and his unwelcome companion had now left him, and what he really wanted to do was to get away to France. To his annoyance the hotel management refused to allow him to check out until the bill for £140 was settled. He wrote to George Alexander thanking him for a cheque for £300, and asking if he could have the balance as soon as possible, as he had been served with writs for £400, and wanted to leave the hotel, which he described as 'loathsome'.[8]

On 28 February Oscar went into the Albemarle Club and the porter handed him the open envelope, labelled by the porter with the date and time it had been handed in. Oscar took out the card and read it. On the card the Marquess, whose erratic spelling betrayed anger, or drunkeness, or both, had written 'For Oscar Wilde posing as somdomite'.[9] Oscar returned at once to the Avondale Hotel and wrote to Bosie, asking him to meet him on the following day. He also wrote to Robert Ross, asking him to call on him at 11.30 p.m. He added that he saw no alternative but a criminal prosecution, and that his life was being spoilt by the Marquess.

Robbie duly arrived, and the two friends discussed the situation into the small hours of the morning. Next day when Lord Alfred Douglas arrived all three went to see Humphreys, the solicitor whom Oscar had already consulted about Queensberry's conduct towards him. Humphreys asked Oscar whether there was any truth in Queensberry's allegations. Oscar assured him that there was not, whereupon Humphreys expressed the opinion that Oscar should succeed. Oscar later claimed that had it not been for Bosie's taunts of cowardice, he would not have taken the final step. He took refuge in the fact that he had no money; but at this point Bosie interposed and said that his family, who had been made miserable by the Scarlet Marquess for years, would be only too glad to defray the cost. Both Lady Queensberry and Bosie's elder brother, Percy, were conveniently out of the country, but Oscar took Bosie's assurance at face value, and borrowed £500 from Ernest Leverson, husband of the Sphinx, to defray court costs. Humphreys was able to proceed, and a warrant was taken out for Queensberry's arrest.

Constance, meanwhile, had returned to London. On or about 1 March she received a brief note from Oscar, who was still staying at the Avondale Hotel. It was written hastily in pencil and read:

Dear Constance,

I think Cyril better *not* come up. I have so telegraphed to Mr Badley.

I am coming to see you at nine o'clock. Please be in – it is important.

Ever yours,

Oscar[10]

Constance would certainly have complied with such a request, and presumably at that point Oscar broke the news to her of the action he had decided to take against the Marquess. Queensberry was arrested on Saturday 2 March 1895 at Carter's Hotel in Albemarle Street, where he was staying. He claimed to have been trying to find Oscar for days. The arresting officers took him to Vine Street Police Station, where he was charged before being taken before the magistrate at Great Marlborough Street. The case was adjourned and he was released on bail.

Whatever Constance's opinion of the actions which Oscar had decided on, she cannot have been happy about what happened next. Incredibly, at Bosie's insistence, Oscar now took the young man off to Monte Carlo, where they spent a week together. It was the height of folly, as Oscar seems to have later realized:

The warrant once granted, your will of course directed every-thing. At a time when I should have been in London taking wise counsel, and calmly considering the hideous trap in which I had allowed myself to be caught – the booby-trap, as your father calls it to the present day – you insisted on my taking you to Monte Carlo, of all revolting places on God's earth, that all day, and all night as well, you might gamble as long as the Casino remained open. As for me – baccarat having no charms for me – I was left alone outside to myself. You refused to discuss even for five minutes the position to which you and your father had brought me. My business was merely to pay your hotel expenses and your losses. The slightest allusion to the ordeal awaiting me was regarded as a bore. A new brand of champagne that was recommended to us had more interest for you.[11]

Though Oscar now knew that Constance was ill and still feeling the effects of her fall downstairs, he again failed to leave her a forwarding address. On 12 March Constance wrote to Robert Ross:

Dear Robbie,
    I don't know Oscar's address, so I will send this to you to take charge of. If you write to him tell him that I am going to stay with my aunt Mrs Napier, and as I am forbidden to walk I shall not be able to come over to Oakley Street, but I will leave directions about his mother having everything that she needs. I

am going to have an operation (not a serious one!) performed on me next week, and hope after that to be better.

Very sincerely yours

Constance Wilde.[12]

Constance's concern for her mother-in-law's well-being in the midst of all her own troubles was quite touching, as was Robbie's typical response. He replied immediately by telegraph giving Constance her husband's address, and obviously concerned for her state of health. Constance wrote to him from her aunt's house at 31 Lower Seymour Street, assuring him that the operation would not be serious. 'If Oscar comes home on Tuesday, and wishes to stay in Tite Street, I shall probably put it off until the case is over,'[13] she added. Clearly, she was prepared to go back to the House Beautiful to look after Oscar, despite her illness, if he needed her. Robbie also asked whether he might call and see her on the following Monday, a prospect which Constance welcomed. She had greater need of friends about her than she realized, for the terrible processes of law which were to bring ruin to her husband and herself had already begun.

On 9 March, shortly before their ill-judged holiday in Monte Carlo, Bosie and Oscar, together with Bosie's elder brother, Lord Hawick, had driven together to the court in Great Marlborough Street, where for the first time Oscar had taken the stand as Queensberry's prosecutor. The courtroom was crowded, but the proceedings were fairly short, and at the end of them the Marquess was committed for trial. He was released on bail of £5,000.

Their tour abroad left Oscar and Alfred Douglas rather short of time for the necessary consultations with Oscar's legal advisers. Humphreys offered the brief to Sir Edward Clarke, Q.C.,M.P., a man with a formidable reputation and an impeccable character. At his preliminary meeting with Oscar, Clarke made it clear that he could only undertake the case if Oscar could assure him that there was and never had been any truth in the allegations which had been made against him. Oscar made the necessary declaration without the smallest hesitation. Two junior counsel, William Mathews and Travers Humphreys, son of Oscar's solicitor, were also briefed.

Queensberry's counsel was no less eminent. He was Edward Carson,Q.C.,M.P., who had known Wilde slightly at Trinity

College, Dublin. Although a fellow countryman, he had never much cared for Oscar. His junior counsel in this case was Charles Gill. Unlike his opponents, Queensberry had remained in close contact with his advisers, and had been doing everything he could to rake up information likely to prove damaging to Oscar. The private detective he had employed for some time past had been singularly unsuccessful. At a fairly late stage in the proceedings all the 'evidence' which Queensberry could produce in his favour was contained in two letters, obtained via the would-be blackmailers, which Oscar had written to his son and the internal interpretation of Oscar's published works. This alone was unlikely to impress a jury

Suddenly, however, fortune favoured Queensberry. Charles Brookfield, that disgruntled minor actor and playwright who had lampooned *Lady Windermere's Fan*, decided for reasons known only to himself to pass on the names and addresses of men who knew more of Oscar's private life than he would care to have raised in open court. His information led the detective to a homosexual circle centred round a man called Alfred Taylor, whose rooms Oscar had sometimes visited. Other names followed. It now became clear that if these men gave the testimony which was now envisaged, they would lay themselves open to criminal charges, and since the Crown was not instructing in this case, there could be no question of legal immunity. It is appropriate to speculate upon the motives which might have induced these men to come forward to incriminate themselves in circumstances which could clearly lead to their imprisonment. The range of possibilities is small, and would not include such altruistic motives as public duty, private conscience and morality. The unsavoury odours of corruption did not reach the carefully averted nostrils of Edward Carson. He was above all that.

Oscar and Bosie were also engaged in seeking advice at this important juncture. While Queensberry busied himself with lawyers and detectives, they went along to the Sibyl of Mortimer Street, Mrs Robinson, and had their palms read. Their elation when she 'prophesied complete triumph and was most wonderful'[14] confirms the conclusion that the two men had long since lost all touch with reality.

On All Fools' Day Oscar and Bosie went to the Domino Room of the Café Royal where they met Frank Harris by arrangement to talk about the case. Bernard Shaw was also there, but his presence was purely coincidental, for he was not intimately acquainted with

Oscar, but was lunching with Harris by prior appointment. At Oscar's invitation he stayed and listened to the whole conversation. Oscar had hoped to recruit Harris as a prosecution witness to the artistic merit of his work, and of *The Picture of Dorian Gray* in particular. He was rather wounded when Harris declined. Harris' advice to Oscar on that occasion was absolutely sound. No jury in the country, he pointed out, would give a verdict against a father seeking to protect his son, however mistaken he might be. In his considered opinion Oscar ought to go abroad, and as his ace of trumps, he ought to take Constance with him. He advised him at the same time to write a letter to *The Times*, saying that he was a maker of beautiful things, not a fighter, and that he refused to fight under those circumstances.

At this juncture Bosie arrived, somewhat late, and they went over the ground again. Harris later noted:

> To my astonishment Douglas got up at once, and cried with his little white, venomous, distorted face:
> 'Such advice shows you are no friend of Oscar's.'
> 'What do you mean?' I asked in wonderment; but he turned and left the room on the spot.[15]

To Harris' amazement Oscar stood up and repeated the same idiotic formula, and hurried after his friend. Suddenly Harris realized that from start to finish Bosie had simply been manipulating Oscar for his own selfish ends. Shaw told him that he had nothing to reproach himself for in the matter, but he continued to brood over it:

> Left to myself I was at a loss to imagine what Lord Alfred Douglas proposed to himself by hounding Oscar on to attack his father. I was still more surprised by his white, bitter face. I could not get rid of the impression it left on me. While groping among these reflections I was struck by a sort of likeness, a similarity of expression and of temper between Lord Alfred Douglas and his unhappy father. I could not get it out of my head – that little face blanched with rage and the wild, hating eyes; the shrill voice, too was Queensberry's.[16]

Shaw also gave an account of that meeting, and evaluated Harris' friendship with Oscar:

He was one of the few men of letters who really appreciated Oscar Wilde, though he did not rally fiercely to Wilde's side until the world deserted Oscar in his ruin. I myself was present at a curious meeting between the two when Harris prophesied to Wilde with miraculous precision exactly what immediately afterwards happened to him and warned him to leave the country. It was the first time within my knowledge that such a forecast proved true. Wilde, though under no illusion as to the folly of the quite unselfish suit-at-law he had been persuaded to begin, nevertheless so miscalculated the force of the social vengeance he was unloosing on himself that he fancied it could be stayed by putting up the editor of the *Saturday Review* (as Mr Harris then was) to declare that he considered *Dorian Gray* a highly moral book, which it certainly is. [17]

Some thirty years later Douglas wrote to Frank Harris on the subject of that meeting and acknowledged his terrible fear that Oscar might weaken and throw up the sponge. This was the reason why he hurried Oscar out of the restaurant. Both he and Oscar had by now seen Queensberry's plea of justification in its amended form, and Bosie realized that neither of their companions were aware of the new witnesses who were about to come forward. 'I did not tell you our case for fear I might not convince you,' he wrote, 'and that you and Shaw might, even after hearing it, argue Wilde out of the state of mind I had got him into.' [18]

That evening, Oscar took Constance and Lord Alfred Douglas out to dinner and then to his box at the St James's Theatre to see *The Importance of Being Earnest*. Under any other circumstances Constance would have been elated by the huge audience and the general acclaim of her husband's latest and finest play. As matters stood, the evening must have been an ordeal, especially in view of her state of health and the operation she had recently undergone. Douglas, who never saw her again, reported that she appeared very agitated, and that when they said goodnight at the end of the evening, her eyes were filled with tears. He said that although he confidently expected Oscar to beat his father, he felt dreadfully sorry for her, as he realized that the business must be a terrible ordeal for her. [19]

During the interval Oscar went backstage and talked to George Alexander, who was less pleased to see his author than usual. He felt that it was an error of judgment for Oscar to be seen at the theatre at such a time, and urged him to go abroad.

'Everyone wants me to go abroad. I have just been abroad. And now I have come home again,' Oscar replied. 'One can't keep on going abroad, unless one is a missionary, or, what comes to the same thing, a commercial traveller. But make your mind easy, my dear Alec. I have consulted Mrs Robinson, the palmist, and she assures me that I shall win.'

'Do you really believe in palmists?'

'Always . . . when they prophesy nice things.'

'When do they ever prophesy anything else?'

'Never. If they did no one would believe in them, and the poor creatures must earn a living somehow.'

'Oh, you're impossible!'

'No, not impossible, my dear fellow . . . Improbable . . . yes . . .I grant you improbable.'[20]

And with those words, he rejoined Constance and Lord Alfred Douglas in the box, and laughed all the way through the rest of the play.

13

Revelations

Lord Illingworth: The Book of Life begins with a man and
a woman in a garden.
Mrs Allonby: It ends with Revelations.

A Woman of No Importance

Lord Queensberry's trial for criminal libel of Oscar Wilde began on
Wednesday 3 April 1895 at the Old Bailey.[1] The case had
attracted widespread public interest on account of the fame of the
two protagonists, and because of the nature of the accusation that
Lord Queensberry had made. The courtroom was filled to capacity,
and many who had hoped to get in were turned away.

Lord Queensberry arrived before Oscar, and looked unimpressive
in his light blue hunting stock. Oscar, predictably, was immaculate
in a frock coat, and even sported a flower in his buttonhole. Mr
Justice Collins, though slightly late, got briskly down to business,
and the jury were sworn in. Constance was not in the courtroom to
hear the Scarlet Marquess plead not guilty on the grounds that the
words of which her husband complained were true and published for
the good of the public. Indeed there were no ladies in the court at
all; the nature of the case precluded that, for this was Victorian
England at its most hypocritical.

Initially Oscar seemed confident in court; but his witticisms after
a time began to alienate the jury, who were incapable of rising to
Oscar's level of intellect. On only one trifling point did he make an
error. When asked his age, he said that he was thirty-nine.

This gave Edward Carson, opening for the defence, his first
chance to score in cross-examination. Oscar, born on 16 October
1854, was over forty, and Carson produced a copy of his birth
certificate to prove it. This was the level of trivia to which he had to
sink in order to gain the sympathy of the jury. A series of questions
concerned with Oscar's literary works and his interpretation of

morality ensued. Many of the questions centred on *The Picture of Dorian Gray*, and Oscar was asked about the morality of Dorian. He was also, quite improperly, called on to account for the moral tone of *The Chameleon*, an Oxford undergraduate magazine which had published Oscar's introduction to the book, 'Phrases and Philosophies for the Use of the Young', as a separate article. A story called 'The Priest and the Acolyte', which appeared in the same issue, a badly written and immoral story, was used to attack him though he had had nothing to do with its creation or its publication.

On the following day Oscar looked more subdued. Carson's opening questions centred round a man called Alfred Taylor, whose rooms were considered to be furnished in a decadent style, with lighted candles and curtains that were never drawn back. Taylor, whose father owned a limited company, was a gentleman. He had been educated at Marlborough, and later by a private tutor at Preston near Brighton. He went into the army but gave it up. In 1883 he had inherited £45,000. Oscar was questioned about his friendship with Taylor; whether he realized that Taylor was under police surveillance, and whether he knew that he had been arrested. Oscar replied that he had read it in the newspaper. He was asked whether he had then dropped the acquaintance. He replied that he had not, for Taylor had assured him of his innocence and the magistrate had dropped the case.

The defence asked about various young men of Oscar's acquaintance, including Charles Parker, an out-of-work valet who had been arrested with Alfred Taylor, and his brother, who was a groom. Carson indicated that the name of one young man might be left out of the proceedings. It was a delicate thought. The young man was Maurice Schwabe, whose aunt happened to be married to the Solicitor-General.

When Sir Edward Clarke began his re-examination he dealt extensively with the letters Lord Queensberry had written to his son. His object was to show that Oscar's association with Taylor, the Parkers and others was innocent. But to his dismay, in the lunch adjournment Oscar asked him whether he could be examined about any matters they chose. Clarke explained that this was indeed the case, and that his introduction of fresh evidence in the shape of the Queensberry correspondence had given the other side the opportunity to widen the scope of the questioning. They could in fact ask about anything which the judge did not object to. Asked what was troubling him, Oscar told him that he had once been turned out of the Albemarle Hotel with a boy in the middle of the night. Clearly it would be embarrassing if this came up in court.

Finally, Edward Carson announced his intention of calling into the witness-box a number of young men, including the blackmailer Wood, who had returned from America, and Charles Parker, who would reveal 'shocking' acts which he was led by Oscar to perform in the Savoy Hotel under the influence of iced champagne.

It was probably after the adjournment that Constance received a brief letter from Oscar, delivered to her by hand at Tite Street, telling her to allow nobody to enter his bedroom or sitting-room except the servants, and to see no one but her friends. Her state of mind at this juncture was of extreme bewilderment and distress. Full accounts of the trial had appeared in the newspapers and it was clear that things were not going well for her husband. Still she clung to the desperate hope that Oscar would win and return home triumphant. Obediently she locked up his rooms, and told the servants that she was not at home to callers.

That evening Frank Harris called at Oscar's home hoping to find him there, and with the intention of advising him to flee the country. The house appeared deserted, but after he had been knocking and ringing for some time, Arthur, the butler, opened the door. Mr Wilde was not at home. He did not know when he would be back; indeed, he thought that he might not return at all.

Clarke was now decidedly uneasy about the progress of the case. On mature consideration he felt that Oscar should now withdraw from the prosecution. Mathews, one of the two junior counsel, was in favour of a fight to the finish, for he felt that the witnesses would be discredited as criminals. Clarke's great fear, however, was that if the trial was allowed to run to its full conclusion and Oscar lost the case, he might be arrested on order of the judge in open court.

On the third day of the trial, Oscar, having listened gravely and quietly to Sir Edward Clarke's advice, agreed to be guided by him and withdraw from the prosecution. He need not appear in court, Clarke said, and he hoped that he would take the opportunity to leave the country. After Carson had opened the proceedings by going through a list of some of the witnesses he proposed to call, Sir Edward Clarke asked for a few moments with Mr Carson. He then stood up and announced to the court that his client now thought it better to withdraw the prosecution and submit a verdict of 'not guilty'. He could not resist the verdict of 'not guilty' since the Marquess had not made a direct accusation, but had used the phrase 'posing as'; and this, he trusted, would make an end of the matter.

The jury consulted briefly and a verdict of 'not guilty' was formally given, with costs to be paid by Oscar. The judge made no effort to bring the courtroom to order as cheering broke out. Lord Queensberry left the courtroom in triumph. On the streets outside the riff-raff shouted ribald comments and treated Queensberry as a hero. Prostitutes danced on the pavements. Oscar was spared this sight, at least. He had slipped quietly out by the side door.

Until his dying day, Lord Alfred Douglas blamed Clarke for not calling him into the witness-box. He always maintained that had he been allowed to make the court aware of his father's callousness to his family, of his insane behaviour which amounted to nothing short of persecution, Oscar would have won the case. He failed to see that all this was totally irrelevant. The point at issue was not whether Queensberry treated his family well or ill, not whether he cared for them or not, but quite simply whether or not he was guilty of libelling Oscar Wilde. Clarke fully realized this, and made the right decision. By maintaining his refusal Clarke effectively robbed Bosie of the one thing he had looked to in all this, the chance to confront the father he hated in open court.

On two other issues Sir Edward Clarke's judgement was, however, faulty. As an experienced counsel he should have seen from the outset the significance of that little word 'posing' on the Marquess's card, and should have appreciated the danger. The Marquess's allegation was an indirect one, and it was never necessary for him to prove Oscar guilty of the so-called crime. True, Oscar had assured Clarke of his innocence, but he should have pursued his enquiries beyond that point. Had he asked Oscar more about his life-style, he would surely have seen that there were elements in it which made it likely that Queensberry, acting out the part of aggrieved father, would have all the court's sympathy. He should have advised Oscar from the outset not to sue.

His second fault was in advising Oscar to drop the case on the third day of the trial without first ensuring that his client was also prepared to flee the country. Since the object of his advice was to avoid Oscar's being arrested in open court no benefit could be gained unless Oscar actually escaped to safety. Given that he was not willing to do this, it would have been better to see the thing through to the bitter end, in the hope that the criminal backgrounds of Queensberry's witnesses would have disinclined the jury to believe their allegations.

Meanwhile, the Marquess of Queensberry had not done his worst. Immediately after his acquittal, in order to avoid any possibility that the Director of Public Prosecutions might turn a blind eye, he instructed his solicitor to send him a copy of all the witnesses' statements and shorthand notes of the trial. He also wrote to Oscar, saying, 'If the country allows you to leave, so much better for the country! But if you take my son with you, I will follow wherever you go and shoot you!'[2]

Oscar left the Old Bailey at noon in a brougham, accompanied by Lord Alfred Douglas and Robert Ross. They drove first to the Holborn Viaduct Hotel, where Oscar wrote the following letter to the *Evening News*:

> It would have been impossible for me to have proved my case without putting Lord Alfred Douglas in the witness box against his father. Lord Alfred Douglas was extremely anxious to go into the box, but I would not let him do so. Rather than put him into so painful a position I determined to retire from the case, and to bear on my own shoulders whatever ignominy and shame might result from my prosecuting Lord Queensberry.[3]

After this Oscar and Bosie went to Oscar's friend, the solicitor Sir George Lewis, and asked him what could now be done. He had no advice to offer at this juncture. Had Oscar consulted him in the first place, he would have told him to throw Queensberry's card in the fire and leave it at that. Oscar and Bosie then went to the Cadogan Hotel, where the latter was staying, and had lunch. Reggie Turner joined them there. Robbie had been dispatched to cash a cheque for £200 at the bank for Oscar. He noticed that he was followed by a detective. Reggie and Robbie, who returned to the Cadogan Hotel at about a quarter to two, now did all that they could to persuade Oscar to leave the country.

Constance, who by now was in a state of extreme agitation, had gone to her Aunt Mary Napier in Seymour Street. It was Robbie who came to her in the early afternoon and broke the terrible news to her at Oscar's request. Her distress was most painful and pitiable.

There was no way of softening such a blow, and it was probably the most difficult task that Robbie was called upon to perform during that terrible day. Constance asked Robbie to beg her husband not to risk arrest, but to flee instead to the Continent.

Constance's pleadings were as useless as those of his friends. Oscar seemed glued to his chair, and had lost all power of action. He simply drank hock and seltzer in almost total silence. At four o'clock Bosie's cousin, George Wyndham, arrived. Bosie had gone out, and he asked to see Oscar; but Oscar could not bear the prospect of further reproaches, and asked the faithful Robbie to see him instead. Wyndham expressed the opinion that it would be better if Bosie and Oscar were kept apart, whereupon Robbie pointed out that Oscar's friends had been trying to separate them for years without success. If he could manage to keep his cousin away, he would be doing Oscar an inestimable service. Wyndham grew more amenable at this, and dropped his aggressive attitude. He suggested that Oscar leave the country at once to avoid a further scandal, whereupon Robbie pointed out that Oscar had refused his friends' repeated entreaties to do so. When Bosie returned, he and Wyndham went out to see if they could use their influence on Oscar's behalf.

The Director of Public Prosecutions had decided in favour of a warrant for Oscar's arrest. The details were taken by hand to the House of Commons, where they were seen by Asquith, the Home Secretary, and the Law Officers. Asquith said that Oscar should be stopped wherever he might be found. A detective inspector and a Treasury lawyer now applied at Bow Street to the presiding magistrate for a warrant. It would appear that the magistrate, who checked the time of the last boat train, deliberately procrastinated in order to enable Oscar to catch it if he so wished; but by this time Oscar was totally incapable of further action.

The warrant was signed shortly after five o'clock, and almost immediately afterwards a *Star* reporter called Marlowe came to interview Oscar, who was unable to see him. He told Robbie that a message had arrived at the newspaper office to the effect that a warrant had now been issued. Robbie passed this information on to Oscar, who blanched at the news but said nothing.

A few minutes later Oscar asked Robbie for the two hundred pounds he had cashed for him, and Robbie handed it over, believing that he had now decided to make good his escape. Immediately

afterwards, however, he settled back in his chair and reiterated his
intention of seeing it out. From time to time he asked querulously
after Bosie, but nobody knew where he was. At ten past six two
detectives called and arrested him. Oscar asked where he was to be
taken, and whether he would be granted bail. The detective said
that he would be taken to Bow Street, and held out virtually no
hope of bail that night.

Oscar was allowed, before leaving, to dash off a line to Bosie,
telling him that he had been taken to Bow Street and asking him to
persuade his brother Lord Hawick, the actor-producer George
Alexander and the actor Lewis Waller to attend next morning to
give bail. He also begged him to come to see him. Neither
Alexander nor Waller was prepared to go bail for their friend,
despite the personal profit each expected to gain from Oscar's plays.

Robbie now hastened to Tite Street. Constance had not returned,
but together he and Arthur, the loyal servant, managed to burst
open the door to Oscar's bedroom and study and pack an overnight
bag. At the door of the police station he found a mob shouting
indecencies. The overnight bag was refused. He returned to Tite
Street and removed a quantity of Oscar's letters and manuscripts,
but could not find A Florentine Tragedy and the enlarged version of
'The Portrait of Mr W. H.'. Afterwards, having done all he could
for his friend, he returned to his mother, who gave him £500 for
Oscar's defence and then induced him to go to Calais, where he was
ultimately joined by Bosie. The latter also, distraught by the turn
events had taken, did what he could to persuade the police to allow
comforts to be brought to Oscar, but without success.

That evening Constance's Aunt Mary did her best to enlist help
for the Wilde family. Laura Hope recorded in her diary: 'A most
trying visit from Mrs William Napier in a most frantic state about
her poor niece Constance Wilde as the whole verdict has gone
against her monstrous husband — the whole episode most terrible.'
Next morning she reported: 'Adrian has had a most painful
interview with Lord Alfred Douglas, who came to implore him to
go bail for that fiend O.W. which was of course impossible.'[4]

Constance, despite all her distress, rallied sufficiently to think of
her children. It was painfully clear to her that they could not remain
at their preparatory schools, and she accordingly arranged for them
to return to London without delay. Above all she wanted to keep
from them the news of the scandal surrounding their father. Yet

despite all her precautions, Cyril read the headlines on a placard at Baker Street, and although he did not understand the meaning of the terms used, he did not rest until he had found out. His opportunity occurred soon afterwards when he was sent to stay with the Hemphills in Ireland, where it was initially intended that Vyvyan should join him. Newspapers were left about and before long the whole tragic business was clear to him.

It is difficult to say which of the boys suffered worse, Cyril who knew the truth and was permanently saddened by it, or Vyvyan, who was eighteen years old before he learned what had happened to his father. Instead Vyvyan found his secure, happy childhood converted to a strange nightmare in which he was unable to comprehend other people's attitudes towards himself and his brother. For a time Vyvyan remained at Tite Street with his mother; but it quickly became apparent to Constance that something else would have to be found for the boys. As she pored over the newspapers day after day with tears spilling from her violet eyes she saw that they could not escape from the painful publicity even in Ireland. She therefore hastily engaged a French governess, who knew little English, and sent the children with her to the Continent, remaining in England herself in order to be of help to her husband.

A few days after Oscar's arrest, Constance took refuge with her great friend and confidante Lady Mount-Temple at Babbacombe. Oscar had persistently and unjustly been refused bail, which he needed desperately, not only to help rebuild his shattered morale, but also to attend to the thousand and one things required to get his defence together. He had one stroke of great good fortune. Sir Edward Clarke offered to defend him free of all charge, an offer which Oscar gratefully accepted, particularly since it also carried with it the free services of the two junior counsel. But other circumstances weighed heavily against him. The Queensberry letters had contained damaging allegations about Lord Rosebery; and the name of Maurice Schwabe, nephew of the wife of the Solicitor-General, also seemed likely to crop up. It was therefore essential that there should be no suspicion of covering up a scandal which might involve these people. Oscar was finally committed for trial on 19 April, and the first hearing at the Old Bailey was scheduled for 26 April.

Constance, like Oscar, had also consulted the palmist, Mrs

Robinson. On the day when Oscar was committed for trial, she wrote to her:

My dear Mrs Robinson,
What is to become of my husband who has so betrayed and deceived me and ruined the lives of my darling boys? Can you tell me anything? You told me that after this terrible shock my life was to become easier, but will there be any happiness in it, or is that dead for me? And I have had so little. My life has all been cut to pieces as my hand is by its lines.
    As soon as this trial is over I have to get my judicial separation, or if possible my divorce in order to get the guardianship of the boys. What a tragedy for him who is so gifted.
    Do write to me and tell me what you can.

Very sincerely yours

Constance Wilde

I have not forgotten that I owe you a guinea[5]

Five days later Oscar's creditors sent the bailiffs into the House Beautiful to sell up everything the couple owned. The way in which the auction of their effects was carried out was an outrage. Vast quantities of valuable property were stolen, and the rest sold at scandalously low prices. Oscar's entire library of rare and auto-graphed first editions was bundled up in lots of twenty or thirty books and sold off for two or three pounds per lot. Somebody boasted of getting a Whistler for a shilling. Constance used to keep all her letters from Oscar in a little blue leather case, but somebody was heartless enough to steal the case and its contents. Various manuscripts and personal letters belonging to Oscar vanished without trace, and all the children's toys were sold off for thirty shillings. For months afterwards the boys asked for their trains and tin soldiers, and wondered why this always made Constance cry. They knew nothing of the sale. In the eyes of the public, Oscar was guilty before his trial. His books were accordingly withdrawn from sale. For a short time his plays limped on, with the author's name removed from the boards, but soon they, too, faced with falling audiences, had to be taken off.
    Constance had now lost virtually everything. Her husband was in

jail, her children exiled; her home and all her belongings had been sold over her head. The family name was disgraced, and she faced the sad prospect of divorce. As if this was not enough, she was still ill, and steadily growing worse.

14

Separation

Ah! hadst thou liked me less and loved me more,
Through all those summer days of joy and rain,
I had not now been sorrow's heritor,
Or stood a lackey in the House of Pain.
                                    'Quia Multum Amavi'

When Oscar appeared at the Old Bailey on 26 April 1895 he did not
stand trial alone. With him in the dock was Alfred Taylor, who
could have bought immunity from prosecution if he had agreed to
turn Queen's evidence against his friend; but he would not. They
faced twenty-five counts alleging gross indecency and conspiracy to
procure the commission of acts of indecency by Wilde, and Taylor
additionally stood charged with having acted as procurer for Wilde.
As witnesses against them the prosecution had lined up a group of
self-confessed blackmailers, all of whom had been promised
immunity from prosecution and had had their palms well covered
by Queensberry for their testimony.

Bosie was not in court. He had fled to Calais on the previous day.
He was not alone in this. The trials of Oscar Wilde had led to a
mass exodus of prominent wealthy people who had suddenly
realized to their horror that haunts which they had always
considered safe were in fact regularly under the surveillance of the
police.

Oscar looked decidedly the worse for his long weeks in Holloway
prison as he faced his accusers. One by one the witnesses were
paraded before him: Charles Parker, who alleged that Alfred Taylor
had procured him and his brother for Oscar, whom Clarke proved
was a blackmailer; Alfred Taylor's landlady, who thought that she
had once heard him talking to someone called Oscar; a neighbour of
Parker's, who thought she had once seen Oscar leaving his lodgings;
and Alfred Wood, introduced to Oscar by Lord Alfred Douglas,

who claimed to have received gifts and money from Oscar, and to have committed indecencies with him at Tite Street. Quite apart from his attempt to blackmail Oscar with the set of letters from the pocket of the suit given him by Lord Alfred Douglas, he was shown to have joined in a blackmail conspiracy with Allen and Parker which had netted them some £300. Of this his personal share had been £175. Even more sensational was Fred Atkins, who claimed to have surprised Oscar in Paris in bed with the nephew of the Solicitor-General's wife. This man was exposed by Sir Edward Clarke as a professional blackmailer who had extorted £200 from a Birmingham gentleman some four years previously. Sidney Mavor, the next witness, had spent a night with Oscar at the Albemarle Hotel, but denied any misconduct.

A chambermaid at the Savoy claimed that when Oscar and Bosie occupied adjoining rooms, she had seen a sixteen-year-old boy in Oscar's bed. Edward Shelley, from Oscar's publisher's office, accused Oscar of kissing him and inviting him into his bedroom, though he agreed that although this had degraded him, he had continued to accept Oscar's invitations to dinner. Indeed, when he was arrested for assaulting his father, it was Oscar who persuaded the father to go to the police station and withdraw the charges against him.

The trial now moved into its fourth day. To the surprise of the spectators the proceedings opened with an announcement that the prosecution had decided to drop the conspiracy charge. Sir Edward Clarke protested immediately at the tardiness of the decision, for he pointed out that it was predjudicial to the interests of each of the accused for the cases to be tried together. The publicity already given made it exceedingly difficult for the jury to approach the matter with an open mind, and these difficulties were increased by the association of the two defendants in the minds of the jurors. He also put it to the jury that Oscar's voluntary airing of the matter in public by charging the Marquess of Queensberry with criminal libel was a clear indication of his innocence.

Oscar now took the stand. The prosecution, in the person of Charles Gill, asked him about *The Chameleon*, and whether Lord Alfred Douglas was a contributor to it. Oscar assented, and agreed that he had admired the poems his friend had had published there. The prosecution then read out Douglas' poem entitled 'In Praise of Shame':

> Unto my bed last night, methought there came
> Our lady of strange dreams, and from an urn
> She poured live fire, so that mine eyes did burn
> At sight of it. Anon the floating flame
> Took many shapes, and one cried, 'I am Shame
> That walks with Love, I am most wise to turn
> Cold lips and limbs to fire; therefore discern
> And see my loveliness, and praise my name.'
>
> And afterward, in radiant garments dressed
> With sound of flutes and laughing of glad lips,
> A pomp of all the passions passed along,
> All the night through; till the white phantom ships
> Of dawn sailed in. Whereat I said this song,
> 'Of all sweet passions Shame is loveliest.'[1]

Gill now began to ask Oscar for his comments on the poem. To this Clarke objected, since it was not by the accused. Oscar explained that it was not for him to interpret the work of another, but he pointed out that the word 'shame' in this context meant modesty. When Gill claimed that the poem would be unacceptable to a reader with an ordinary balanced mind, Oscar replied that this was strictly a matter of individual taste and judgement. Next Gill read out a portion of another of Bosie's poems:

>   'Sweet youth
> Tell me why, sad and sighing, thou dost rove
> These pleasant realms? I pray thee tell me sooth
> What is thy name?' He said 'My name is Love.'
> Then straight the first did turn himself to me
> And cried, 'He lieth, for his name is Shame,
> But I am Love, and I was wont to be
> Alone in this fair garden, till he came
> Unasked by night; I am true Love, I fill
> The hearts of boy and girl with mutual flame.'
> Then sighing said the other, 'Have thy will,
> I am the Love that dare not speak its name.'[2]

Asked whether the last line referred to unnatural love, Oscar replied that it did not; it was the affection of the older man for the younger, as between David and Jonathan, and such as is described in the sonnets of Shakespeare and Michelangelo. It was not unnatural, but intellectual.

Finally, Oscar said that he could not be responsible for what hotel servants had said years after he had left the hotel, and that there was no truth in the allegations of indecency that had been made.

The examination of Alfred Taylor was quite short by comparison. When the judge finally summed up, he wrote down four questions which the jury needed to ask themselves: whether Wilde committed indecent acts with Edward Shelley and Alfred Wood and with a person or persons unknown at the Savoy Hotel, or with Charles Parker; whether Taylor procured or attempted to procure the commission of these acts or any of them; whether Wilde or Taylor or either of them attempted to get Atkins to commit indecencies; and whether Taylor committed indecent acts with Charles Parker or William Parker.

After four hours of deliberations the jury were unable to agree a verdict, nor could there be any possibility of agreement, except that they found them not guilty in regard to question three. A formal verdict was recorded on this point only. There would now have to be a retrial, and although the judge was not prepared to grant bail, he saw no objection to a fresh application to a judge in chambers.

Next morning Clarke appealed for Oscar to be released on bail and this time the application was granted, but was set at the almost prohibitive sum of £5,000 of which half was to be put up by Oscar himself. As he was virtually bankrupt by this time, it was probably Constance in fact who supplied the money. Lord Hawick put up half the remainder, leaving the question of finding one more person to go bail for £1,250. At this stage a City friend of Oscar's, who was prevented from helping him as he wished by his articles of association, asked the Reverend Stewart Headlam, founder of the Church and Stage Guild, to stand bail on his personal assurance that he would cover the sum of money involved. 'I was surety not to his character but for his appearance in court to stand his trial. I had very little personal knowledge of him at that time. I think I had only met him twice,'[3] he said afterwards.

When Oscar was released on bail he no longer had a home of his own to go to. He drove to a hotel where friends had taken rooms for him, and was about to sit down to dinner when the manager came

Constance, about 1894

Oscar *(left)* and Lord Alfred Douglas in about 1894

The Marquess of Queensberry

Reading Gaol

Oscar's grave at Bagneux

in to say that he had learned his identity, and that he must leave immediately. He drove to another hotel, where the whole sorry process was repeated, and thereafter moved from one hotel to another, only to be refused admittance. Queensberry's bloodhounds had done their work well. They had followed him from the instant he left the prison walls, and threatened to wreck any hotel whose manager took in Oscar Wilde.

Finally Oscar, tired and hungry, knocked at his mother's door in Oakley Street. His brother opened the door. 'Willie, give me shelter, or I shall die in the streets,'[4] he said, and staggered pale and dishevelled into the hallway. In many ways his mother's house was quite the worst place for Oscar to seek refuge in the present crisis. Speranza's strong sense of the dramatic led her to look on this in some curious way as a fight for Ireland. She threatened to disown him if he left the country now. Willie, intemperate as ever, took the same line. No doubt he meant well, but deep inside he probably rather enjoyed the discomfiture of his younger brother, whose preaching in recent years he had resented bitterly.

Yeats was one of Oscar's callers in Oakley Street. Willie received him rather pompously and asked his name. 'Are you urging him to flee?' demanded Willie as the poet handed him a note for his brother. 'Because if you are, I won't let him have the note.' 'I think that the whole family – Irish pride being aroused – felt that the cowardice of running away would be a far greater disgrace than the disgrace of a conviction and imprisonment,'[5] Yeats said later. Ellen Terry also called at the house, heavily veiled, and left a horseshoe with a bouquet of violets and the words 'For luck' written on the card.

Another early caller was Frank Harris, who descended on the house and took Oscar out to dinner. Willie, whose air of theatrical insincerity annoyed Harris, met him at the door. 'He cannot go out,'[6] said Willie, but Harris would not take no for an answer. Sherard was with Oscar, who began to brighten at the prospect of an outing. They went to a little-known restaurant in Great Portland Street where they booked a private room. Over the meal they discussed the progress of the trial and the new one which was to follow. One of the aspects they discussed was the evidence of the staff at the Savoy Hotel. Oscar said, 'They are mistaken, Frank. It was not me they spoke about at the Savoy Hotel. It was Bosie Douglas. I was never bold enough. I went to see Bosie in the morning in his room.'[7]

Harris asked why Sir Edward Clarke had not brought that out at the trial. Oscar replied that the lawyer had wished to do so but he had forbidden it. 'I must be true to my friend. I could not let him.'[8] Harris also tried to reassure him about Shelley's evidence, which he felt sure would be ruled out at the next trial. He recorded Oscar's reply:

'Oh, Frank,' he said, 'you talk with passion and conviction, as if I were innocent.'
  'But you are innocent,' I cried in amaze, 'aren't you?'
  'No, Frank,' he said, 'I thought you knew that all along.'[9]

Harris, though dumbfounded, declared that this made no difference to their friendship, and offered to arrange to charter a boat in which he could escape to the Continent. Oscar refused. He had given his word to his mother and to Stewart Headlam, who had stood bail, and he intended to keep it.

Two ladies were of special help to Oscar in the crisis. Adela Schuster, referred to by Oscar as 'the Lady of Wimbledon', hearing of his bankruptcy sent £1,000 towards his defence. The other was Ada Leverson, who called at Oakley Street and realized at once that this was not the right place for Oscar at such a trying time. She and her husband, Ernest, took him to their home in Courtfield Gardens, in South Kensington, and turned over the nursery floor to his use. He remained discreetly upstairs until six o'clock each day, when he descended to dinner, carefully dressed and sporting a flower in his buttonhole.

When Constance learned that he was there, she came to see him and spent a couple of hours trying above all to persuade him to leave the country. Her own solicitor urged this course of action, for he felt sure that the next trial would ruin him. To her absolute despair, he refused to go. She implored, she wept, she urged him to think of the boys, but his mind was made up. She had travelled up from Babbacombe to see him, and brought a message from Lady Mount-Temple to the effect that he could stay at Babbacombe between trials if he so wished; but he preferred to stay in London.

On 20 May 1895 Oscar Wilde and Alfred Taylor stood once more in the dock at the Old Bailey. The Solicitor-General, Sir Frank Lockwood, appeared for the prosecution, with Charles Gill and Horace Avory. Sir Alfred Wills was the presiding judge, and to him

Sir Edward Clarke immediately applied for the two cases to be heard separately, since the conspiracy charge had been withdrawn. Nevertheless, Wills refused to allow the cases to be heard in reverse order, acquiescing in the Solicitor-General's decision to take the case of Taylor first. Inevitably this was predjudicial to Oscar's defence. Predictably, Taylor was found guilty on counts of indecent behaviour with the Parker brothers, although he was not found guilty of procuring. The sentence was deferred until Oscar Wilde's case had been heard.

Oscar's trial began on 22 May. There were now only eight counts, four alleging acts of gross indecency with Charles Parker, two of indecency with unknown persons in the Savoy Hotel, one of indecency with Shelley, and the other with Wood at Tite Street. Under Clarke's questioning Shelley was quickly exposed as a neurotic young man with a history of violence and fantasies. The servant at the Savoy was demonstrated to be unable to recognize people without the aid of her glasses, which she had not been wearing at the time she claimed to have seen a man in Oscar's bedroom with him. Two other servants had been hastily found and persuaded to testify about the events of many months previously, and owned to having been asked to testify only on the preceeding Friday. There was nothing to corroborate Wood's statement that he had been to Tite Street.

Oscar, having once more denied all the charges of indecent acts, was asked about his relations with Bosie and the nature of the letters. The foreman of the jury interrupted the proceedings to ask whether a warrant had ever been issued for the arrest of Lord Alfred Douglas, or whether such a warrant was ever contemplated. He was told that this was irrelevant since the jury had only to deal with the matter of the prisoner in the dock. The foreman of the jury was, however, persistent. He pointed out that if the jury members were to look on the correspondence between Oscar and Bosie as evidence of guilt, the latter was as guilty as the former. Mr Justice Wills said that the supposition that Lord Alfred Douglas would be spared because he was Lord Alfred Douglas was one of the wildest injustice. It was hopelessly impossible. In the event, of course, Bosie was never charged.

The judge's summing up was fairly reasonable, and the Solicitor-General remarked to Sir Edward Clarke while the jury were considering the verdict that he expected Oscar to be acquitted.

But when the foreman read over their verdict, they found Oscar guilty of all charges but the one relating to Edward Shelley. In passing sentence Mr Justice Wills said:

> It is no use for me to address you. People who can do these things must be dead to all sense of shame, and one cannot hope to produce any effect upon them. It is the worst case I have ever tried. That you, Taylor, kept a kind of male brothel it is impossible to doubt. And that you, Wilde, have been the centre of a circle of extensive corruption of the most hideous kind among young men, it is equally impossible to doubt.
>
> I shall, under such circumstances, be expected to pass the severest sentence that the law allows. In my judgment it is totally inadequate for such a case as this. The sentence of the court is that each of you be imprisoned and kept to hard labour for two years. [10]

The savagery of the sentence after the relatively mild summing-up stunned the crowded courtroom. The first to react were those who, sickened by the monstrous verdict and the decision of the learned judge cried 'shame'. Oscar tried to speak, but the judge motioned to the officers to take him away. He swayed a little in the dock before hands reached out and led him away to an unjust and inhuman punishment. There had been no evidence that Oscar had corrupted anybody. He had been convicted on the unsupported testimony of blackmailers, for 'crimes' which ten years ago had been no crime, and which were not regarded by any other European country of the day as criminal. Once the verdict of the jury was made known, the judge allowed all his predjudices to surface, and reacted with a brutality which was perhaps predictable. He had shown the world that he regarded homosexuality as disgusting and obscene and, despite his remarks about Lord Alfred Douglas, must have been well aware of the immunity from prosecution that privelege and influence would buy. As Oscar was borne away to his solitary confinement in Pentonville Prison, the rabble danced with glee on the streets outside.

For Constance the news was shattering. Her always gentle heart was torn alternately by love and anger at the betrayal of her trust. She clung with even greater tenacity now to her notions of motherhood, and in the months that were to follow was consumed by doubts about her future. Happiness, she feared, was now a thing of the past for her. Duty to her children was all that she had to console her. Had she been childless, perhaps her decisions would have been easier to make; had her children been daughters perhaps the need to remove them from all possibility of contact with their father's friends might have seemed less urgent. André Gide once wrote of Lord Alfred Douglas, 'I was questioning him one day about Wilde's two sons; he laid great stress on the beauty of Cyril (I think) who was quite young at the time, and then whispered with a self-satisfied smile, "He will be for me."'[11] Many of Gide's tales about Wilde have subsequently been exposed as untrue, and there may or may not be a firm foundation for this story. If it is true, there is no doubt that Oscar, had he been aware of it, would have reacted violently, for he loved Cyril more than any other human being. Nevertheless, the sordid little tale puts into words exactly the kind of fear of his friends which obsessed Constance, and all her protective instincts now came to the fore.

What made matters harder to bear was that she still loved Oscar and would never cease to love him. Oscar came in time to think that she might possibly one day find happiness in marriage to another; yet the notion was clearly impossible. The woman who had been Oscar Wilde's wife could settle for no one less, and Oscar was unique.

The other major problem was that the family and friends of the couple were now firmly divided into two camps, and had their own notions as to what was now right for the pair. It is interesting that both Constance and Oscar were capable of inspiring extreme and partisan affection. Constance's friends now rallied around her. A few rare spirits, like her brother Otho and Lady Mount-Temple, seemed to understand her deeper feelings and did not try to railroad her into a divorce which she clearly did not wish. But others, like the Napiers, no less well-meaning, reacted towards Oscar with bitter hatred and would settle for nothing less than his complete expulsion from their family circle. In their efforts to wipe their lives clean of all past association with him, they even cut his name from the front of those of his books which lined their shelves, and the name Wilde was forbidden within their walls.

Oscar's friends were further subdivided. One camp was occupied almost exclusively by Bosie, who quickly re-emerged in his true colours after a brief period of mourning his champion's defeat at the hands of the father he hated. Soon he lost even Oscar's sympathy; his letters swiftly ceased altogether and he began pawning Oscar's gifts and selling news stories about their friendship to the papers. Oscar had to ask his friend Robert Sherard to prevent Bosie from publishing his letters to him from prison in the *Mercure de France*. He saw that Bosie was now wearing their friendship like a flower in his buttonhole, and he resented it bitterly.

In another camp were Oscar's friends like Robbie Ross, More Adey and Robert Sherard, who wanted to see an end to Oscar's association with Douglas and his reunion with his wife and family; but their primary interest was Oscar, whose welfare they placed above all other considerations. They were well-meaning, and disposed to see the couple reunited under happier circumstances, but unfortunately their efforts to take care of Oscar's tangled affairs only led to increased problems between himself and Constance.

15

Mrs Holland

I think his fate is rather like Humpty Dumpty's, quite
as tragic and quite as impossible to put right.

Constance in a letter to Otho of 26 March 1897

After the terrible ordeal of the trial and the many consultations with
Mr Hargrove, old John Lloyd's solicitor, and a few days of
recuperation at Babbacombe with Lady Mount-Temple, Constance
hurried to join her children at Glion, on Lake Geneva, where they
had been taken by their hastily recruited governess. On the very day
of her arrival at the Hotel Righi-Vaudois, Mademoiselle had seen fit
to take them in a hired rowing boat to St Gingolph, on the other
side of the lake. A storm had sprung up, with the result that she
and Cyril were sick, and though the boatman remained calm, she
seemed to think that her last hour had come. A devout Roman
Catholic, Mademoiselle lit her bedroom with a hundred francs'
worth of lighted candles, and presented Constance with the bill.
She was not pleased. On investigation she found that the governess
had failed to provide proper food for the children *en route* to
Switzerland, had abandoned them in a Paris Hotel room while she
went out on an assignation of her own, and had caused trouble in
the hotel. Eventually she was dismissed, though not until some
three months had passed and her behaviour with the hotel staff had
made it quite impossible for her to be kept on.

On Constance's arrival they had transferred to the Hotel du Parc
in Glion, where Constance resolved to stay for three months.
Shortly after her arrival she wrote to her friend Emily Thursfield:

People have been so kind to me, but you know I am quite
broken-hearted. It is so terrible to be here free in the heavenly
air, and to think of those four walls round him. I have to sue for
divorce because the boys must be free, and I cannot get a

separation. I have not the legal claims for that, and on account of the way he has behaved about money affairs no-one would trust him to look after the boys if anything should happen to me, and if he got control of my money. I have got to come back in December or January in order to give evidence in Court but I shall not settle in England until next April. I am more likely to settle in London than anywhere else but I am quite vague and waiting for something to turn up as an inducement.[1]

She described her plans for preparing Cyril for a naval career, and added that his headmaster at the English preparatory school had felt that the Navy would have provided him with the kind of discipline which his character required. Vyvyan was more of a problem. He was still only eight yet it seemed to trouble Constance a little that a career had not yet been chosen for him. She described him as a perfect baby, 'much sharper and quicker than Cyril, very affectionate and tremendously self-willed, an exceedingly clever boy'.[2]

When he had completed his first three months in prison, Oscar was entitled to write one letter and receive one visitor. He received a letter from Otho Lloyd, telling him that if he wrote to Constance it seemed to him likely that she would abandon all notions of getting a divorce. Oscar took his brother-in-law's advice and wrote to Constance at once. His expression of regret about the trouble he had brought upon her and the boys and his wish to be reunited with them were wholly sincere. Robert Sherard, who was the first visitor to Wandsworth Prison, where he had been transferred at the end of July, also wrote to Constance, giving her a pitiable account of his life and the privations which Oscar had daily to undergo. He was greatly depressed and prone to tears, and had been deterred from suicide only by the lack of means to accomplish it. His hands were disfigured, his nails broken and bleeding from the rough work he was put to, and his face emaciated and unrecognizable.

Constance was touched by this news of her husband. It was clear that she still loved him, as Otho, who was staying with her at the Hotel du Parc, well knew. Despite all the advice that her solicitor had given her, she weakened, and a reply was sent to Oscar encouraging him to hope that a divorce was not inevitable.

At the beginning of September 1895 Constance planned to spend a month at Yverdon, near Neuchatel, to take the baths and be massaged, which she hoped would help her illness. Two problems intervened, however. Mademoiselle had finally had to be dismissed, and Constance needed a replacement urgently as she could not leave the boys until she had someone to look after them; and she received a visit from her solicitor.

The visit began very mysteriously. At luncheon Constance was told that a Mr Erroll had telephoned from les Avants and had left word that he would call and see her. Knowing nobody of that name, Constance was puzzled. When she realized the true identity of her caller she was terrified, for the letter which had been sent to Oscar on the day before was in direct contradiction to all the advice he had given her. She asked Otho to be with her for moral support, fully expecting a difficult interview. To their amazement, Mr Hargrove began by showing them a letter from Oscar to Constance, which had been sent through him, and which he had opened as her legal adviser. He found it one of the most touching and pathetic letters he had ever read. He now admitted the possibility, in view of this humble and penitent letter, that Constance might be disposed to forgive Oscar. At this juncture Constance produced Robert Sherard's letter, and told him that she had resolved not to proceed with the divorce. Naturally the solicitor pointed out to her that she would probably have to reconcile herself to beginning life afresh with the boys under new identities on the other side of the world, but she was prepared for that.

Besides writing to Oscar, Constance had written also to the prison governor, saying that she would like to see her husband. A friend called Miss Boxwell, in whose company Constance had been taking boat excursions on Lake Geneva and generally taking advantage of the superb countryside and mountain air, was due to return to London on 18 September. Constance now proposed to defer her visit to Yverdon, taking advantage of Miss Boxwell's suggestion that they should travel together and that Constance should stay with her. Perhaps it was significant that she did not elect to stay with the Napiers. Inevitably, kind though they were, they would have disapproved strongly of any contact between Constance and Oscar, and even more of any talk of reconciliation. Constance would remain in London for a week and at the end of that time would go to Yverdon for the waters. As for the boys, they would go to Otho and his wife at Bevaix.

The prison governor replied to Constance that as Oscar had

already had a visitor he would not be allowed another until three more months had elapsed. She therefore made an urgent application to the Prison Commissioners, who gave a special dispensation. The visit took place on 21 September 1895, under the most degrading conditions. As soon as she got back to Miss Boxwell's apartment, Constance wrote to Robert Sherard to tell him what had happened.

c/o Miss Boxwell
12 Holbein House
S.W.

Sept. 21. 1895

My dear Mr Sherard,

It was indeed awful, more so than I had any conception it could be. I could not see him and I could not touch him. I scarcely spoke. Come and see me before you go to him on Monday at anytime after 2 I can see you. When I go again I am to get at the Home Secretary through Mr Haldane and try to get a room to see him in and touch him again. He has been mad these last three years, and he says that if he saw Alfred Douglas he would kill him. So he had better keep away and be satisfied with having marred a fine life. Few people can boast of so much.

I thank you for your kindness to a fallen friend; you are kind and gentle to him and you are, I think, the only person he can bear to see.

Yours most truly

Constance Wilde[3]

Before she left England Oscar had to submit to a further humiliation. On 24 September he was removed from the prison and taken to the Bankruptcy Court by public transport, guarded by two policemen. His clothes were ill-fitting, his hair was cropped convict-style. He looked haggard and ill. The sight of a prisoner in handcuffs seemed an entertaining spectacle to the crowds who saw him; but worse was to follow, for Oscar was recognized, and then the hoots of the crowds shamed him beyond description. Only one action lightened the terrible indignities he had to bear. In the crowded corridor outside the courtroom Robbie Ross stood waiting, and gravely raised his hat to the prisoner as he was hustled past him with bowed head.

The bankruptcy hearing was adjourned because Oscar's counsel told the court that there was good reason to believe that the debts outstanding could be covered by subscriptions from Oscar's friends. Those debts totalled £3,591. As he went over his financial affairs with the Bankruptcy Receiver he realized that he had spent, between the autumn of 1892 and the date of his arrest, some £5,000 on Lord Alfred Douglas.

> Though it may seem strange to you that one in the terrible position in which I am situated should find a difference between one disgrace and another, still I frankly admit that the folly of throwing away all this money on you, and letting you squander my fortune to your own hurt as well as to mine, gives to me and in my eyes a note of common profligacy to my Bankruptcy that makes me doubly ashamed of it.[4]

Shortly before her departure for England, Constance had experienced some unpleasantness at the hotel in Glion, for the proprietor suddenly realized their true identity and told them that they were no longer welcome. This decided Constance that for all their sakes they would have to change their names. They were at Bevaix when the formal documents arrived. Constance and her brother called the boys into the study and told them that in future their surname would be Holland. There were papers to be signed by each member of the family, and all their belongings were gone through and relabelled. Vyvyan had more changes than the rest, for his Christian names were altered also. The name Oscar was dropped altogether and his first name was now to be spelt Vivian. It was not until much later in his life that he reverted to the original spelling; but none of them ever resumed the name of Wilde.

As she told her boys that they must forget for ever that they had once borne the name of Wilde, Constance's heart was leaden. Vyvyan was puzzled by the occasion, but accepted it in the dumb, uncritical fashion of the very young. It was Cyril's response that upset Constance the most. He was, for a start, older than his brother, and hence more likely to react. He also knew the details of his father's disgrace, having been well primed by the Irish Press, and having subsequently talked to his mother about the whole terrible business. He understood enough to try and spare his little brother a kind of suffering which they all judged him too young to bear, but he had suffered greatly himself in the process. Now he ran off to the summerhouse in the garden, and there he remained, refusing to speak or eat, until eventually Constance's tears prevailed; then, at last, for the sake of his gentle mother, he came back into the house.

Holland was a family name. It was Otho's middle name from Holland Watson, his great-great-grandfather. When the name was officially changed, it was backed by an imposing Royal Warrant, with seals, in a red morocco case, and it included a grant of arms into the bargain. But nobody cared to take advantage of that.

Back in Bevaix, Constance wrote to her friend Emily Thursfield of her feelings and her plans for the future:

> I do not wish to sever myself entirely from Mr Wilde who is in the very lowest depths of misery. And he is very repentant and minds most of all what he has brought on myself and the boys. It seems to me (and to many others too) that by sticking to him now, I may save him from even worse, and I believe that he cares now for no-one but myself and the children. This is the opinion of the prison authorities and no-one can just now know him so well. At the same time I am quite aware that I am running a certain, possibly a very great risk. But I have my own money over which I have now perfect control and the life-interest has been renounced by Mr Wilde in favour of the boys, so if I find it impossible to live with him I can always leave him. But, dearest Emily, I think we women were meant to be comforters and I believe that no-one can really take my place now, or help him as I can.[5]

Hand in hand with her decision to stand by Oscar came the realization that England was no place for her, and she told her friend that she thought she would never live in England again. She wanted to send the boys to English schools when they were older. Vyvyan she thought would turn out to be very clever, but Cyril did not care for books, though he had the Irish gift of speaking well.

Had it not been for her many troubles, life would have seemed positively idyllic to Constance now in this lovely place. They were half a mile from Lake Neuchatel, and here the boys spent many happy hours trying to catch fish. Their idea was not to eat their catch, but to stock the large pond in the garden of their uncle's rented chalet.

The grape harvest was a time of great excitement for the boys, who spent many happy hours working alongside the local children picking grapes to fill their small casks, and eating many more in the process; but there were lessons too, for Otho became their tutor in everything except arithmetic, which Constance taught them herself. Of late Constance had fancied signs of delicacy in Cyril's constitution, reporting that he seemed to have outgrown his strength. He was, she said, growing crooked, which she feared might put an end to all notions of the Navy as a career.

Lovely though their surroundings were, Constance feared the onset of winter in this essentially cold climate, and as the rain set in and the nights grew chill, she longed to escape to the sun. The opportunity came when her great friend Lady Margaret Brooke, the Ranee of Sarawak, pressed Constance to join her in Italy. The Ranee had led an interesting life. In 1869, at the age of twenty, she had married Charles Brooke, the English Rajah of Sarawak, and had moved with him to that country (now an independent state in the Federation of Malaysia). A lively girl fond of dancing, she was forbidden by the Rajah to dance or wear low-cut gowns. Her first three children died of cholera on a voyage to England. She had three more sons. After her health failed she went to live in England, rarely returning to Sarawak. She was a talented pianist and a close friend of Princess Alice of Monaco, who was also a friend of Oscar and Constance. By now Constance was fearful of being left alone, even with the children; so a compromise was reached, and the Ranee found her an apartment at Sori, a few miles from her own home, large enough to accommodate not only herself and her children, but Otho and his wife Mary and their two children into the bargain.

Constance and the children had already paid one visit to the Ranee's lovely villa on the outskirts of the village of Nervi, on the Italian Riviera. The date of that earlier visit is difficult to place, though it had been at some time in the summer, before Constance had visited Oscar in prison. Constance was always more cheerful in the presence of the Ranee, to whom she was much attached. Again, it was an instance of an affection for a woman much older than herself, as were her friendships with Lady Sandford and Lady

Mount-Temple. Her affection for Speranza was different, yet basically her attitude towards all of them was almost filial. It seems that she was happier in the company of older women, who may have compensated to some extent for something which was lacking in her own mother.

The journey through the St Gothard Tunnel was an adventure for the boys, but one which they had made on two previous occasions. This allowed them to feel quite superior towards their cousins, who had never before experienced the noisy, grimy half-hour in the winding tunnel. Though the boys enjoyed it, the journey must have been a considerable ordeal for Constance, whose spine and arm were still very painful, but the apartment at Sori, with its view over the sea and its temperate climate, was worth the effort of the journey. There was a garden, steep, rocky and romantic, with a rickety wooden stairway down to the beach. In wet weather the children could play on a covered patio; and in the afternoons they could go down to the village and watch the fisherman, or down to the side of the railway and watch the Rome to Genoa express thunder by. There was also the pasta factory, where the boys were actually allowed to go in and watch how the various types of pasta were made.

Problems still loomed on the horizon, even in these ideal surroundings. In November 1895 she received a letter from her sister-in-law, telling her that More Adey had been to see Oscar in prison. Adey was a close friend of Oscar and of Robbie Ross, whose business partner he later became. Constance was exceedingly upset by the news, and regarded it as a betrayal of Oscar's promise to give up his old associates. She immediately wrote to him:

> I hear with horror that Mr More Adey has been to see you. Is this your promise to lead a new life? What am I to think of you if you still have intercourse with your old infamous companions? I require you to assure me that you will never see him again, or any people of that kind.[6]

Constance's exact objections to Adey, a kindly and responsible individual, are nowhere stated, and can only be surmised. He was a past friend of Oscar's, a close associate, and she leapt to a number of conclusions about him which were erroneous. What she had failed to realize was that Oscar's true friends, of whom Adey was undoubtedly one, had long wished to separate him for his own sake from Lord Alfred Douglas, whose wholly destructive influence was apparent to them all.

She had taken her decision not to divorce Oscar, and in this, and in the practical way in which she rallied and coped with her family responsibilities, had shown her true mettle. Any woman suddenly left alone with two small boys to provide for has to face up to major difficulties. But in Constance's case she had to cope with scandal, exile and the whole web of legal and financial problems that Oscar's disgrace had brought upon her. The courage she had already shown was remarkable, particularly considering her rather quiet and gentle nature which shrank from anything which brought pain and distress to others. Her love of Oscar, which she was now sometimes tempted to deny, was still plainly apparent, and she suffered as much from the knowledge of the terrible effect of imprisonment on him as from the day-to-day difficulties in her own life.

16

Incomprehension

From the beginning Wilde performed his life and
continued to do so even after fate had taken the plot out
of his hands.

W.H.Auden: *Forewords and Afterwords*

The year 1896 did not begin well for Constance. She had become
virtually imobilized by the terrible spinal condition which had
affected her ever since that unlucky fall down the stairs of Tite
Street. Early in the new year she went to Genoa, where it appears
that she sought medical advice and possibly underwent an operation
to restore her mobility. This was by no means altogether successful.
Nevertheless her typical optimism and courage did not desert her.
To Emily Thursfield she wrote: 'I am better and I hope I shall begin
gradually to walk about when I get back to Sori. I want to see all the
villages which seem to be so pretty with their houses nestling down
to the sea and the gardens with their orange groves and palms and
pergole.'[1]

She had plans for returning to England with the boys in May, and
Emily had suggested rooms near her home which she thought
might suit them. Constance seemed excited at the prospect, and
hoped that when she came her friend's husband might take her once
more to hear the nightingale, which she had first heard while
staying with them in 1889. This simple incident seems to have
made a great impression on Constance. She was alert to beauty in all
its forms, and no doubt as she listened to the nightingale in those
far-off days she recalled Keats' famous ode. Poetry continued to be a
major consolation for her, and that little volume of Keats' poems
which had been at her bedside since she was a girl of nineteen had
never left her.

The prime object of Constance's visit seems to have been to find suitable schools for the boys. She still looked to a career in the Navy for Cyril, and had arranged courses of massage and exercises plus tablets of maltine and phosphate of chalk to correct the 'crookedness' which she fancied she had remarked in him. Her aim was to return him to his naval preparatory school in Haywards Heath. She felt it would be a mistake for the boys to be educated together, and had identified a school in Berkhampstead to which she wished to send Vyvyan. In the event she had to make a much earlier and briefer visit, and these plans came to nothing.

Shortly after the proceedings in which Oscar was officially made bankrupt he was transferred to Reading Gaol. Not long after his arrival his mother fell seriously ill with bronchitis. She had encouraged Oscar to stay and face his trials, and not to flee the country, which she would have regarded as an act of cowardice. Of course, she had believed Oscar entirely innocent of all the charges against him. His imprisonment was a terrible shock to her. She was also at the same time deprived of the devotion which Constance had always lavished on her but could no longer give her now that she was virtually in exile. There was never any question of a breach between the two women. Constance was much too fair-minded to blame Speranza for what had occurred, and regarded her as a victim also. She knew what suffering she had gone through during her son's trial and imprisonment, and her love and respect for the old lady never lessened in any degree.

Speranza had entertained vague hopes that Oscar's first letter from prison might have been to herself. To Ernest Leverson she wrote on 29 August 1895:

> Accept my grateful thanks for your kind attention in bringing me news of dear Oscar, as I am myself very poorly and unable to see friends or to leave my room . . . I thought that Oscar might perhaps write to me after the three months, but I have not had a line from him, and I have not written to him as I dread my letters being returned.[2]

Early in 1896, conscious that her end was near, she wrote to the prison authorities asking that he might be released to visit her for the last time. This dying wish was refused. Speranza died on 3 February 1896. It is said that when she heard that her request to see Oscar had been refused, she simply turned her face to the wall and died. That night, Oscar claimed, he dreamed that she came to him in his prison cell. On being asked to take off her hat and cloak, she shook her head in sorrow and then vanished away.

Constance learned of the death of her mother-in-law from Lily Wilde, Willie's second wife. Constance's personal grief was considerable, but her prime regard was for Oscar, to whom she knew this would be a death-like blow. She immediately wrote back to her sister-in-law:

Dearest Lily,

I have written to Mr Haldane for leave to see O. I quite agree with you that it must be broken to him and I believe it will half kill him. Poor Oscar has been bitterly punished for breaking the laws of his country. I am not strong but I could bear the journey better if I thought that such a terrible thing would not be told to him roughly. I am indeed sorry for you and Baby. I daresay you know the Lilleys have got a little girl now.

I will let you know when I am in London. I shall not start for about 10 days as I must wait till I get an answer from Mr Haldane but as the House will meet soon I hope that he will be in town. I shall most likely be at the Grosvenor Hotel, but 12 Holbein House is the safest address to send to.

Yrs ever

Constance.[3]

Before she left for England, Constance sent for the boys singly and broke the news of Speranza's death to them. She had been very fond of both the boys, especially Cyril, and had shown many little acts of kindness towards them. Her house was well equipped with toys including a rocking-horse, which she had purchased to keep them amused on their visits to her; but both her house and her person were somewhat dark and forbidding to a child. Once the boys had started boarding school they had seen little of the frail old lady. Cyril was the first to be told. He listened without shedding a tear, but there was a set look about his face as he came and told his brother that their mother wanted to see him in her room. Vyvyan, being younger, had not been as close to their grandmother as Cyril, but he was just as upset by her death. Constance now explained to Vyvyan that she had to return to England to break the sad news to their father. This was the first time in all those long months that she had voluntarily mentioned his name in speaking to her younger son. Not altogether unexpectedly, the small boy now asked his father's whereabouts, and why they never saw him now. These were questions that Constance must long have feared, and she had probably rehearsed her reply over and over again in her own mind. She said that he had been unwell and had had a great deal of trouble. Perhaps she realized the terrible misgivings that seized the small boy's heart as he digested this fresh piece of information. Their sudden flight from England, their mother's many absences, the absence of all news of their father and finally the ominous change of the family name were all part of a pattern which proved beyond doubt to Vyvyan that some terrible catastrophe had befallen their father. Above all, he noted the heavy burden of sorrow that weighed so heavily on his mother, and wished with all his heart that he could do something to lighten the load for her.

Oscar wrote of his mother's death and of Constance's visit in *De Profundis*:

Her death was so terrible to me that I, once a lord of language, have no words in which to express my anguish and my shame. Never, even in the most perfect days of my development as an artist, could I have had words fit to bear so august a burden, or to move with sufficient stateliness of music through the purple pageant of my incommunicable woe. She and my father had bequeathed me a name they had made noble and honoured not merely in Literature, Art, Archaeology and Science, but in the public history of my own country and its evolution as a nation. I had disgraced that name eternally. I had made it a low byword among low people. I had dragged it through the very mire. I had given it to brutes that they might make it brutal, and to fools that they might turn it into a synonym for folly. What I suffered then, and still suffer, is not for pen to write or paper to record. My wife, at that time gentle and good to me, rather than that I should hear the news from indifferent or alien lips, travelled, ill as she was, all the way from Genoa to England to break to me herself the tidings of so irreparable, so irredeemable a loss.[4]

Oscar also described his conversation with Constance on that day:

When I last saw my wife – fourteen months ago now – I told her that she would have to be to Cyril a father as well as a mother. I told her everything about your mother's mode of dealing with you in every detail as I have set it down in this letter, only of course far more fully. I told her that the reason of the endless notes with 'Private' on the envelope that used to come to Tite Street from your mother, so constantly that my wife used to laugh and say that we must be collaborating on a society novel or something of that kind. I told her that she should bring him up so that if he shed innocent blood he would come and tell her, that she might cleanse his hands for him first, and then teach him penance or expiation afterwards. I told her that if she was frightened of facing the responsibility of the life of another, though her own child, she should get a guardian to help her.[5]

That visit brought the couple closer together than they had been at any time since Oscar's imprisonment, and had their wishes been respected, things might have turned out very differently for them. But that dreadful partisan element that led their families and friends to decide what was best for them and to separate Constance from an influence they felt evil virtually extinguished all hope of that.

On 10 March 1896 Oscar wrote to Robbie Ross explaining that he wished no impediment to be placed in the way of his wife's acquiring his life interest in the marriage settlement, in return for which she had agreed to settle one third on him in the event of her predeceasing him. He felt that he had brought such ruin on her and his children that he had no right to go against her wishes in anything. He asked Robbie to write to Mr Hargrove, Constance's solicitor, to that effect immediately.

By the time this letter was sent, Constance had already returned to Italy. She had not arrived in England in time to attend Speranza's funeral. Willie arranged the burial in Kensal Green Cemetery and sent out impressive memorial cards; but no headstone was ever erected and after seven years, no fees having been paid, the body was removed to an unknown grave. Oscar bore the full cost of the funeral expenses, and his brother's default in the matter seems to have driven the final wedge between them. Oscar had paid the cost of Lily Wilde's confinement with his brother's only child, but after this period Oscar refused to speak of either of them by name.

Constance was back in Nervi in time for the great event of the year, the festival of flowers. The Ranee of Sarawak had taken a suite in the Hotel Nervi for the occasion and invited Constance and the boys to watch the event from this prime position. The hotel was rather splendid and was frequented by the beau monde of Russia, Austria and other European countries. Though the day was a joyful one, Constance, who had stayed at the hotel soon after she had begun her exile, was immediately recognized by the manager, who kept referring to her as 'Mrs Wilde'. Cyril said nothing for a while, but eventually found himself driven to point out that his mother was now Mrs Holland. This only led to further embarrassment, for he now assumed that she was a widow who had remarried, and began a flow of felicitations, until the Ranee changed the subject.

Constance's intention was still to send the boys back to school in England, and with this in mind she wrote to Cyril's old headmaster at Haywards Heath and asked when the summer term was due to begin. Something intervened, however, which decided her against sending the children back to England. Possibly Cyril's headmaster advised against such a course of action; he may even have refused to take Cyril. Perhaps they had missed too much formal schooling to catch up with the other boys. At this time Constance referred to them teasingly as 'nice backward boys who care for nothing but play, but very affectionate'. Be this as it may, Constance now left Sori for Germany, where she sent the boys to a boarding school in Freiburg im Breisgau and went to stay with her friends Carlos and Carrie Blacker, who lived nearby. This arrangement was singularly short-lived. On the second or third day after their arrival, the class teacher set about Vyvyan with a ruler for a minor offence. This brought to the fore all Cyril's protective instincts, and he promptly kicked the teacher on the shins, simultaneously punching him in the stomach. Vyvyan, delighted at the arrival of reinforcements, immediately attacked from behind. It was an unfortunate incident in one sense, for it led to their immediate expulsion; but at least it had highlighted the unsuitable nature of the school in question. They were next sent to a small school for about fifteen boys where the masters were kindlier and showed greater understanding; but this did not, unfortunately, apply to the rest of the pupils, whose anti-British sentiments so riled the two newcomers that they challenged all the rest to a fight. Despite being greatly outnumbered, Cyril and Vyvyan routed the natives, and were once more expelled.

At this juncture Constance moved on to Heidelberg, which had the attraction of a flourishing English community, and here at the end of April the boys were sent to the Neuenheim College, where all the pupils were expatriate Britons and the staff, too, were almost exclusively English, except for the language teaching. The whole atmosphere of the school was British, with the boys playing Rugby and cricket, and rowing on the Neckar, and wearing Eton jackets on Sundays. For Cyril it proved a relatively satisfactory establishment; but Vyvyan was an altogether different case. Once more he found himself the youngest boy in the school and, despite Cyril's attempts to protect him, he was mercilessly bullied by the other boys. Once he was even pushed into a locker and left there, until finally his cries attracted the attention of a master. This incident left him a permanent sufferer from claustrophobia.

When the cricket season arrived and the boys got out their whites, they discovered to their horror that their old names were still in them. Cyril frantically hacked the names out with his penknife, and all the old sense of disaster flooded over the boys. Despite all Constance's efforts to shield them, she could not prevent the occasional failure of this kind; nor could she do very much to alleviate the terrible mental distress they suffered whenever they thought of their father and the old life that was now so far behind them.

Though the couple had reached an apparently amicable agreement during Constance's visit to the prison, new problems soon arose. The weight of Oscar's affairs had decided him to split them into roughly two categories; the literary and the legal matters. The former he decided to entrust to Robbie Ross and the latter to More Adey, helped, of course, by a solicitor. At once a pressing matter arose. Bosie was proposing to dedicate a volume of poetry to Oscar. Oscar immediately wrote to Robbie and asked him to stop him from doing so, and also to get back from him all his letters – some of which Bosie had previously had to be restrained from publishing in the *Mercure de France*. In the event of Oscar's death he instructed Robbie to destroy them all for the sake of Cyril and Vyvyan. 'Though my unfortunate children will never of course bear my name, still they know whose sons they are and I must try and shield them from the possibility of any further revolting disclosure or scandal,'[6] he wrote. He was aware that Bosie had been pawning his gifts, but he now wished Robbie to get back for him such jewellery and other gifts as still remained in his possession. Significantly, he now referred to him simply as 'Douglas'.

In trying to straighten out Oscar's tangled affairs Adey and Ross employed the services of two solicitors. Humphreys, who had acted for Oscar in the bankruptcy proceedings, had done nothing except put in his bill for £150, and Oscar felt he could no longer entrust any of his business to him. The two men whose advice Adey took were Clifton and Hassell, who were no less disastrous than Humphreys. On their advice, Adey made an offer of £50 to the Official Receiver for the interest in the marriage settlement, in contradication of Oscar's instructions to allow Constance to acquire it. In doing so they told Mr Hargrove, Constance's solicitor, that a major fund had been set up by Oscar's friends, and that they would acquire the interest whatever it cost.

This had a most unfortunate effect, in that it alienated Constance completely and led her to raise again the issue of a divorce. It also led her to suppose that Oscar would have very substantial means at his disposal, and would need no help from her. The acquisition was duly made without Oscar even being aware of it. In their eagerness to get an income for him, they had overlooked the elementary fact that if Constance divorced him the settlement would immediately be void and he would have no income at all. Constance's confidence in Oscar was now still further eroded, and she was once more at the mercy of those of her relatives who wished her to break with him completely.

In June Robbie wrote to Constance and assured her of his wish to remain her friend. She replied that God and his conscience would judge whether his affection and friendship were genuine, and went on:

I have gone through too much and too much has crumbled beneath my feet for me to be at all now able to judge of the genuiness of anyone's professions on any subject. I have always had a great affection for you which I once thought and hoped that you returned. The business matters of which you speak are quite incomprehensible to me.[7]

Constance's bewilderment and her inability to put her trust in anyone was understandable. However, her exposition of the situation showed that she had not lost her grasp of the financial implications. Robbie claimed that the Marquess of Queensberry was rumoured to be trying to acquire the life interest in the marriage settlement, and that it was for this reason that Oscar's friends had taken such a step. Constance knew nothing of such an attempt nor of Oscar's alleged intention of settling most of the money on the children. She said that she would not accept such a gift for the boys, and that if the life-interest were acquired over her head in this way she would withdraw her offer to pay Oscar £150 a year. Clifton had told Mr Hargrove that Oscar's friends had raised some two or three thousand pounds for him, and she felt that he should invest this properly in an annuity. She added:

> I am obliged to live abroad and the boys will be forced to make their own way in life heavily handicapped by their father's madness for I can consider it nothing else. I have no feeling but one of the most intense pity for him as anybody with any heart must have when they contemplate such a terrible wreck.[8]

This thorny question of the marriage settlement dragged on for months, poisoning relations between Constance and Oscar. On 4 July 1896 Oscar applied formally to the Principal Secretary of State for the Home Office for permission to see More Adey in the Solicitors' Room at Reading Gaol. More Adey would be discussing on Constance's behalf issues connected with the guardianship, education and future of the children, and the marriage settlements, with particular reference to Oscar's bankruptcy. The Home Office agreed, but left the length of the interview to the discretion of the Governor.

Adey was shocked at Oscar's condition when he saw him, and at once wrote to Constance to tell her about his visit and what took place. She wrote back immediately from Heidelberg:

> Dear Mr Rady (sic),
>   I am much shocked at your account of Mr Wilde's condition and will write both to the Home Secretary and to Mr Balfour to see what can be done about his liberation when I have the assurance that I shall be left free to bring up my children and when Mr Wilde's unwise friends withdraw from their opposition to my buying the Life-Interest in my settlement. If Mr Wilde has

already expressed in writing a wish to this effect I consider that these friends are acting wickedly in going against his desire. A written statement that the offer at present in the hands of the Official Receiver will be withdrawn must be lodged in the hands of my lawyer and this must be notified to me before I will write the letters that you wish.

Yours sincerely,

C.M. Holland[9]

For the first time, there are indications of Constance's new tough line, and the letter is so carefully phrased that it seems probable that it was written under the direction of Mr Hargrove.

As regards the other pressing legal issues, Oscar was against the notion of a divorce, although he clearly realized that he was entirely in Constance's hands. There was also the important question of the children's future. Though he would have liked to have retained control over their future, he was sufficiently realistic to realize that this was probably impossible. He seems to have favoured the notion of guardianship, though in many ways this was a risk to his own relationship with Cyril and Vyvyan. Probably he was influenced throughout by his inside knowledge of Lady Queensberry's disastrous relationship with Lord Alfred Douglas; her efforts to bring him up without a guardian were in some measure responsible for her son's warped and vicious nature. What Oscar did fight against was any notion of a guardian from Constance's own family, for he felt that the boys for their own sakes ought not to be brought up to look on him with hatred or contempt. In this Constance was with him. Above all she wanted the children's tender susceptibilities protected from further hurt.

Oscar himself would have liked his solicitor, Arthur Clifton, as guardian, if he felt able to undertake it. Initially he seems to have got along reasonably well with Constance. He visited Oscar at Reading Gaol in October 1896 to discuss business matters. Oscar was dressed in ordinary clothes for the interview, but his hair was rather long and he looked painfully thin. Meeting him in these conditions was a painful experience; Oscar seemed quite brokenhearted and cried a great deal. He did not express any very decided ideas on business matters, but he hoped that some portion of the settlement, perhaps a third, would be retained for his use. Such was

Oscar's depressed state that there were serious fears that he might not last out his punishment.

Constance was in England during October. It seems likely that she travelled with the Ranee of Sarawak, who was on a visit to Miss Schuster, the 'Lady of Wimbledon' as Oscar always called her. Clifton saw Constance about these business matters and reported that she was quite agreeable, so that he foresaw little difficulty. But finally in December 1896 Constance's solicitor, Mr Hargrove, was informed by the Official Receiver that he had decided to sell half Oscar's interest in the marriage settlement to his friends, and as a result Constance withdrew her offer to pay Oscar £150 a year on his release from prison. Oscar seems to have gone along with the purchase at that particular juncture. What seems to have incensed him was Constance's proposal that he should continue to receive the same amount after her death if she predeceased him. This he considered cruel and heartless. It seems that under the arrangements Constance proposed, each of the boys would get approximately £700 per annum, while he was left in virtual poverty. During this period Constance wrote a number of letters, no longer extant, that cut him to the quick, and in the end he wrote to More Adey that he felt Constance did not realize his mental condition, or the suffering, both mental and physical, that her letters were inflicting on him. He said that since his imprisonment the only two people who had tried to distress him by terrible letters were Constance and Lord Queensberry. He asked Adey to go to the Ranee of Sarawak, who had once been a great friend of his, and ask her if she would intercede with Constance on his behalf.

That summer Constance had discovered a charming hotel in Heidelberg called the Schloss Park, and here she spent much of the latter part of 1896. It was situated on the heights behind the town and stood in extensive private gardens. Though remote enough to be undisturbed by noisy traffic, it was reached by funicular from the town, so that in Constance's state of health, which had failed to improve, it was ideal. Herr Köhler and his wife, who owned it, soon assumed the status of personal friends, and Constance and Frau Köhler spent many happy hours together, sewing and improving their knowledge of each other's language. Constance's natural gift for modern languages was apparent, and she quickly added German to the list of foreign languages in which she had attained fluency. Herr Köhler, meanwhile, spent a great deal of time with the boys, who admired his huge stamp collection. Often he took them out for walks, which was a great help to Constance in her handicapped state. The degree of friendship between them quickly advanced to the point where, when business summoned her to England, Constance was able to leave the children in the care of the couple.

That Constance and the boys missed their friends in England was clearly apparent, and there were few people on the Continent at that time with whom Constance still felt able to communicate. Among the friends remaining from former years were Carlos and Carrie Blacker. They now kindly invited Constance and the boys to spend Christmas with them in Freiburg, and she accepted gratefully. There was thick snow on the ground and the boys loved the chance to go tobogganing and skating. In the evenings Carlos Blacker entertained his guests with a seemingly endless repertoire of conjuring tricks. He and Carrie managed to raise Constance's spirits; unfortunately they could not conjure away the heavy weight of the legal, personal and financial problems which bore on Constance at this time. It was clear that the following year would prove no less difficult.

17

The Last Summer

Like two doomed ships that pass in storm.
We had crossed each other's way,
But we made no sign, we said no word,
We had no word to say.
The Ballad of Reading Gaol

The Christmas holiday had given Constance the opportunity to talk to Vyvyan about his future. Clearly he was unhappy at Neuenheim College, where the bullying continued almost unabated. Cyril, so loyal a defender of his little brother, was beginning to grow away from Vyvyan a little. It was all part of the process becoming adult but Vyvyan could not be expected to know that, and he was much hurt by it. Constance now decided that it would be better to send Vyvyan to a different school, one where he would not be entirely at the mercy of boys so much older and bigger than himself.

There was a further factor. The whole family had been attracted to Roman Catholicism and recently, under the influence of Herr Köhler and Carlos Blacker, Vyvyan's interest had increased. When Princess Alice of Monaco, who had protested at the inhuman treatment Oscar had received, suggested to Constance that Vyvyan be sent to the Jesuit school in the tiny principality, Constance was enthusiastic. Monaco was not far from Nervi, where Constance wanted to return; and Princess Alice also said that she would keep a bit of an eye on Vyvyan. Vyvyan was consulted in the matter, and visibly brightened at the prospect of leaving Neuenheim College; and so the matter was settled.

In January 1897 Constance went with Vyvyan to the Collegio della Visitazione, as his new school was called, and stayed in Monte Carlo for a few days, seeing her little boy every day and also calling on the Princess. It was a welcome relief from the renewed legal battles which had been going on in the meantime.

Constance's action regarding custody of the children was heard in the Chancery Division on 12 February 1897 by Mr Justice Kekewich, who awarded custody to Constance and made her legal guardian of the boys jointly with Adrian Hope. Oscar seems temporarily to have forgotten his request that the guardian should not be from Constance's own family and wrote of the choice in *De Profundis* in terms of approval: 'She has chosen Adrian Hope, a man of high birth and culture and fine character, her own cousin, whom you met once at Tite Street, and with him Cyril and Vyvyan have a good chance of a beautiful future'.[1] Hope, who had been Secretary to the Hospital for Sick Children in Great Ormond Street seemed, indeed, ultra respectable; yet his appointment as guardian was a positive disaster for both Oscar and the boys. He took no part in the day-to-day lives of the children, and never foresaw seriously an occasion when he would be called on to do so. From the very outset he had been hostile towards the Wildes in general and Oscar in particular, though it would appear that Constance failed to realize this. He was now in a position to prevent Oscar and his sons from ever meeting again.

On 26 March 1897 Constance wrote to her brother from Italy:

I have again had pressure put upon me to persuade me to go back to Oscar, but I am sure you will agree that it is impossible. I am told that I would save a human soul, but I have no influence over Oscar. I have had none, and though I think he is affectionate, I see no reason for believing that I should be able now to perform miracles, and I must look after my boys and not risk their future. What do you think I should do? The Ranee thinks that he has fallen and cannot rise. That is rather like Humpty Dumpty, but then I think his fate is rather like Humpty Dumpty's, quite as tragic and quite as impossible to put right.[2]

The folly of trying to fight Constance in the matter of the marriage settlement was only now beginning to strike More Adey. He had genuinely struggled to help his friend, but had somehow, through a failure in elementary logic, been unable to come to grips with the situation. Oscar was now in a terrible situation. He had lost custody of his boys; Constance had withdrawn her offer of financial help; and the question of a divorce was once more a live issue. What Adey had failed to realize was the true nature of the threat of divorce. It was now too late for Constance to cite the offences raised in the trials as grounds for divorce, for after this lapse of time she was deemed to have condoned them. If she wished to proceed, she would have to furnish a whole new set of evidence against Oscar. The implications of this were terrifying. Any such evidence would leave Oscar open to further prosecution, a new criminal trial, and fresh imprisonment. For such a prosecution to be brought against Oscar it would not matter that the 'crimes' pre-dated his original arrest and imprisonment; any additional offences which came to light could be used against him in this way.

Oscar's solicitor friend from whose good graces he had fallen after the scandal erupted, Sir George Lewis, had been attempting to pressurize Constance into taking divorce proceedings against Oscar from the outset, and now Constance began to feel that she was forced to do it. Oscar's view was that he must defer to his wife's wishes in this, as in all matters. He had been erroneously advised by his lawyer, Mr Holman, that if Constance did predecease him, his sons would be left penniless if he relinquished his share in the marriage settlement. The sum finally paid out to the Official Receiver for it was £75, for his friends had been obliged to increase their original offer of £50. Oscar now decided that the only right and proper course for him to take was to make Constance a present of it, and he wrote to More Adey to this effect, adding:

Whether I am married or not is a matter that does not concern me. For years I disregarded the tie. But I really think that it is hard on my wife to be tied to me. I always thought so. And, though it may surprise some of my friends, I am really very fond of my wife and very sorry for her. I sincerely hope she may have a happy marriage, if she marries again. She could not understand me, and I was bored to death with married life. But she had some sweet points in her character, and was wonderfully loyal to me.[3]

Oscar now persistently blamed his friends for the incredible state of his affairs, which he said was directly attributable to their failure to carry out his wishes, and to their persistent failure to appreciate Constance's true character. She was invariably described by him as sweet and loyal, strictly honourable in all matters involving business and money, and generous where no generosity could be

expected of her. His estimate of Constance's character was wholly
accurate. She had met crisis after crisis with courage and,
incredibly, loyalty. Only two major factors had influenced all her
decisions: her love of her husband and her devotion to her children.
Ultimately she saw her duty to her sons as the higher obligation,
and from first to last her actions revolved around their welfare. She
sought at the same time to preserve her loyalty to Oscar intact, but
this had to be the secondary consideration. Had they been childless,
there is little doubt that she would have remained Oscar's wife.

In the end, Constance dropped the idea of divorce, but felt
legally obliged to apply for a separation. On 17 May 1897 Hassell,
Oscar's solicitor, was due to call at Reading Gaol to collect Oscar's
signature on the deed of separation. Constance, on one of her
frequent visits to London to visit her solicitors, now begged that she
might accompany him and, if possible, get a glimpse of Oscar
without his being aware of her presence there. Oscar's warder later
gave an account of what happened:

> The saddest story I know of Wilde was one day when his solicitor
> called to see him to get his signature, I think, to some papers in
> the divorce proceedings then being instituted by his wife – a suit
> which, of course, Wilde did not defend.
>
> Unknown to Wilde his wife had accompanied the solicitor but
> she did not wish her husband to see her. The interview with the
> solicitor took place in the consultation room, and Wilde sat at a
> table with his head on his hands opposite the lawyer.
>
> Outside, in the passage with me, waited a sad figure in deepest
> mourning. It was Mrs Wilde – in tears. Whilst the consultation
> was proceeding in the 'solicitor's room', Mrs Wilde turned to me
> and begged a favour. 'Let me have one glimpse of my husband,'
> she said, and I could not refuse her.
>
> So silently I stepped to one side, Mrs Wilde cast one long
> lingering glance inside, and saw the convict-poet, who, in deep
> mental distress himself, was totally unconscious that any eyes
> save those of the stern lawyer and myself witnessed his
> degradation. A second later, Mrs Wilde, apparently labouring
> under deep emotion, drew back, and left the prison with the
> solicitor.
>
> I fancy Wilde, when she saw him, was putting his final
> signature on the divorce papers . . .[4]

On 18 May 1897 Oscar left Reading Gaol under guard of two prison officers and travelled by the London train to Westbourne Park. Here they transferred to a cab which took them to Pentonville, where Oscar spent the last night of his cruel sentence. Next morning shortly after six o'clock he was released.

It was at this point that Constance made a terrible mistake. What she should quite clearly have done was to collect her husband at the gates of the prison and accompany him into exile. That she did not do so was one of the results of the years of uncertainty. Mentally she was now exhausted. Her state of mind was absolutely consistent with that of any person used to definitive thought and positive action who is suddenly faced with a crisis too great to handle. Her great problem lay in the impossibility of finding a clear-cut solution and acting accordingly. Busying herself with the future of her sons was virtually the only thing that helped her stave off severe mental illness. Whatever she decided, there would always be uncertainties. Would Oscar return to her? Would he henceforth behave like a model husband and father? Or would he return to his old ways, betraying her trust and influencing the boys to evil effect, wasting their money into the bargain? Even Arthur, their former butler in Tite Street, had suffered mental collapse under the strain of what happened to the family. It is said that twenty years later he was still in an asylum. Constance's strength of mind in surviving her ordeal with her personality intact was remarkable.

Unfortunately Constance now listened to her family and her legal advisers. She did not rule out the possibility of resuming married life at some time in the future, despite the legal separation; but she allowed herself to be persuaded that a trial period must first elapse, during which Oscar could demonstrate his remorse and his determination to lead a new life. The decision was fatal to the marriage, and to any real possibility of the re-establishment of family life.

When he left Pentonville, Oscar was taken in a cab by More Adey and Stewart Headlam, the clergyman who had gone bail for him, to Headlam's home in Bloomsbury. Oscar had now decided that he wished to convert to the Catholic faith, and wrote a letter to a Roman Catholic retreat, asking if he might come there for six months. To his dismay he was told that he could not be accepted for at least a year.

Instead he went to Newhaven with More Adey and crossed by the night boat to Dieppe. Here, at half-past four in the morning, the faithful Robbie Ross and Reggie Turner waited for him on the jetty. Oscar's tall figure was readily identifiable as he towered above the other passengers. He looked as he had done in his days as an undergraduate at Oxford. His luggage bore the initials S.M. for he had decided to call himself Sebastian Melmoth in future – 'not Esquire, but Monsieur', as he was careful to point out to Ada Leverson. They stayed at the Hotel Sandwich in Dieppe. 'Reggie Turner is staying here under the name "Robert Ross", Robbie under the name "Reginald Turner". It is better they should not use their own names,'[5] he added.

Within five days of his release from prison Oscar had embarked on one of those acts of compassion which Constance most cared for in his personality. Martin, his warder, had been dismissed from his post for the sin of having given biscuits to a small child prisoner. Oscar wrote immediately, a long, wise letter which the *Daily Chronicle* published on 27 May 1897, appealing for greater understanding in the punishment of children, and for clemency towards those who, like Warder Martin, were moved to pity by the plight of the pathetic child detainees.

The present treatment of children is terrible, primarily from people not understanding the peculiar nature of a child's nature. A child can understand a punishment inflicted by an individual, such as a parent or guardian, and bear it with a certain amount of acquiescence. What it cannot understand is a punishment inflicted by society . . . The child consequently, being taken away from its parents by people whom it has never seen, and of whom it knows nothing, and finding itself in a lonely and unfamiliar cell, waited on by strange faces, and ordered about and punished by the representatives of a system that it cannot understand, becomes an immediate prey to the first and most prominent emotion produced by modern prison life – the emotion of terror. The terror of a child in prison is quite limitless. I remember once in Reading, as I was going out to exercise, seeing in the dimly lit cell right opposite my own a small boy. Two warders – not unkindly men – were talking to him, with some sternness apparently, or perhaps giving him some useful advice about his conduct. One was in the cell with him, the other was standing outside. The child's face was a white wedge of sheer terror. There was in his eyes the terror of a hunted animal. The next morning I heard him at breakfast-time crying, and calling to be let out. His cry was for his parents. From time to time I could hear the deep voice of the warder on duty, telling him to be quiet. Yet he was not even convicted of whatever he had been charged with. He was simply on remand . . . Justices and magistrates, an entirely ignorant class as a rule, often remand children in prison for a week, and then perhaps remit whatever sentence they are entitled to pass. They call this 'not sending a child to prison'.

From Berneval, a resort a few miles along the coast from Dieppe, Oscar wrote on 1 June to Robbie and asked him to send Constance a copy of the *Daily Chronicle*. He knew her well enough to understand that she would be pleased to find him devoting his talent to a cause which was so noble, and making use of his experiences to help society to understand and reform where necessary the evils of the prison system. To Warder Martin he wrote, 'I have spoken highly of your character and intellect. Let me beg of you to deserve all I have said of you. You have, I think, a good chance of a good place, so you must be as sound and straightforward and as good a fellow as possible.'[6]

Constance, meanwhile, had returned to Italy but was exceedingly ill. She was now very lame, and could hardly write. She found a typewriter which she managed to use with difficulty. The Ranee of Sarawak had lent her a house until the end of June, after which she went to Otho at the Maison Benguerel, at Bevaix in Switzerland. On 22 July she moved on to Basle where Vyvyan was due to arrive on the following day from his school in Monaco. She took the opportunity of going to see an exhibition of pictures by Bochlin, about whom she was, as she described it, 'crazy'. The Blackers pressed her to go and stay with them, but she was not able to join them immediately. But as soon as Vyvyan had joined her and was sufficiently rested she took him with her to Freiburg. Here Cyril joined them when term ended.

Constance's physical condition was now pitiable. Not yet forty years old, she was virtually immobilized by her spinal condition. She never complained, but she was now quite unable to walk. To Carlos Blacker she wrote that she would like to see something of Freiburg if he did not mind driving with her. Her visit was specifically to see the Blackers, to whom she had become deeply attached. It was Carlos who took two rooms for her at a local hotel where she and the boys could stay in comfort.

At the beginning of August Constance went back to Basle, and then moved on immediately to the Black Forest. Höchenschwand, the little village where they stayed, was a delightful place, very much off the beaten track. Constance had engaged a German governess to look after the boys for a month, as was absolutely necessary in view of her own incapacity. She did her best, with characteristic courage, to behave as though nothing was wrong, and said nothing to alarm the boys. Still, she regretted being unable to join them as they wandered through cool woods and meadows ablaze with colour. She was always in the boys' thoughts, and each day when they returned they brought armfuls of flowers to decorate her room.

Despite the isolation of the village, the hotel was crowded. There were even two English girls staying there; but Constance did not care for them very much, though with characteristic gentleness she blamed herself for want of amicability. She established her own routine, however, and found a little shop that sold everything, which she liked to visit. Her doctors had advised her to take ten minutes' walk each day in order to try and preserve some degree of mobility. But writing letters continued to be a problem, for her arm was still semi-paralysed. The month was noted for frequent thunderstorms, some of them quite terrifying to Constance, who always disliked storms because they gave her a headache. The first rumblings of thunder, however distant, sent her back to her room to lie down. Only a couple of days after they arrived in Höchenschwand there was a storm so terrible that the villagers crowded into the church, for they thought that the Day of Judgment must be at hand. There was no interval at all between the flashes of lightning, for the storm was right overhead. Two houses in the village were struck by lightning and gutted inside. Though Constance, as always on such occasions, shut herself away in her room, the two boys revelled in the storm and watched as the lightning played round the lightning-conductors on the spire of the church. Cyril told Constance later that he wished every day could seem as long.

While they were staying in the village, Cyril taught Vyvyan to ride a bicycle. One day Vyvyan lost control of the machine and crashed into a wooden fence on a bend; he hurtled over the handlebars into a field of corn, but luckily escaped with a few bruises. The bicycle, however, was a complete write-off. Nor was it easy to replace it. Constance's cousin, one of the Napiers, chose a new one, but it turned out to be too small, for Cyril was big for his age and needed a full-sized one.

From Höchenschwand they travelled to Basle and then on to Freiburg, where they spent their days with the Blackers until it was time to send the boys back to their respective schools. Constance stopped over in Milan on the way back, but she found the journey very tiring, and was glad to get back to the Hotel Nervi. The weather continued hot and sunny, much to Constance's delight. She was much preoccupied with the problem of Cyril's bicycle. She had the address of the vendor, and had been trying to replace it after Vyvyan's accident; but her cousin, who had chosen a model suitable for a fourteen-year-old, had now returned to India, and Constance had nobody to attend to the matter on her behalf.

Shortly after her return to Nervi, Constance wrote to Carlos Blacker, 'Not a sign of Oscar or a word from him, but I have an idea he will turn up some day without writing'.[7] It was perhaps a deep-felt wish which she scarcely cared to put into words.

On the following day Constance wrote to Carlos Blacker again. This time there was a complete change in the tenor of her letter. She had sent Oscar photographs of the boys in Eton collars, taken in Freiburg, which he had not acknowledged. What seemed to Constance even worse was that he failed to acknowledge the boys' little remembrances. But most important of all, Constance had had word that he had met up with Bosie again.

Initially when Oscar came out of prison Constance wrote to him every week, and once even sent him a photograph of herself. But on 14 July he had written somewhat enigmatically to Robbie, 'Hansell's letter is most satisfactory, except his communicating with Hargrove, which means of course a possible estrangement with Mrs Holland.'[8] At the end of the month he received a letter from Carlos Blacker, telling him of the terrible spinal paralysis from with Constance was suffering, and of which she made so light. He replied that he was very distressed about the news, and had had no idea that it was so serious. He had wanted her to join him in France, but now realized that this was out of the question. He had only a manservant, and he now perceived that she needed the services of a

maid; also that the journey would be too much for her. On 4
August he wrote again to Blacker, 'I don't mind my life being
wrecked — that is as it should be — but when I think of poor
Constance I simply want to kill myself.'9 He added that he
thought it would be better for him and Constance to meet, but
conceded that his friend's judgement was probably best.

On 4 September, much disappointed at Constance's continued
refusal to let him see Cyril and Vyvyan, and fearing that he might
never see them again, he finally jeopardized his prospects of a
reconciliation with Constance by meeting Lord Alfred Douglas in
Rouen. It was a tearful reunion, and they spent much of the day
walking about arm in arm together. Oscar returned to Berneval
only long enough to pack his gear and arrange the necessary finance
before joining Bosie in Italy. To Robbie he wrote from Naples
telling him of their reunion, which he said was psychologically
inevitable. He said that while he was alone at Berneval he had felt
suicidal, but now he hoped to be able to write again. On 23
September he received a letter from Carlos Blacker, forwarded from
Paris. He replied that he would go and see Constance in October.
'Had Constance allowed me to see my boys, my life would, I think,
have been quite different. But this she would not do. I don't in any
way venture to blame her for her action, but every action has its
consequence.'10

He and Bosie set up home together in a lovely villa overlooking
the Bay of Naples. They were both working hard, perhaps because
it was essential to earn enough cash to enable them to resume their
relationship where it had broken off. In defending his decision to
return to Bosie, Oscar wrote to his friends praising the young man's
poetic abilities, and expressing the hope that they might never be
separated. To Leonard Smithers, with whom he was in negotiation
over the publication of *The Ballad of Reading Gaol* he wrote that
Constance's letter agreeing to see him had come too late. He had
waited in vain for four months, to be invited to visit her only after
his sons had gone back to school, by which time the situation was
irretrievable.

On 26 September Constance wrote to Oscar asking him whether
he had been to Capri and whether he had met Bosie, whom she
called, in a letter of the same date to Carlos Blacker, 'that appalling
individual'.11 She also reproached him for not acknowledging
the boys' photographs. On the same day she received a letter saying

that he intended to visit her next month; and Constance confided in another letter to Blacker that if Oscar came at all, it must be as her husband. She was tired of a life of lies and deceptions, and the staff at the Hotel Nervi, where she was staying, knew that she had only one brother. In her heart she was convinced that he had been to see Bosie, for nobody ever visited Capri at that time of the year, though it was well known as a haunt of wealthy homosexuals.

Any hopes that Constance had entertained that Oscar had not returned to his old ways were ended when Carlos sent her a letter he had had from Oscar admitting all that had happened. She was much grieved by his conduct and despised his weakness. Not surprisingly, she wrote back angrily to Oscar, and the terms of her letter made matters even worse. To Robbie, who had written three angry letters to him about the folly of returning to Bosie, Oscar now wrote:

> I am awaiting a thunderbolt from my wife's solicitor. She wrote me a terrible letter, but a foolish one, saying '*I forbid you* to do so and so: I will not *allow* you' etc.: and '*I require* a distinct promise that you will not' etc. How can she really imagine that she can influence or control my life? She might just as well try to influence and control my art. I could not live such an absurd life – it makes one laugh. So I suppose she will now try to deprive me of my wretched £3 a week. Women are so petty, and Constance has no imagination. Perhaps, for revenge, she will have another trial: then she certainly may claim for the first time in her life to have influenced me. I wish to goodness she would leave me alone. I don't meddle with her life. I accept the separation from the children: I acquiesce. Why does she want to go on bothering me, and trying to ruin me? Another trial would, of course, entirely destroy me. On the whole, dear Robbie, things are dark with storm.
>
> The solitude of our life here is wonderful, and no one writes to either of us. It is lucky that we love each other, and would be quite happy if we had money, but of course Bosie is penniless as usual – indeed he has nothing at all to speak of, and unless Pinker gets me £300 we will not be able to get food. Up to the present I have paid for almost everything. [12]

The letter Oscar wrote to Constance on the subject of his cohabitation with Lord Alfred Douglas has not survived, but she sent it to Carlos Blacker to look at. Despite her brave words to him it is clear that the letter distressed her a great deal:

> Had I received this letter a year ago . . . I should have minded, but now I look upon it as the letter of a madman who has not even enough imagination to see how trifles affect children, or unselfishness enough to care for the welfare of his wife. It rouses all my bitterest feelings, and I am stubbornly bitter when my feelings are roused. I think the letter had better remain unanswered and each of us make our own lives independently.
>
> I have latterly (God forgive me) an absolute repulsion to him.[13]

Despite everything that had happened, Constance seems still to have hoped that Oscar would return to her. As soon as Vyvyan had gone back to school and she was once more alone she rented the Villa Elvira at Bogliasco, just outside Nervi. Thinking that Oscar might turn up at any time, she moved into her new home in great haste, even borrowing linen from the Hotel Nervi, where she had been staying with Vyvyan. Her hopes remained unfulfilled.

On 16 November Oscar received a letter from his own solicitor saying that as he was living with Bosie, who qualified as a 'disreputable person', he would forfeit his allowance from Constance. He also claimed that Oscar was creating a 'public scandal' by being with Bosie. Oscar told Robbie Ross that he had replied that Bosie did not merit this description, since no charge had been made against him, and that he could not prevent journalists from writing about him. He added:

> If I were living with a Naples renter I would I suppose be all right. As I live with a young man who is well bred and well born, and who has been charged with no offence, I am deprived of all possibility of existence . . . I could not live alone, and so inevitably I took the love and companionship that was offered to me. It seemed to me to be the only gate to any life, but I did it conscious of all the new ruin it might bring on me.[14]

A couple of days later Constance wrote to Otho:

> I have stopped O's allowance as he is living with Lord Alfred Douglas, so in a short time war will be declared! His legal friends

in London make no defence and so far make no opposition, as it was always understood that if he went back to that person his allowance would stop. They have bought a villa in Naples and are living there together.[15]

Oscar bombarded Adrian Hope with letters in an effort to persuade him to get Constance to relent, but he did not reply. By the manner of his return to Bosie, Oscar had also alienated many of his friends. Even Robbie and More Adey recognized that Oscar had forfeited his right to his allowance from Constance, and under the strain of Oscar's angry letters their patience had worn thin. Robbie wrote to Leonard Smithers, who was to publish *The Ballad of Reading Gaol*:

> I regret to inform you that I have ceased to be on intimate terms with Oscar Wilde or to enjoy his confidence in business or any other matter . . . Alfred Douglas has written to a common friend that I have tried to prevent any considerable sum being obtained for the poem.[16]

Constance stood firm in the matter of the allowance. Though Oscar offered to agree not to live under the same roof as Bosie if his allowance was restored, he was not prepared to refuse to remain on friendly terms with him. But in the end Bosie's faults of character achieved what Constance could not. When he invited Oscar to join him in Italy, he had plainly expected that he would quickly make money on the old grand scale and place his profits at Bosie's disposal. Oscar hoped from the American rights of *The Ballad of Reading Gaol* to receive advances of £300 or more. This proved to be false optimism. Once it had been easy to sell anything that bore the name of Oscar Wilde. Now, regrettably, few people were interested. When Oscar's cash ran out, Bosie left him. Two instalments of £100 were paid to Oscar by Lady Queensberry in respect of sums Oscar had previously incurred on the family's account, though she would not hand over this money until Bosie and Oscar had split up.

Robbie Ross and More Adey eventually patched up their differences with Oscar. Adey wrote:

> Mrs Wilde did act strictly within her legal rights by appealing to the arbitrator according to the agreement; your friends, as the other parties to it, had therefore nothing to do but submit to his

decision. There was no ground on which to oppose Mrs Wilde; it would have been a purely vexatious opposition, worse than useless to you, and we had no money to pay solicitors for carrying on fruitless correspondence merely to gain time.[17]

Bosie's reactions after leaving Oscar were typical. He accepted no particle of responsibility for what happened, and tried to shift the blame on to Constance:

I hate appearing to attack Mrs Wilde, whom I liked and admired and respected, but as I am writing this book more as a defence of Oscar than anything else . . . I am obliged to say that I think that Mrs Wilde in the long run let him down rather badly.'[18]

He amplified this remark on another occasion;

If she had treated him properly and stuck to him after he had been in prison, as a really good wife would have done, he would have gone on loving her to the end of his life . . .Obviously she suffered a great deal and deserves every sympathy, but she fell woefully short of the height to which she might have risen, and while I feel deeply for her I cannot but blame her for the attitude she took up after his conviction. She was far from generous to him in the matter of money, and apart from that she wrote to him a letter [now lost] which he received very soon after he came out of prison which was calculated, as she must have known perfectly well, (knowing his character as she did), to exasperate and embitter him, and to make impossible the reunion which she professed to desire.[19]

Bosie claimed that a letter from Constance to Oscar finished all chance of reconciliation and killed all that remained of his love for her. He also placed the entire blame for Oscar's reconciliation with him in Naples on her shoulders, for he claimed that if she had not written that fatal letter to Oscar he would never have gone to Naples. He saw Constance's actions as a profound disservice to himself, for he felt that his relationship with Oscar not only stood between him and his father's allowance, but also damaged him in the eyes of society. No wonder Constance referred to this unfortunate specimen in terms of loathing and disgust.

18

Requiescat

She that was young and fair
Fallen to dust.

'Requiescat'

Despite all these renewed problems with Oscar, and her rapidly worsening state of health, Constance's life somehow seemed in general more tranquil. Oscar never crossed the threshold of the Villa Elvira, but she took immense pleasure in her new home, which she had taken on a two year lease. It was a very pretty villa, and she could now put down roots for the first time since the sale of the House Beautiful.

The house was run by an Italian servant who was absolutely devoted to Constance and saw that everything was done to her liking. The Ranee came to see her almost every day, and she built up a little circle of friends who paid frequent calls. In the Christmas holidays Cyril came home to her, though Vyvyan had to stay in Monaco for the religious ceremonies.

As Vyvyan had not been able to go home to the Villa Elvira for Christmas, Constance went in mid-February to Monaco, where she stayed as usual at the Hotel Bristol. She asked special permission for Vyvyan to sleep away from the school, and he shared her room at the hotel. She was if anything even sweeter to him than usual. Their week together went all too quickly, and when the priest came and took Vyvyan away at the end of the brief holiday, she cried a little. Vyvyan could not know that they would never see each other again.

In February 1898 *The Ballad of Reading Gaol* was published. Constance wrote to Otho:

I am frightfully upset by this wonderful poem of Oscar's of which so far I have only seen the extracts in the *D.C.* [Daily Chronicle]. I hear that it was sold out the day it was published and that orders are pouring in, and that is a good thing as it means money! It is frightfully tragic and makes one cry.[1]

On the following day Oscar sent Constance a copy. He even sent one to Otho, and the two corresponded quite cordially. Oscar also wrote to Robbie Ross:

> I am going to write to Constance to say that really now my income, such as it is, must be restored. Bosie and I are irrevocably parted — we can never be together again — and it is absurd to leave me to starve. Will you suggest this to her, if you write?[2]

Oscar's behaviour in regard to money and to Lord Alfred Douglas had been outrageous, and it is difficult to see how he could expect to be forgiven. But Oscar was Oscar, and though she was still prudently cautious, Constance restored his allowance almost in its entirety. She also arranged for it to be continued if she predeceased him, ostensibly because she did not want the boys to have to contribute to his support. In early March she wrote and gave Oscar's address to Carlos Blacker, who was going to Paris, in the hope that he would give Oscar the intellectual stimulus she felt he needed. Constance offered to send Carlos a copy of the *Ballad*, if he had not got one, and asked him to tell Oscar that she thought it exquisite. Her great hope was that he would continue to devote himself to writing. 'I hear that he does nothing now but drink and I heard that he had left Lord A. and had received £200 from Lady Q. on condition that he did not see him again . . .'[3]

Constance was now managing to fill her days with various pastimes in spite of her illness. Perhaps rather surprisingly, she had taken up photography, and did her own developing and enlarging into the bargain. She was able to continue to work at her enlargements long after she had become effectively housebound. As always, she spent a lot of time embroidering and now added macramé work to her list of skills. She also planned to learn lace-making at some time or another. Carrie Blacker wrote and suggested that they should try and spend the summer holidays together, and this idea greatly appealed to Constance. She had been thinking of spending the major part of the summer in Lucerne, as she had heard of a very nice family there who could help Cyril with his French. His headmaster had written to her saying that he knew she would be very pleased with his half-term report. Vyvyan had had influenza, but was stronger than a year ago. This she put down to the excellent climate in Monte Carlo.

No sooner had Carlos Blacker made contact with him than Oscar began demanding money from Constance, as of right. Hearing that he was in desperate straits, she had already sent Robbie £40 for him; but this question of money was clearly a permanent bone of contention now. Constance wrote:

> I know that he is in great poverty, but I don't care to be written to as though it were my fault. He says that he loved too much and that that is better than hate! This is true abstractedly, but his was an unnatural love, a madness that I think is worse than hate. I have no hatred of him, but I confess that I am afraid of him.[4]

Although Carlos Blacker's account of Oscar was pitiful, Constance felt that he was better off in Paris, where he would get the continual intellectual stimulus that he needed. She felt that he would have been bored to death by family life, even by the children, much as he loved them. She asked Carlos to look out for a copy of *Dorian Gray* in French, as she had lent her copy and it had not been returned to her. Despite all that had happened, her belief and pride in Oscar's genius remained unchanged. She also wrote to Carlos Blacker of Robbie Ross:

> Your church does sometimes produce marvellous instances of exceeding unselfishness, of which one should be more than grateful in this selfish world, and for which I am indeed grateful. I have never seen anything in a man like him (women are as a rule more unselfish than men) and at first as you know was the case with me one scarcely believes it. But now I not only believe it, but admire and am astounded by it.[5]

Robbie had wisely decided to dole out the £40 Constance had sent in instalments, and around this time Carlos Blacker received another letter from Oscar complaining that Constance was refusing to pay him 'arrears' of his allowance, and adding that he had an idea she wanted him dead, and would be relieved to hear that his body had been identified in the morgue. Constance had had to face financial struggles of her own since Oscar's arrest. She had borrowed £150 from Sir Edward Burne-Jones at that time, but had never borrowed a penny since. 'No words can describe my horror of that BEAST, for I will call him nothing else, A.D.,'[6] she wrote. Constance said that if only she knew where he was staying, she could arrange to pay Oscar's hotel bill direct, at, say, ten francs a day full board. She felt he ought really to go to a pension to reduce his expenses. She herself had paid four marks a day in Heidelberg, but knew that Oscar would think that horrible.

She was also much concerned about Vyvyan's wish to become a Roman Catholic. She had clearly anticipated that this situation might arise when she had decided to send him to a Jesuit school. In principle she was fully prepared for it but she hesitated a little in case, when he went back to school in England, in two years' time, she might be unable to find a Roman Catholic school with a comparable academic standard. The other consideration which made her pause was the fact that she was not sole guardian. Clearly she suspected that Adrian Hope would be hostile to the idea, and she now wondered whether it was possible for Vyvyan to become a Roman Catholic without Hope's permission, and indeed his knowledge. Perhaps at this point she may have wondered whether she had been altogether wise in taking legal action to secure a second guardian for the children.

Towards the end of March Oscar wrote to Robbie asking him to find out from Constance whether the money he had received was meant for arrears, or for his current allowance. He said that he feared Constance found his letters unwelcome; and indeed it is very likely that she did, if the subject was always money. At the same time Constance had a letter from Carrie Blacker in which she indicated that her husband also wished to be free of Oscar. Constance wrote back telling Carrie of Oscar's total inability to grasp money matters, and his urgent need of someone with a strong will to look after him. 'If he had plenty of money he would drink himself to death and do no work, so that would be useless,'[7] she wrote. Oscar had written a letter, which had been published in the *Daily Chronicle*, totally condemning the prison system, which clearly impressed Constance. Whenever Oscar produced literary work, Constance was enraptured; but when he wrote about social and humanitarian matters, she almost forgot the trouble he had brought on her. Solid Christian virtues still had a great influence on

Constance, and to some extent it would seem that Oscar was aware of this, and made use of it to gain his wife's sympathy.

Constance now prepared a codicil to her will so that Oscar's allowance could continue after her death. She positively refused, however, to make herself in any way responsible for Oscar's debts. She noted with approval that he had moved to two rooms in the Hotel d'Alsace, in the Rue des Beaux Arts, Paris, which would be far more economical than his former style of living. 'It may interest your husband and disgusted me to hear that A.D. is received in society by the embassy at Rome and by private persons in Nice,' she wrote to Carrie Blacker. 'So much it is with a bourgeois nation to be of the aristocracy!'[8]

On 30 March she wrote to Carlos Blacker enclosing copies of Oscar's letter to the *Daily Chronicle*, and also the *Saturday Review*. She was clearly impressed by Oscar's writings on the prison system, and felt that he ought to write a book on the subject. Doubtless she was aware that Oscar had had an accident in a *fiacre* a few days previously, for he had written to tell Carlos Blacker all about it; but she made no mention of it. Her letter was full of pride in Cyril's achievements at school. He had passed an examination and come top not only of his own form but of boys in the form above. He was also going in for a race, being one of only four juniors chosen to run. Perhaps it was for him that Constance asked Carlos to get one of the new Swiss fifty-centime pieces, which she thought very lovely, and which were difficult to come by.

For some time past Constance had been using a typewriter for her letters, but now she seems to have made a conscious effort to write in her own hand; at the beginning of April Vyvyan received a long epistle in her own handwriting, which clearly cost her a great deal of effort. 'Try not to feel harshly about your father; remember that he is your father and that he loves you. All his troubles arose from the hatred of a son for his father, and whatever he has done he has suffered bitterly for.'[9]

Almost immediately after this typically stoical endeavour she went into a nursing home in Genoa for an operation to relieve the pressure on her spine. She had been in severe pain during the last months and all attempts to relieve the condition without resorting to the surgeon's knife had failed. The operation was unsuccessful, and she died on 7 April 1898. The Ranee of Sarawak and Otho, Constance's brother, both maintained that she had no idea that she might die, but that last letter to her son seems to indicate only too clearly that she foresaw that her death was imminent. She had remained uncomplaining to the very end. Vyvyan, who was now eleven years old, was at school when the news of her death was broken to him. He cried a little, and then asked about his father. The priest said that he did not know. Then, with one of those flashes of insight which come to children when grown-ups hide the truth, Vyvyan asked whether he had been in prison. Father Stradelli said that this was so, though he was now free. He also asked whether his mother, being a Protestant, would go to Heaven, and was reassured about this.

On 13 April Vyvyan wrote to Carlos Blacker:

When I wrote to you first they had not told me that Mother was dead but they told it to me little by little so that it should not shock me too much but now I do know it and I am very unhappy.

Do not talk to Cyril about Mother being dead because perhaps they have not told him yet but as soon as he knows I will tell you . . . [10]

He ended with uncertainties about his future life, and hoping that he might be allowed to stay on at his school. He added that he had a guardian who was nice although he scarcely knew him. His touching concern for his brother showed a far greater maturity than Cyril's, though he was the younger of the two. But Cyril, too, was shocked, even though he wrote of having fun at the theatre and playing with his new revolver. He wrote to Vyvyan: 'Isn't it awful? Poor, poor Mother! It's hard to realise. One's so used to having her. What shall we do in the holidays with no Mother? . . .Think of Mother always and remember she sees everything you do.'[11]

It was Otho who arranged Constance's funeral. She was buried in the corner of the Campo Santo in Genoa set aside for Protestants. The cemetery was a beautiful garden in the hills that surround Genoa. A more peaceful spot could scarcely be imagined. Otho chose a marble cross with dark ivy leaves inlaid in a pleasing pattern. The name Wilde did not appear at all. It read simply. 'Constance Mary, daughter of Horace Lloyd, Q.C.' followed by a verse from *Revelations*.

Bosie still had occasional contact with Oscar, and he later claimed that Oscar had told him that on the night of Constance's death he dreamed that she came to see him. He kept telling her to go away and leave him in peace; and the next day a telegram came to say that she had taken him literally. Oscar was prone to such claims, which could well have been genuine. But in fact, he was not informed of Constance's death until 12 April, when Otho sent him a telegram. He telegraphed back: 'Am overwhelmed with grief. It is the most terrible tragedy. Am writing.'[12] He also telegraphed to Robbie Ross with the news, and begged him to come to him at once. To Carlos Blacker he wrote:

> It really is awful. I don't know what to do. If we had only met once, and kissed each other.
> It is too late. How awful life is . . .[13]

Robbie responded immediately, joining Oscar in Paris as quickly as he was able. His letter to Leonard Smithers shows his assessment of Oscar's emotions:

> You will have heard of Mrs Wilde's death. Oscar of course did not feel it at all. It is rather appalling for him as his allowance ceases and I do not expect his wife's trustees will continue it. He is in very good spirits and does not consume too many . . . Oscar has only seen Douglas once. I went to see his lordship. He is less interested in other people than ever before, especially Oscar. So I really think that alliance will die a natural death.[14]

In February 1899 Oscar, who was going to stay with a friend at Gland on Lake Geneva, made a detour for a pilgrimage to Constance's grave. He drove out to the cemetery in a ramshackle little green cab, bearing an armful of flowers. When he saw her name on the tombstone he broke down in grief and remorse, praying and sobbing violently. As he strewed the grave with scarlet roses he vowed everlasting fidelity to her. He left the cemetery exhausted with weeping. Afterwards he was seized by a mood of reckless hilarity; but this was a simple reaction to the terrible nervous ordeal he had just undergone.[15]

It was Robert Sherard who wrote the best tribute to his friend's wife:

> Constance Wilde, who had long been ailing, and who had never recovered from the horrible shock of the catastrophe which

shattered her home, was released, from a world so full of cruel surprise to the simple and gentle, by death. She died in Genoa about one year after her husband had left prison. She was a simple, beautiful woman, too gentle and good for the part that life called upon her to play. She was a woman of heart whom kindlier gods would never have thrown into the turmoil and stress of an existence which was all a battle. Her death was to Oscar Wilde's affectionate heart a sorrow which accentuated his despair. His love for her . . . was pure, deep and reverent. [16]

Constance had brought to her marriage a dowry of special qualities that few women possess. She had never lost that childlike quality and shy youthful beauty that had claimed Oscar's heart. Yet though she had retained her looks, she had thrown off that naïvety which characterized the early years of her married life. Her courage and loyalty to Oscar never faltered, even in the darkest days of disillusionment. She faced up to her problems with a courage and determination remarkable for one of her gentle nature. Whatever she suffered, she suffered in secret, and she bore the pain and disablement of her final illness without complaint.

Socially and politically, Constance Wilde was a woman of some importance. To her two sons she had been supremely important. In intellect she had not been the equal of her remarkable husband; yet she had enormous respect for his genius, and had avoided the mistake of trying to bury it in conventional domesticity. She had nurtured his gifts as perhaps no other woman of her era could have done. Towards the end of his imprisonment Oscar had paid her the outstanding tribute of comparing her to his own mother, and indeed she had some of Speranza's virtues and none of her faults. She did not love blindly; she loved with all her being, and in the full knowledge that her idol had feet of clay.

Oscar did not outlive his wife for very long. While he was in prison, he had fallen and severely damaged his ear. Initially no treatment was given, and this neglect had resulted in permanent deafness. On 10 October 1900 he had an operation on the ear, possibly for the removal of a mastoid. The operation kept him in bed for a fortnight. On the day after his first outing he caught a cold and suffered severe pain in the ear. Soon it became clear that a second abcess had formed in the ear.

Between them Robbie and Reggie Turner nursed Oscar. Robbie, not realizing the full seriousness of the situation, left Paris on business and had to be sent for. It was he who summoned a priest and arranged for him to be received into the Roman Catholic Church. Oscar was by now scarcely conscious, so that it is doubtful whether he really understood what was going on; but he had long wished to take this step, and it is beyond all doubt that this is what in his heart he really wished.

Oscar died on 30 November 1900. Robbie, Reggie and the hotel-keeper, who had been a good friend to him, were with him when the end came. Robbie's own rosary was about Oscar's neck when he was buried at Bagneux on 3 December 1900.

Epilogue

After Constance's death, Cyril and Vyvyan were removed from the schools where they had been happy and brought back to England. Adrian Hope did not wish to bring them up himself, and handed them over to the care of Constance's aunt, Mary Napier. Effectively it was her daughter Lizzie who acted as guardian. She was an exceedingly kind woman, but she shared the Napiers' bourgeois morality and never mentioned Oscar's name. Both she and Aunt Mary spoke frequently of Constance, whom they had both adored.

It was probably a relief to Constance's family when Oscar died. Vyvyan learned of the event from the Rector of Stonyhurst, where he was sent to school. His brother read it in the newspapers. Among the funeral arrangements which he made for his friend, Robbie Ross was careful to include flowers in the name of the children. Afterwards he wrote a letter jointly to Cyril and Vyvyan, to which the elder replied; the younger never saw Robbie's letter.

Bosie interrupted his round of social pleasures long enough to be chief mourner at the funeral. Two years later he contracted a runaway marriage with the poetess Olive Custance, an heiress, who soon found that even her substantial fortune was insufficient to keep Bosie in the style to which he was accustomed. Robbie had sent him Oscar's letter, *De Profundis*, which he had written while in Reading Gaol, and Bosie had been so angry at its contents that he destroyed it. Fortunately Robbie had sent him only a typescript.

As Oscar's literary executor, Robbie set to work zealously on behalf of his dead friend. One of his first acts was to approach the Official Receiver in an attempt to buy the copyright of Oscar's works. He was lucky enough to acquire them without laying out the vast sum which they were worth because the Receiver regarded them as unsaleable. He had to get the permission of Adrian Hope, who as trustee of Constance's estate was one of the principal creditors. To Adela Schuster, Oscar's 'Lady of Wimbledon', he wrote:

It is arranged that if obtainable the rights shall be purchased by *me*, and Mr Hope was kind enough to say that they would prefer that I should possess them. If ever there is any remuneration I would of course hand it over to Mr Hope for the benefit of the children if the Paris debts were by that time cleared off and I notified my intention to Mr Hope, but he would not permit me to write any promise to that effect as he says the children must not have any official benefit from their father's works . . .[1]

Adrian Hope's death in 1904 effectively lifted this embargo. In 1905 Robbie published a shortened version of *De Profundis*, and despite a hostile reaction the book went into five editions in the first year alone. The first collected edition of Oscar's works followed in 1908. A year later, having paid off Oscar's debts in Paris, Robbie obtained £2,000 from Mrs James Carew and was finally able to arrange for Oscar's body to be transferred from the Bagneux cemetery to Père Lachaise, where Epstein sculpted a splendid monumental tomb. The coffin had to be officially opened for formal identification, and it is said that Robbie personally descended into the open grave and reverentially assisted in the removing of the remains.

After Hope's death there was no longer any reason why Robbie Ross should not make himself personally known to Cyril and Vyvyan, who were now able to enjoy the rich fruits of Oscar's works which Robbie had been able to harvest on their behalf. He proved as true a friend to the young men as he had been to their father.

Lord Alfred Douglas, meanwhile, viewed Robbie's activities with mounting hostility, and when in 1913 the young Arthur Ransome published a book about Oscar, Bosie sued him for libel, hoping in this way to involve Ross. The latter had judged Bosie's character well when he had sent him a typescript of *De Profundis*, and not the handwritten original. This latter he had lodged in the British Library on condition that it remain sealed for fifty years; but during the libel action it was produced and read out to the court. Douglas lost, and now it was his turn to be bankrupted. His wife left him and his father-in-law obtained custody of his only child, a boy who suffered from schizophrenia and died in 1964. Bosie, who seems to have had a talent for getting involved in lawsuits, was himself sued for libel by Winston Churchill in 1923. He ended up in Wormwood Scrubs, where he served a six months' sentence.

Cyril, unfortunately, died in action in the First World War. He never really got over the terrible catastrophe that befell his family. Vyvyan, though haunted in his early years by events which were kept hidden from him, or that he did not really understand, seems to have adjusted to life much better than his elder brother. He married and had a son. He lived the life of a man of letters and produced many fine books. Most of them are translations, for he inherited Constance's love of languages; but fortunately for posterity, he published his own recollections of his childhood and later years, giving us a glimpse into the house in Tite Street and a privileged view of his remarkable father and mother and the circle in which they moved.

Now that his 'crimes' are no crimes, and men's achievements are judged for their intrinsic worth, Oscar's genius is enjoyed throughout the world. It has often been said that his conversation was far more wonderful than anything he wrote, and the opinion of so many men of wit and imagination cannot lightly be disregarded. In any event, the dialogue of his plays hints at it.

In due course Constance's family rectified the earlier omission by adding to her tombstone the words 'Wife of Oscar Wilde'. Her life was sad and rather brief; and yet I doubt she would have lived her life differently if she had had to choose again. Of course she would have avoided the pain if she could; yet not at the cost of her great and enduring love. Her proper role in life was simply to be Mrs Oscar Wilde.

Bibliography

Manuscript Sources

The largest collection of Constance's autograph letters is in the Library of William Andrews Clark Jnr at the University of California, Los Angeles. There are further autograph letters in the British Library. The most important private collection is the typescript of Constance's correspondence with Carlos and Carrie Blacker belonging to H. Montgomery Hyde.

I have also drawn on the large collection of autograph letters of Speranza (Lady Wilde) in typescript in the Library of the University of Reading.

Published Sources

BETTANY, F.G., *Stewart Headlam: A Biography*, London 1926
BRAZOL, Boris L., *Oscar Wilde: The Man – the Artist*, London 1938
BRAYBROOKE, Patrick, *Lord Alfred Douglas: His Life and Works*, London 1931
BRÉMONT, Anna Comtesse de, *Oscar Wilde and His Mother*, London 1911
BYRNE, Patrick, *The Wildes of Merrion Square*, London 1953
Cheiro's Memoirs: The Reminiscences of a Society Palmist, London 1912
CORKRAN, Henriette, *Celebrities and I*, London 1902
CROFT-COOKE, Rupert, *Bosie*, London 1963
DOUGLAS, Lord Alfred, *Sonnets*, London 1909
———, *Oscar Wilde and Myself*, London 1914
———, *Autobiography*, London 1929
———, *Without Apology*, London 1938
———, *Oscar Wilde: A Summing Up*, London 1940
DOUGLAS, Lord Alfred, and HARRIS, Frank, *A New Preface to The Life and Confessions of Oscar Wilde*, London 1925
DOUGLAS, Francis A.K. (Marquess of Queensberry) and COHEN, Percy, *Oscar Wilde and the Black Douglas*, London 1949
FIELD, Michael (i.e. Katherine Bradley and Edith Cooper), *Works and Days: From the Journal of Michael Field*, edited by T. and D.C. Sturge Moore, London 1933
GIDE, André, *If It Die (Si le grain ne meurt)*, translated by Dorothy Bussy, London 1951
HARRIS, Frank, *Oscar Wilde: His Life and Confessions*, London 1910; *Oscar Wilde:*

His Life and Confessions, Including the hitherto unpublished Full and Final Confession by Lord Alfred Douglas and My Memories of Oscar Wilde by Bernard Shaw, New York 1930 (this book ran through various editions with substantial variations. Where other editions are quoted these are indicated in the Notes).

————, *Mr and Mrs Daventry* [a play based on Wilde's scenario], edited by H. Montgomery Hyde, London 1956

HICHENS, Robert, *The Green Carnation*, London 1894

HOLLAND, Vyvyan, *Son of Oscar Wilde*, London 1954

————, *Oscar Wilde and His World*, London 1960

————, *Time Remembered After Père Lachaise*, London 1966

HYDE, H. Montgomery, *Cases That Changed the Law*, London 1963

————, *Oscar Wilde: The Aftermath*, London 1963

————, *The Other Love*, London 1970

————, *Oscar Wilde*, London 1976

LAMBERT, Eric, *Mad With Much Heart: A Life of the Parents of Oscar Wilde*, London 1967

LANGTRY, Lillie, *The Days I Knew*, London 1925

LE GALLIENNE, Richard, *The Romantic Nineties*, with an introduction by H. Montgomery Hyde, London 1951

LOWNDES, Marie Belloc, *Diaries and Letters 1911-1947*, edited by Susan Lowndes, London 1971

MASON, Stuart, *Oscar Wilde Three Times Tried*, London 1912

Minutes of the Proceedings of the Institution of Civil Engineers, Volume 78 (1883–4), London

PEARSON, Hesketh, *The Life of Oscar Wilde*, London 1946

POMEROY, Frances (Lady Harberton), *Reasons for Reform in Dress*, London 1885

RANSOME, Arthur, *Oscar Wilde: A Critical Study*, London 1912

Robert Ross: Friend of Friends. Letters to Robert Ross, Art Critic and Writer, Together with Extracts from His Published Articles, edited by Margery Ross, London 1952

ROBERTSON, Graham, *Time Was*, London 1931

ROTHENSTEIN, William, *Men and Memories*, London 1931

SHERARD, Robert Harborough, *Oscar Wilde: The Story of an Unhappy Friendship*, London 1905

————, *The Life of Oscar Wilde*, London 1906

————, *The Real Oscar Wilde*, London 1917

————, *Oscar Wilde Twice Defended*, Chicago 1934

————, *Bernard Shaw, Frank Harris and Oscar Wilde*, London 1937

The Story of Oscar Wilde's Life and Experience in Reading Gaol, By His Warder, New Jersey 1963

TERRY, Ellen, *Memoirs*, London 1933

The Trials of Oscar Wilde, edited by H. Montgomery Hyde, London 1948

TROUBRIDGE, Laura, *Life Amongst the Troubridges*, edited by Jaqueline Hope-Nicholson, London 1966

VYVER, Bertha, *Memoirs of Marie Corelli*, London 1930

WHISTLER, James McNeill, *The Gentle Art of Making Enemies*, London 1890

WHITE, Terence de Vere, *The Parents of Oscar Wilde*, London 1967

WILDE, Constance, 'There Was Once': Grandma's Stories, London 1889
———, A Long Time Ago, London 1892
WILDE, Jane Francesca Speranza (Lady Wilde), Social Studies, London 1893
WILDE, Oscar, Complete Works, with an introduction by Vyvyan Holland, Collins; London 1966
———, Oscariana, edited by Constance Wilde, London 1895
———, Letters, edited by Sir Rupert Hart-Davis, London 1962
———, Letters to the Sphinx, With Reminiscences of the Author by A. Leverson, London 1930
———, A Collection of Original Manuscripts, Letters and Books of Oscar Wilde, Including His Letters Written to Robert Ross from Reading Gaol and Unpublished Letters, Poems and Plays Formerly in the Possession of Robert Ross, C.S. Millard (Stuart Mason) and the Younger Son of Oscar Wilde, Dulau & Co. Ltd, London 1928
Wilde and Wildeiana (5 vols), collated and compiled by Robert Ernest Cowan and William Andrews Clark Jr, The Library of Williams Andrews Clark Jr: San Francisco 1922-31
WYNDHAM, Horace, Speranza, London 1951
YEATS, J.B., Letters to W.B. Yeats, edited by J.M. Hone, London 1944
YEATS, W.B., Autobiographies, London 1955
———, Letters, edited by Allen Wade, London 1956
———, Memoirs, edited by Denis Donoghue, London 1972

Notes

Blacker = typescript of the correspondence with Carlos and Carrie Blacker shown to me by H. Montgomery Hyde

Clark Library = autograph letters in the Library of William Andrews Clark Jnr at the University of California, Los Angeles

Complete Works = *The Complete Works of Oscar Wilde*, with an introduction by Vyvyan Holland (Collins; London 1966)

Harris = *Oscar Wilde: His Life and Confessions* (New York 1910), by Frank Harris

Hyde = *Oscar Wilde* (London 1976) by H. Montgomery Hyde

Letters = *The Letters of Oscar Wilde* (London 1962), edited by Sir Rupert Hart-Davis

Chapter 1: Many Relations

1   further details of John Horatio's career may be found in *Minutes of the Proceedings of the Institution of Civil Engineers, Volume 78 (1883 – 4),* (London), pp.450 – 4.
2   Register of Baptisms, Christ Church, Cosway Street, London NW1.
3   ibid.
4   ibid.
5   autograph letter of Constance Wilde to Emily Thursfield, 10 October 1895, Clark Library.
6   London 1916, p.587.
7   New York 1930, p.443 and note.
8   ibid.
9   14 April 1874.
10 Henriette Corkran, *Celebrities and I* (London 1902), p.139.

Chapter 2: The Aesthete

1   Harris, p.82.
2   *Complete Works*, p.776.
3   from a typescript in the Library of the University of Reading: acc.559, no.8.
4   ibid., no.15.
5   ibid.
6   ibid., no.16.
7   ibid., no.18.

8 ibid., no. 19.
9 Harris, p.3.
10 *Letters of J.B. Yeats to W.B. Yeats*, edited by J.M. Hone (London 1944), p.277.
11 R.H. Sherard, *The Life of Oscar Wilde* (London 1906), pp.27 – 8.
12 Harris, p.44.
13 Sherard, op. cit., pp.33 – 4.
14 autograph letter of 10 July 1876 in the Library of Magdalen College, Oxford.
15 ibid., 20 July 1878.
16 Sherard, op. cit., pp.33 – 4.
17 *Letters*, p.23.
18 Laura Troubridge, *Life Amongst the Troubridges* (London 1966), p.152.
19 ibid., pp.164 – 5.

Chapter 3: Loved by a Poet

1 Hyde, p.47.
2 ibid., p.53.
3 *Letters*, p.92.
4 ibid.
5 ibid.
6 Troubridge, op. cit., pp.164 – 5.
7 *Letters*, p.153.
8 ibid.
9 ibid., note.
10 Lillie Langtry, *The Days I Knew* (London 1925), p.74.
11 *Letters*, p.154.
12 26 December 1883.
13 Hyde, p.93.
14 Hesketh Pearson, *The Life of Oscar Wilde* (London 1946), p.110.
15 ibid., p.111.
16 ibid.
17 ibid.
18 ibid.
19 ibid.
20 Sotheby's Catalogue, 10 April 1924.
21 autograph letter of Constance Lloyd to Mrs Harris, 30 March 1884, Clark Library.
22 *The Life of Oscar Wilde*, pp.255 – 6.
23 31 May 1884.
24 *The Life of Oscar Wilde*, p.257.
25 *The World*, 4 June 1884.
26 *Letters*, p.159.
27 *Lady's Pictorial*, 7 June 1884.

Chapter 4: Honeymoon

1 Sherard, *The Life of Oscar Wilde*, p.258.
2 8 June 1884.
3 'I like this woman – I like a woman who is self-effacing and affectionate'. *Letters*, pp.157 – 8 note.
4 undated autograph letter, Clark Library.
5 *Letters*, p.159.
6 ibid., p.158.
7 *Lady's Pictorial*, 19 July 1884.
8 ibid., p.165.
9 ibid., p.166.
10 for a full account of what happened, see H. Montgomery Hyde, *Cases that Changed the Law* (London 1951).

Chapter 5: The House Beautiful

1 *Letters*, p.166.
2 5 January 1885.
3 Hyde, p.104.
4 *Letters*, p.172.
5 Hyde, p.104.
6 Vyvyan Holland, *Time Remembered After Père Lachaise* (London 1966), p.129.
7 *Today*, 24 November 1894.
8 ibid.
9 ibid.
10 *Complete Works*, p.809.
11 p.70: the book was published under the pseudonym 'Michael Field'.
12 Anna, Comtesse de Brémont, *Oscar Wilde and His Mother* (London 1911), pp.88 – 9.
13 *Diaries and Letters of Marie Belloc Lowndes 1911 – 1947*, edited by Susan Lowndes (London 1971), pp.13 – 14.
14 R.H. Sherard, *Oscar Wilde Twice Defended* (Chicago 1934), pp.10 – 11.
15 Harris, pp.186 – 7.

Chapter 6: The Modern Woman

1 autograph letter from Constance Wilde to Emily Thursfield, 1 September 1889, Clark Library.
2 Harris, pp.88 – 9.
3 op. cit., p.85.
4 *Lady's Pictorial*, 23 July 1887.
5 e.g., *Rational Dress Society Gazette*, April 1889.
6 *A Collection of Original Manuscripts . . . of Oscar Wilde, etc.* (London 1928), p.87.
7 ibid., pp.7 – 8.

8   Bertha Vyver, *Memoirs of Marie Corelli* (London 1930), p.92.
9   ibid.
10 *Lady's Pictorial*, 8 January 1887.
11 Horace Wyndham, *Speranza* (London 1951), p.119.
12 *Rational Dress Society's Gazette*, April 1889, p.7.
13 ibid.
14 Jane Francesca Speranza Wilde, *Social Studies* (London 1893), p.96.
15 Henriette Corkran, *Celebrities and I* (London 1903), pp.139 – 40.
16 ibid.
17 no. 49, 1889.
18 autograph letter from Constance Wilde to Mrs Stopes, British Library Add. mss. 58454.
19 no. 49, 1889.
20 'Councilloresses and Alderpersons', *Top Copy*, Christmas 1976.
21 London County Council Minutes, 11 April 1889.
22 ibid., 30 April 1889.
23 ibid., 21 May 1889.
24 autograph letter of Constance Wilde to Emily Thursfield, 1 September 1889, Clark Library.
25 autograph letter, Clark Library.
26 British Library Add. mss. 44488, f.20.
27 ibid., f.154.
28 ibid., f.218.
29 de Brémont, op. cit., p.39.
30 *Lady's Pictorial*, 30 July 1887.
31 Pearson, op. cit., p.109.
32 undated autograph letter, Clark Library.
33 Pearson, op. cit., p.109.
34 ibid.

Chapter 7: Family Life

1   Hyde, p.116.
2   W.B. Yeats, *Memoirs*, edited by Denis Donoghue (London 1972), p.21.
3   *Diaries and Letters*, p.13.
4   Vyvyan Holland, *Son of Oscar Wilde* (London 1954), p.35.
5   Harris, pp.175 – 6.
6   Hyde, p.107.
7   *Letters*, p.215.
8   *The Life of Oscar Wilde*, p.159.
9   *Letters*, p.219.
10 *Sun*, 17 November 1889.
11 *Letters*, p.256.
12 Richard Le Gallienne, *The Romantic Nineties* (London 1951), p.144.
13 *Son of Oscar Wilde*, pp.34 – 5.
14 *Oscar Wilde: A Critical Study* (London 1912), p.80.

15 ibid.
16 Pearson, op. cit., p.184.
17 ibid.

Chapter 8: The Decadent

1 *Letters*, pp.254 – 5.
2 Patrick Braybrooke, *Lord Alfred Douglas: His Life and Works* (London 1931), pp.33 – 4.
3 ibid., p.34.
4 30 June 1890.
5 *Daily Chronicle*, 2 July 1890.
6 Pearson, op. cit., p.147.
7 ibid.
8 *Complete Works*, p.27.
9 ibid., p.21.
10 ibid., p.25.
11 ibid., p.20.
12 ibid.
13 ibid., p.174.
14 ibid., p.176.
15 ibid.
16 *The Life of Oscar Wilde*, p.315.
17 27 June 1891.
18 *Complete Works*, p.169.
19 *Letters*, p.273.
20 ibid., p.274.
21 ibid., p.288.
22 autograph letter, Clark Library.
23 Hyde, p.127.
24 ibid., p.135.

Chapter 9: The Gilt-headed Youth

1 autograph letter from Constance Wilde in Torquay to Mrs Fitch, Clark Library.
2 Hyde, p.139.
3 ibid., p.140.
4 ibid.
5 Lord Alfred Douglas, *Oscar Wilde: A Summing Up* (London 1940), p.97.
6 *Letters*, p.314.
7 ibid., p.316.
8 ibid.
9 autograph letter of 3 September 1892, Clark Library.
10 ibid.
11 ibid.

12 *Complete Works*, p.876.
13 *Letters*, p.326.
14 autograph letter from Campbell Dodgson to Lionel Johnson of 8 February 1893, British Library Add. mss. 580796.
15 ibid.
16 *Letters*, p.333.
17 autograph letter from Campbell Dodgson to Lionel Johnson of 8 February 1893, British Library Add. mss. 580796.
18 undated autograph letter, Clark Library.
19 *Complete Works*, p.880.
20 *Letters*, p.336.
21 *Complete Works*, p.880.
22 Hyde, p.152.
23 autograph letter, Clark Library.
24 ibid., 16 April 1893.
25 ibid., 13 May 1893.
26 undated autograph letter, Clark Library.
27 Hyde, p.156.

Chapter 10: Deception

1 Hyde, p.158.
2 *Cheiro's Memoirs: The Reminiscences of a Society Palmist* (London 1912), pp.56 – 7.
3 Hyde, p.159.
4 Rupert Croft-Cooke, *Bosie* (London 1963), pp.56 – 7.
5 Pearson, op. cit., p.184.
6 *Complete Works*, pp.880 – 1.
7 ibid.
8 undated autograph letter, Clark Library.
9 Pearson, op. cit., p.109.
10 undated autograph letter, Clark Library.
11 Hyde, p.167.
12 *Complete Works*, p.883.

Chapter 11: The First Attack

1 Harris, pp.188 – 9.
2 ibid., p.47.
3 Hyde, p.153.
4 undated autograph letter, Clark Library.
5 Pearson, op. cit., p.166.
6 Hyde, p.169.
7 Pearson, op. cit., p.272.
8 ibid., pp.272 – 3.
9 Harris, pp.188 – 9.

10   Hyde, p.194.
11   *Letters*, p.358.
12   *Complete Works*, p.887.
13   ibid.
14   ibid., p.888.

Chapter 12: The Constant Wife

1   Douglas, *Oscar Wilde: A Summing Up*, p.98.
2   autograph letter of 18 March 1894, Clark Library.
3   ibid., 15 October 1894.
4   *Lady's Pictorial*, 12 January 1895.
5   autograph letter of 28 January 1895, Clark Library.
6   ibid., 1 February 1895.
7   Oscar Wilde, *Letters to the Sphinx, With Reminiscences of the Author by A. Leverson* (London 1930), pp.26 – 7.
8   *Letters*, p.383.
9   Hyde, p.196.
10   *Letters*, p.384.
11   *Complete Works*, p.879.
12   autograph letter of 12 March 1895, Clark Library.
13   ibid., 15 March 1895.
14   *Letters*, p.385.
15   Harris, p.200.
16   ibid., pp.200–1.
17   ibid., p.201.
18   Frank Harris, *Oscar Wilde His Life and Confessions Including the Hitherto Unpublished Full and Final Confessions by Lord Alfred Douglas and My Memories of Oscar Wilde by Bernard Shaw* (New York 1930), p.xxiii.
19   Douglas, *Oscar Wilde: A Summing Up*, p.97.
20   Pearson, op. cit., p.288.

Chapter 13: Revelations

1   for a full account of both trials, see *The Trials of Oscar Wilde*, edited by H. Montgomery Hyde (London 1948).
2   Hyde, p.222.
3   5 April 1895.
4   Hyde, p.227.
5   *Letters*, p.389.

Chapter 14: Separation

1   Harris, p.551.
2   ibid.
3   F.G. Bettany, *Stewart Headlam: A Biography* (London 1926), p.130.

4 Pearson, op.cit., p.304.
5 W.B. Yeats, *Memoirs*, edited by Denis Donoghue (London 1972), pp.79 – 80.
6 Harris, p.282.
7 ibid., p.285.
8 ibid.
9 ibid., p.286.
10 Hyde, p.293.
11 André Gide, *If It Die (Si le grain ne meurt)*, translated by Dorothy Bussy, (London 1951), p.277.

Chapter 15: Mrs Holland

1 autograph letter of 25 June 1895, Clark Library.
2 ibid.
3 R.H. Sherard, *The Real Oscar Wilde* (London 1917), p.173.
4 *Complete Works*, p.877.
5 autograph letter of 12 October 1895, Clark Library.
6 *Letters*, p.681.

Chapter 16: Incomprehension

1 autograph letter of 5 January 1896, Clark Library.
2 *Letters*, p.398.
3 copy letter, undated, in the handwriting of Mrs More Adey, Clark Library.
4 *Complete Works*, p.905.
5 ibid., p.944.
6 *Letters*, p.400.
7 autograph letter of 21 June 1896, Clark Library.
8 ibid.
9 ibid., 3 August 1896.

Chapter 17: The Last Summer

1 *Complete Works*, p.945.
2 *Letters*, p.515.
3 ibid., p.516.
4 *The Story of Oscar Wilde's Life and Experience in Reading Gaol, By His Warder* (New Jersey 1963), pp.16 – 17.
5 *Letters*, p.566.
6 ibid., p.587.
7 Blacker, 25 September 1897.
8 *Letters*, p.622.
9 ibid., p.628.
10 ibid., p.647.
11 Blacker, 26 September 1897.

12   *Letters*, p.685.
13   Blacker, 1 October 1897.
14   *Letters*, p.672 – 3.
15   ibid., p.675.
16   Stetson Sale Catalogue 1920.
17   *Letters*, p.697.
18   Douglas, *Oscar Wilde: A Summing Up*, p.98.
19   ibid., pp.98 – 9.

Chapter 18: Requiescat

1   *Letters*, p.706.
2   ibid., p.707.
3   Blacker, 4 March 1898.
4   Blacker, 18 March 1898.
5   ibid.
6   Blacker, 20 March 1898.
7   Blacker, 26 March 1898.
8   Blacker, undated.
9   Holland, *Son of Oscar Wilde*, p.130.
10   Blacker.
11   Holland, *Son of Oscar Wilde*, p.131.
12   *Letters*, p.730.
13   ibid.
14   ibid., p.729.
15   Pearson, op. cit. p.356.
16   *The Life of Oscar Wilde*, p.375.

Epilogue

1   Hyde, p.379.

Index

Adey, More, 184, 192–3, 200–2, 207–9, 210, 217
Alexander, George, 105, 157, 171
Alice, Princess of Monaco, 105, 191, 206
Allen (blackmailer), 125
Anderson, Mary, 68
Archer, William, 113
Atkins, Fred, 176
Atkinson, Adelaide Barbara, *see* Lloyd, Adelaide Barbara
Atkinson, John, 12–13
Atkinson, Mary, 12–13, 21–2, 37, 81-2
Avory, Horace, 181

Babbacombe Cliff (Lady Mount-Temple's house), 114–20, 125, 156, 172, 181, 185
Backhouse, Trelawney, 128
Ballad of Reading Gaol, The, 217, 220–1
Beardsley, Aubrey, 54
Benson, E. F., 136
Beerbohm, Max, 128
Bernhardt, Sarah, 31, 47, 57, 68, 96, 112–13
Boucicault, Dion, 35–6, 153
Bourget, Paul, 47
Boxwell, Miss, 187–8
Brémont, Anna, Comtesse de, 58, 59, 81
Blacker, Carlos, 205, 212–17, 221–2, 224-6
Blacker, Carrie, 205, 213–14, 221, 223–4
Blavatsky, Madam, 81
Brooke, Charles, Rajah of Sarawak, 191
Brooke, Lady Margaret, Ranee of Sarawak, 80, 105, 191, 198–9, 207, 212, 220, 224
Brookfield, Charles, 114, 153, 161
Browning, Robert, 57
Burnand, Frank, 33
Burne-Jones, Sir Edward, 57, 114, 223

Carew, Mrs James, 230
Carson, Sir Edward, Q.C., M.P., 160–1, 165–7
Chameleon, The, 176–7
'Chiero', 126–7
Clarke, Sir Edward, Q.C., M.P., 160, 166–8, 172, 176, 181–2
Clibborn (blackmailer), 125

Clifton, Arthur, 202–5
Cobden, Jane, 76, 79
Cochrane, Lady, 108
Cochrane, Vice-Admiral Basil, 80
Cochrane, Cornelia, 80
Cochrane, Minnie, 108
Cons, Emma, 76, 79
Collins, Mr Justice, 165
Corelli, Marie, 72–3
Crane, Walter, 57, 91, 153
Cromer, Lord, 111, 134, 136

da Souza, Sir Walter, 79
Decay of Lying, The, 92
De Profundis, 130, 136, 148, 197, 207, 229
Dodgson, Campbell, 119–20
Donoghue, John, 46–7, 55
Douglas, Lord Alfred 'Bosie', 100–1, 103, 108–13, 115–22, 124–5, 128–40, 142–64, 168–71, 175–82, 184, 188, 192, 200–1, 203, 214–18, 221, 223–4, 229–31
Drumlanrig, Lord, 110, 150
Duffy, Charles Gavan, 23

Edward, Prince of Wales (later Edward VII), 111, 128, 154

Florentine Tragedy, A, 116
Fortescue, Emily, 39

Gabrielli, Mme, 49
Garmoyle, Viscount, 39
Gide, André, 183
Gill, Charles, 176–7, 181
Gladstone, William Ewart, 80–1, 110
Godwin, E. W., 31, 50–2, 66, 161–3

Happy Prince and Other Tales, The, 90–1
Harberton, Lady Frances (née Pomeroy), 71, 75
Hare, Charles, 19
Hargrove, Mr, 185, 187, 198, 201–4, 214
Harris, Frank, 15, 21, 61–2, 89, 179–80
Harris, Walter, 56
Hassell, Mr, 201, 214
Hatchard, Mr, 152
Hawick, Lord, 111, 158, 160, 171, 178
Headlam, Rev. Stewart, 178, 180, 210
Hemphill, Barbara Hare, 19
Hemphill, Charles Hare, first Baron, 19, 21, 36–7, 42

Hemphill, John, 19
Hemphill, Stanhope, 19, 37
Heron-Allen, Edward, 56, 103
Holland, Constance Mary, *see* Wilde, Constance Mary
Holland, Cyril, *see* Wilde, Cyril
Holland, Vyvyan Oscar Beresford, *see* Wilde, Vyvyan Oscar Beresford
Hood, Jacob, 91
Hope, Adrian, 31, 54, 56, 108, 171, 207, 217, 223, 228, 229
Hope, C. Beresford, 76–8
Hope, Laura (née Troubridge), 31, 36, 54, 56, 108, 171
House of Pomegranites, A, 105
Humphreys, Arthur L., 152
Humphreys, Charles Octavius, 143, 158, 160, 201
Humphreys, Travers, 160
Hutchinson, Nellie, *see* Lloyd, Nellie

Ideal Husband, An, 130, 134, 153–4
Importance of Being Earnest, The, 147, 156, 163
Irving, Henry, 49, 50, 67–8, 112

Johnson, Lionel, 99–100, 108
Jopling, Louise, 123

King, Adelaide Barbara, *see* Lloyd, Adelaide Barbara
King, Eliza Mary, 16, 82
King, George Swinburn, 16–17, 82
Kirkes, Caroline (née Lloyd), 17, 39, 44, 107
Köhler, Frau and Herr, 204–5

La Sainte Courtisane, 117
Lady Windermere's Fan, 105, 111–12, 114, 117, 130, 153
Langtry, Lillie, 31, 38, 57, 96, 101, 128
La Gallienne, Richard, 93, 106
Leonard, Bibidie, 96
Lane, John, 126, 130
Leslie, Mrs Frank, 82–4
Leverson, Ada, 156, 158
Leverson, Ernest, 158
Lewis, Sir George, 149, 208
Lloyd, Adelaide Barbara, (née Atkinson, later King), 12–13, 16, 69, 82
Lloyd, Caroline (née Watson) 10–11
Lloyd, Constance Mary, *see* Wilde, Constance Mary
Lloyd, Emily, 17–18, 21, 36–8, 43, 49–50, 56, 107
Lloyd, Fabian, 107
Lloyd, Otho jun., 107
Lloyd, Frederick Watson, 12–13
Lloyd, Horace, 12–16, 225

INDEX

Lloyd, Horatio, 18
Lloyd, John, 10
Lloyd, John Horatio, 10–11, 16–18, 21, 33, 36–40, 42, 49–50, 107, 185
Lloyd, Mary (née Watson), 10
Lloyd, Nellie (née Hutchinson), 38, 44
Lloyd, Otho Holland, 12–17, 21–2, 37–40, 42, 49, 60–1, 82, 107, 183, 186–90, 207, 212, 217, 220–1, 224–6
Lloyd's Bonds, 11
Louÿs, Pierre, 126, 128
Lord Arthur Savile's Crime, 102–4
Lowndes, Marie Belloc, 59–60, 86, 96

Martin (Oscar's warder), 209, 211–12
Mathews, William, 160, 167
Mavor, Sidney, 176
Menpes, Mortimer, 61
Melba, Nellie, 97
Meredith, George, 57, 122
Miles, Frank, 31, 50
Mr and Mrs Daventry, 153
Montgomery, Alfred, 113, 136, 143
Mount-Temple, Lady Georgiana, 114–15, 119, 123–4, 156, 172, 181, 183, 185, 192

Napier, Baron, 17
Napier, Eliza, 17, 229
Napier, Hon. Mrs Louisa Mary ('Aunt Mary'), 17, 39, 69, 118, 120, 160–9, 171, 229

Oscariana, 151–2

Parker, Charles, 166–7, 176, 178, 181
Parker, William, 178, 181
Patience, 34–5
Picture of Dorian Gray, The, 100–2, 105, 112, 162–3, 222
Poems (by Oscar Wilde), 112
Portrait of Mr W. H., The, 99

Queensberry, Marchioness of, 108, 110, 119, 129, 134–6, 143, 145, 158, 198, 203, 217, 221
Queensberry, eighth Marquess of, 109–11, 129, 137–9, 143–6, 149–50, 155–63, 168–9, 179, 202

Rational Dress Society's Gazette, 70–5, 152
Reubell, Henrietta, 47–8
Robinson, Mrs, 146, 161, 164, 172–3
Rosebery, Lord, 110, 150, 172

Ross, Robert Baldwin 15, 98–9, 106, 112, 117, 123–4, 153–60, 169–70, 184, 189, 192, 198, 200–2, 211–12, 214–16, 217, 222–3, 226, 228–30
Ruskin, John 57–60

Salome, 112–13, 118, 131, 134
Sandhurst, Lady Margaret, 57, 75–81, 94, 114, 192
Sargent, John Singer, 47, 57
Schuster, Adela, 180, 230
Schwabe, Maurice, 166, 172, 176
Shaw, George Bernard, 110, 113, 161–3
Sherard, Robert Harborough, 30, 36, 43, 45, 57, 61, 91, 103, 184, 186
Sphinx, The, 130
Stopes, Mrs, 71, 76
Story, Waldo, 41, 69

Terry, Ellen, 31, 48, 49, 57, 68, 96, 179
Taylor, Alfred, 161, 166, 175, 178, 181, 182
Thursfield, Emily, 79–80, 185, 190, 194
Tite Street, Number 16, 42, 49–56, 85–6, 98, 107, 115, 123, 125, 143, 150, 152–3, 171, 173, 181
Travers, Mary Josephine, 24–7, 125
Tree, Herbert Beerbohm, 33, 57, 125, 126, 128
Turner, Reginald, 169, 211, 228

Vivian, Herbert, 92–3
Villa Elvira (Constance's house outside Nervi), 217, 220

Watson, Holland, 10–11
Watson, James, 10
Whistler, James NcNeill, 39, 42, 44, 50–1, 55, 57
Wilde, Constance Mary (née Lloyd, later Holland): birth, 12; childhood, 13–18; appearance, 15, 38, 42, 59; meets Oscar Wilde, 21–2, 31–2; courtship, 33, 37–41; marriage, 9, 42–4; honeymoon, 45–9; home life, 49–55; motherhood, 56, 85–92; dress, 58–60, 65, 69, 73, 106; at-homes, 57-60, 69, 85–6; marital relations, 61–2, 120–1, 140; writings, 66–71, 82; politics 75–80; relationship with Lord Alfred Douglas, 108–9, 129–30, 136, 163, 223; holidays at Babbacombe 114–21; European tour of 1893, 118–21; illness, 155, 192, 212–14, 221, 224; exile, 185–225; change of name, 189; prison visits, 196–8, 209; legal separation, 209; death, 224–5
Wilde, Cyril (later Holland), 56, 60, 63–4, 85–93, 104, 108, 117, 119–20, 129–30, 142, 158, 171–2, 183, 185–6, 189–91, 195, 199–200, 203, 206, 212–15, 220, 225, 229, 231
Wilde, Emily, 22–3, 26–7, 74
Wilde, Isola, 24, 26, 65
Wilde, Lady Jane Francesca (Speranza), 18, 22–9, 42–3, 48, 64–6, 74–5, 83, 86, 105, 120, 132–3, 141, 159–60, 179, 192, 196–8, 227
Wilde, Mary, 22–3, 26–7, 74

INDEX

Wilde, Oscar; birth, 24; childhood, 26–8; at Oxford, 16, 28, 29–31, 34; first meeting with Constance, 21–2, 31–2; courtship, 33, 37–41; American tour, 35–6; marriage, 9, 42–4; honeymoon, 45–9; home life, 49–55; parenthood, 56, 85, 92; at-homes, 57–60, 69; marital relations, 61–2, 120–1, 140; relationship with Lord Alfred Douglas, 108 ff.; trials, 165–82; imprisonment, 182–210; release from gaol, 210; reunion with Douglas, 214; final separation from Douglas, 217–18; death, 129

Wilde, Ralph, 24

Wilde, Sophie 'Lily', 133, 196, 198

Wilde, Vyvyan Oscar Beresford (later Holland), 54, 60–4, 85–9, 95, 104, 117, 129–30, 142, 171–2, 186, 189–90, 195–7, 199–200, 206, 212–15, 217, 220–5, 231

Wilde, Sir William, 22–8, 86

Wilde, William Charles Kingsbury (Willie), 21, 23–4, 28–9, 40, 42, 49, 65, 82–4, 103, 120, 133, 141–2, 179, 198

Wills, Sir Alfred, 181–2

Wilson, Henry, 22, 27–9

Woman of No Importance, A, 115–16, 123, 125, 126–8

Woman's World, 68–70, 75, 82, 96

Wood, Alfred, 124–5, 167, 181

Wyndham, George, 143, 170

Yeats, William Butler, 85, 96, 179